Quality Talk About Text

Quality Talk About Text

Discussion Practices for Talking and Thinking About Text

IAN A. G. WILKINSON • KRISTIN BOURDAGE

HEINEMANN
Portsmouth, NH

Heinemann
145 Maplewood Avenue, Suite 300
Portsmouth, NH 03801
www.heinemann.com

Offices and agents throughout the world

The authors and publisher wish to thank those who have generously given permission to reprint borrowed material:

pp. 5–6 Excerpt from "Role of Discussion in Reading Comprehension" by Ian Wilkinson and Kathryn Nelson from *Visible Learning Guide to Student Achievement* edited by John Hattie and Eric Anderman. Copyright © 2020 by Ian A.G. Wilkinson and Kathryn Nelson. Reprinted by permission of the Copyright Clearance Center on behalf of Taylor & Francis Group, LLC.

Figure 3.1 and Figure 3.3 Adapted from "Dialogue-Intensive Pedagogies for Promoting Literate Thinking" by Ian A. G. Wilkinson, Anna O. Soter, P. Karen Murphy, and Sarah C. Lightner from *The Routledge International Handbook of Research and Dialogic Education* edited by Neil Mercer, Rupert Wegerif, and Louis Major. Copyright © 2000. Reprinted by permission of the Copyright Clearance Center on behalf of Taylor & Francis Group, LLC.

Figure 3.2 Adapted from "Instructional Frameworks for Quality Talk About Text: Choosing the Best Approach" by Sarah Lightner and Ian Wilkinson from *The Reading Teacher*, Volume 70, Number 4. Copyright © 2017. Reprinted by permission of the Copyright Clearance Center on behalf of John Wiley & Sons, Inc.

p. 41 Excerpt from *Grand Conversations* by Ralph Peterson and Maryann Eeds. Copyright © 2007 by Ralph Peterson and Maryann Eeds. Reprinted by permission of Scholastic Inc.

pp. 69–70 Excerpt from "Bridging the Gap Between Fiction and Nonfiction in the Literature Circle Setting" by Penny L. Beed and Debbie Stien from *The Reading Teacher*, Vol. 57, No. 6. Copyright © 2004. Reprinted by permission of the Copyright Clearance Center on behalf of John Wiley & Sons, Inc.

pp. 83–84 Excerpt from "Acting Up or Acting Out? Unlocking Children's Talk in Literature Circles" by Caroline Pearson from *Literacy,* Volume 44, Number 1. Copyright © 2010. Reprinted by permission of the Copyright Clearance Center on behalf of John Wiley & Sons, Inc.

Credits for borrowed material continue on page 250.

Library of Congress Control Number: 2020950102
ISBN: 978-0-325-08866-2

Editor: Margaret LaRaia
Production: Patty Adams
Cover Design: Vita Lane
Cover Photography: © wee dezign / Shutterstock; © track5 / Getty Images; © SDI Productions / Getty Images
Typesetter: Shawn Girsberger
Manufacturing: Val Cooper

Printed in the United States of America on acid-free paper
2 3 4 5 GP 26 25 24 23 22
PO 34838

Contents

ONLINE RESOURCES

The forms in the Appendix can also be found under Companion Resources at http://hein.pub/QualTalk.

Foreword | Nell K. Duke

Years ago a group of researchers followed a group of children, from low-income homes, from preschool through fourth grade (Dickinson and Porche 2011). In preschool, among other things, the researchers looked carefully at language use in the children's classrooms. One of the items they coded was how much analytic talk there was, including talk about the meaning of words and the reasons for events or for characters' actions. The researchers found that the proportion of analytic talk in preschool classrooms predicted children's vocabulary in fourth grade! How is this possible? The researchers hypothesized that "[c]hildren in classrooms with teachers who engaged in analytical discussions might have become more attuned to books and more able to engage in and learn from classroom discussions" (882). This is the power of quality talk about text.

In another study, a research team observed eighty-eight middle- and high-school English language arts classes with forty-four teachers in twenty-five schools in four states. Using state test data, researcher Judith Langer (2001) separated the schools into those with typical student achievement compared to other schools with similar demographics, and those that had relatively high student achievement compared to other schools with similar demographics. One of Langer's key findings was that in the classrooms that had relatively high student achievement, "[s]tudents work[ed] together to develop depth and complexity of understanding in interaction with others," whereas in typical classrooms, "[s]tudents work alone, in groups, or with the teacher to get the work done, but do not engage in rich discussion of ideas" (857). This is the power of quality talk about text.

Looking across forty-two studies that examined the impact of specific approaches to discussion of text, mostly at the upper elementary level, researchers found a number of approaches that worked to increase student talk, decrease teacher talk, and improve students' comprehension of text (Murphy et al. 2009). Evidence for the power of quality talk about text has really accumulated.

Given the findings I have just shared, and others, I was eager to have a book on text discussion in the Research-Informed Classroom series. I was thrilled that Ian Wilkinson and Kristin Bourdage agreed to write the book, given their enormous depth of expertise in both research and practice. I had high expectations for the book—and the authors have exceeded them. The book is beautifully written, firmly grounded in research, and yet eminently practical. One of my favorite features of the book is that it enables educators to match the discussion approach they select with their goal for the text discussion: to emphasize personal response, knowledge building, or argumentation. Even within these three discussion purposes, the authors offer multiple approaches to discussion, so that teachers can select just the right approach for their context. Another feature of the book I especially appreciate is the Talk Assessment Tool for Teachers (see the Appendix). It is challenging to facilitate discussion and reflect on the quality of that discussion, but this tool helps make that achievement more attainable. I could go on, but suffice it to say that there is a lot to like about this book. I truly believe that if our field engages deeply with it, we could see substantial improvement in the quality of text discussion and in students' reading comprehension. We can harness the power of quality talk about text.

References

Dickinson, David K., and Michelle V. Porche. 2011. "Relation Between Language Experiences in Preschool Classrooms and Children's Kindergarten and Fourth-Grade Language and Reading Abilities." *Child Development* 82 (3): 870–886.

Langer, Judith A. 2001. "Beating the Odds: Teaching Middle and High School Students to Read and Write Well." *American Educational Research Journal* 38 (4): 837–880.

Murphy, P. Karen, Ian Wilkinson, Anna Soter, Maeghan Hennessey, and John Alexander. 2009. "Examining the Effects of Classroom Discussion on Students' Comprehension of Text." *Journal of Educational Psychology* 101 (3): 740–764.

Acknowledgments

The seeds for this book were planted almost 20 years ago with the award of a research grant to the first author from the Institute of Education Sciences (IES), U.S. Department of Education (R305G020075, 2002-2006) to take stock of the extant research and theory on classroom discussions for promoting high-level comprehension of text. That project provided impetus and direction for much of this book and we gratefully acknowledge the contributions of Anna O. Soter and P. Karen Murphy, Co-Principal Investigators, to that early work. We are also grateful to the numerous graduate students (some of whom are now colleagues) who, either directly or indirectly, helped us update that work and broaden our thinking on classroom discussion and dialogue, notably Sevda Binici, Sarah Lightner, Diana Purwaningrum, Min-Young Kim, and Leiah Groom Thomas.

Many of the ideas contained in this book have their roots in the scholarship of others, and we owe an intellectual debt to Neil Mercer, Robin Alexander, Martin Nystrand, and Alina Reznitskaya. Their scholarship on classroom talk, dialogic teaching, and dialogic pedagogy greatly informed our thinking, as we hope is evident in the pages of this book. Any errors of interpretation are, of course, ours.

The ideas contained in this book were also developed in collaboration with the many classroom teachers we have worked with over the years. We are grateful for the countless hours they spent with us in professional development in classroom talk about text. The knowledge gained from their insights and experience greatly influenced our thinking.

Last, and not least, we thank those who helped nurture the seeds of this book through to fruition. We thank Nell Duke for inviting us, so many years ago, to author a book on classroom discussion about text for the Research-Informed Classroom series, and for her insightful and constructive feedback along the way. Our thanks, too, to our patient and thoughtful first editor at Heinemann, Margaret LaRaia. Thank you, Margaret, for your encouragement, for helping shape the final form, and for reminding us, always, that this is for teachers.

—*Ian A. G. Wilkinson and Kristin Bourdage*

SECTION I

The Big Picture: Different Talk for Different Purposes

1

Why Talk?

Language is a funny thing. It doesn't always work very well. Almost every word, every phrase, every sentence and paragraph carry multiple meanings. Let's take the title of this chapter, for example: "Why Talk?" Even these two simple words have at least two interpretations. One interpretation is *why should we talk to each other?* Another interpretation is *why is talk the focus of this book?* This ambiguity of language becomes even more apparent when we try to interpret the meaning of more complex texts, such as the US Constitution, a Shakespearean play, or a poem. Words rarely elicit precise meaning. Their meanings are slippery, hard to pin down, especially when each one of us brings different stores of knowledge and experience, and, likely, different understandings of the context in which the words are heard or read.

But therein lies the power of language. Because no one of us assigns meanings to words in exactly the same way, understanding what an author or speaker is saying is an act of interpretation (Mercer 2000). Because of the inherent ambiguity of language, where words do not always generate precise meanings in the minds of others when we communicate, the reader or listener may create new understandings different from those intended by the author or speaker (Littleton and

Mercer 2013; Mercer 2013). The very unreliability of language, and the space it creates for different perspectives, is the engine that can generate new ideas!

The Power of Talk

Talk, of course, is one way of using language and it is a powerful tool for teaching and learning. In fact, it is the primary tool for teaching and learning. It is through talk that we conduct most of our teaching, and it is through talk that we think and learn. Let's look at some of the amazing things we accomplish with talk.

First, talk makes our thinking public. We use talk to communicate with each other and to share our thoughts. Of course, as we have just seen, talk is not a perfect window into the minds of others because of the inherent ambiguity of language. And let's not forget that what we say (and don't say!) is usually tailored to our audience. But talk offers a partial window nonetheless. So, in a classroom discussion, for example, we can use talk to share how we interpret the text, and through talk we can learn what others are thinking and how others are constructing meaning. We might learn that there are other ways of interpreting the text and different points of view on the issue at hand. This means that we walk away from the discussion with knowledge of other strategies for making sense of the text and, hopefully, an understanding and appreciation of others' perspectives.

Second, talk is a tool for thinking. Talk is a way of using language to help us organize our thoughts, to reason, to plan, and to reflect on our actions. Think back to the last time you were faced with performing a difficult task, such as trying to assemble a complex piece of furniture that arrived "ready for easy assembly." Faced with such a task, you might have heard yourself talking to yourself in your head, or even out loud, in an effort to make sense of the instructions. Your talk helped you think through and perform the task. Translating this into the context of a discussion about text, the mere fact of having to explain our thinking to someone else helps us to clarify and elaborate our thinking, perhaps finding flaws in our argument or something that we still do not understand. As a result, we walk away from the discussion with a much clearer understanding of our own thinking about the text.

Third, and this is key for discussion about text, talk is a tool for *thinking together*. Talk gives us a tool for combining our intellectual resources to collectively make sense of experience and to solve problems. Neil Mercer, a British psychologist who studies language use in the classroom, calls this use of talk as a social mode of thinking "interthinking" (Littleton and Mercer 2013; Mercer 2000).

Talk is a resource for jointly creating knowledge and understanding. This means that we can walk away from a discussion not just with a good understanding of our own ideas and those of others but having co-constructed new ways of thinking about the text that go beyond the individual capabilities of the participants.

It is in using talk as a social mode of thinking, or interthinking, that the generative power of language really comes to the fore. By wrestling with the text together, offering differing interpretations, and trying to reconcile them, we are using talk to create new understandings and ideas.

So, talk is a medium of communication for sure, but it is much more than that. It is a psychological tool to help us think, and a social or cultural tool that enables us to think together. In all cases, what we take away, or "internalize," (Vygotsky 1978, 1981), is a richer understanding of the text and, ideally, a more sophisticated way of thinking about text in general.

Not Just Any Kind of Talk—Quality Talk

But simply placing students in groups, stepping back, and encouraging them to talk about a text is not enough to promote thinking and learning. In some discussions, students talk a lot but this doesn't always mean there's deeper learning. More important than the amount of talk is the kind of talk (Murphy et al. 2009; Wells 1989). As we will see in the next chapter, we want students to engage in a particular kind of talk we call "quality talk." As its name suggests, quality talk is a type of discourse in discussions about text that reflects and helps promote high-level thinking and comprehension. The richer the discourse in terms of quality talk, the more productive the discussion is and the more likely we are to achieve the outcomes we want for our students.

To illustrate what we mean by quality talk, let's look at an excerpt from a discussion among a small group of students in a fourth-grade class. The teacher and the students are discussing a story called "Victor" by James Howe (1997). The story is about a young boy named Cody, who is lying in a coma in a hospital bed. To help him get through his time in the hospital, Cody creates an imaginary world called "The Land Above" in the ceiling tiles above his bed. During his stay, a mysterious man named Victor visits Cody and tells him stories about what his life will be like when he grows up. The teacher and students are grappling with the question *Who is Victor?*

Michelle: I think Victor's an angel.

Teacher: You think Victor's an angel? Can you tell me why you think so?

Michelle: Because he, well maybe he comes from like the land above, and that's where he's talking to him. And that's why maybe Cody can't see Victor 'cause he's from the land above and he's talking to him from up there.

Nancy: Maybe's he's just a figure, but he always has this thing on his face that he doesn't have . . .

Matt: But he, Cody, kept saying "three tiles up, two to the left."

Teacher: That was interesting.

Andrew: You mean "three tiles down, two to the left."

Nancy: Yeah, he was talking about the ceiling.

Sam: He thought it was a real place where people lived and stuff, but he said the funny thing about it was, he never gave them a name.

Andrew: And also, the reason why I don't think Victor was in the land above, well how could he be talking from the land above because remember when Cody said he could hear him, hear the screeching on the floor from when Victor was pulling up a chair to keep Cody company.

Teacher: So that's—are you saying that's evidence?

Andrew: Yeah.

Teacher: Interesting.

Andrew: So how could he be from the land above? I mean he could be from the land above, but how could he be talking from the land above?

Matt: But how do you know people can't travel from and to [the] land above?

Nancy: This isn't realistic. This isn't like nonfiction, so anything can happen.

(Wilkinson and Nelson 2020, 231–232)

When we look at this excerpt, the first thing we notice is that the students have considerable control over the talk. Michelle states her opinion about Victor, and the teacher asks an authentic question that probes the reason for her opinion ("Can you tell me why you think so?"). This elicits a variety of responses. Most of the contributions come from students and there are several consecutive exchanges among students with only brief, occasional comments from the teacher. These exchanges often involve long, elaborated explanations. Notice, too, that the students have responsibility for constructing their understanding and interpretation of the story. They ask questions, manage turn taking, and evaluate each other's answers. What is not apparent from the transcript is that the students do not raise their hands to speak. They converse with each other much as adults do, waiting for a space to talk and building on each other's ideas.

When we look "inside" the students' utterances, another thing we notice is that they are engaged in some fairly high-level thinking about the story. They engage in inductive reasoning, trying to tie things together to account for Victor's actions ("I think Victor's an angel"), deductive reasoning as to why things happened the way they did ("The reason why I don't think Victor was in the land above. . .") and lots of speculation as to what might be going on ("Maybe he comes from like the land above, Maybe's he's just a figure"). Words such as *I think, I don't think, so, maybe, because, how, why,* and *could* are good clues that some powerful thinking is going on during this discussion.

When we step back and look at the excerpt as a whole, yet another thing we notice is that students are not just reasoning individually, they are also reasoning collectively. They offer alternative perspectives about Victor, challenging and counter-challenging each other's ideas constructively, all the while giving reasons and evidence from the text to support their ideas. Granted that the teacher interjects after her key question, but she does so slightly, almost as if she were just another participant in the discussion. Indeed, the students are engaging in what Mercer (2000) calls "exploratory talk."

The excerpt above is very different from the more traditional recitation or I-R-E (Mehan 1979) style of classroom talk with which you may be familiar. In this style of talk, the teacher *Initiates* a question (e.g., "What was the other big thing that Max sent her?"), a student *Responds* (e.g., "a blue jay"), and the teacher *Evaluates* the response (e.g., "Was it really a bird? No, it wasn't."). In a recitation style, the teacher talks the most—about two-thirds of the time—and controls the topic. She asks the questions, nominates students to answer, and is responsible for evaluating the students' answers. Students typically take a passive role and let the teacher shape the direction of the discussion. Recitation has its place in a teacher's talk repertoire, for recapping what has been covered in a lesson or assessing students' knowledge and understanding, but it is not the type of talk that promotes high-level thinking or comprehension.

What Does the Research Say?

The research evidence on the benefits of discussion that involves quality talk is strong. Research shows that when students engage in such talk they make gains on a variety of learning outcomes. What is surprising in some studies is how large and durable the gains can be. We describe the results of research in later chapters. For now, let's visit four studies for a taste of what the research says.

First is a study of Project Challenge, a project that was conducted from 1998–2003 in one of the lowest performing school districts in Massachusetts (Chapin and O'Connor 2012; O'Connor, Michaels, and Chapin 2015). Each year, the researchers worked with a new cohort of one hundred fourth-grade students and engaged them in a variety of activities that included structured discussion. After one year in the program, results showed that 57 percent of students scored "Advanced" or "Proficient" on the state math test, compared with only 38 percent in the state overall. After three years, 82 percent of students scored "Advanced" or "Proficient," compared to only 40 percent in the state overall. These results held up in a more controlled comparison. Even more interesting was the finding that the benefits lasted beyond the first year in the program and that they transferred to the students' performance on the state English Language Arts test! Several things were involved in Project Challenge, but many of the participating teachers reported that the biggest factor contributing to students' gains was the intensive use of classroom talk.

Second is a recent study conducted in England (Jay et al. 2017). This was a large-scale randomized control trial that checked all the boxes for a rigorous experimental study. The researchers compared an approach called "dialogic teaching" with business-as-usual instruction. Seventy-six schools and almost five thousand Year 5 students participated. Teachers in the dialogic teaching program learned to use different types of talk for particular purposes, including to discuss, reason, argue, and explain (Alexander 2018). After only twenty weeks, students who participated in the program were two months ahead of their control group peers on national assessments in English, math, and science.

Next is a study of a version of Philosophy for Children (P4C), one of the discussion approaches featured in this book. The study was conducted in a Local Educational Authority in Scotland with 177 ten-year-olds in seven classes in six schools. After participating in discussions for just one hour per week over sixteen months, using texts developed to teach basic philosophical concepts, the students showed substantial gains on a measure of verbal, nonverbal, and quantitative reasoning compared to those in a business-as-usual control (Topping and Trickey 2007a). These gains persisted when the students were followed up two years later, after they had moved to high school (Topping and Trickey 2007b).

Last, we go to a low-income middle school in Texas where researchers sought to replicate the Scottish study. This study used the same outcome measure, and the same version of P4C, but for a shorter duration (just six months). One hundred and eighty-six seventh-grade students participated in the discussions in their language arts classes for one hour per week. At the end of the program, results again showed substantial gains in reasoning relative to a control group (Fair et al. 2015a). And once again, when students were followed up, three years later this time, researchers found the gains persisted (Fair et al. 2015b). Tellingly, eighth graders who participated in only four to ten weeks of discussions showed no such gains.

This research is compelling. What we find most encouraging about these findings is how large the benefits for students can be, that they can be sustained, and that they can even transfer from one subject area to another. Something powerful is happening in and through the talk. Another frequent finding to be discussed later in this book is that the benefits of this kind of talk are especially apparent for students who, for many different reasons, are disadvantaged (e.g., Gorard, Siddiqui, and See 2017). Quality talk opens up space for all students to benefit.

Different Talk for Different Purposes

As you may have noticed, there is a theme developing in this book: *different talk for different purposes*. As we have intimated, there are a number of options available to us when it comes to engaging students in talk. Recitation has its purpose if we want to recap with students what we have covered or to assess their knowledge and understanding. Discussion has its purpose if we want to further students' thinking, understanding, and learning—especially if it involves quality talk. There are other types of talk, too, such as exposition (good for explaining and conveying information) and rote repetition (good for drilling facts, ideas, and routines) (Alexander 2017). The important thing to keep in mind is that different kinds of talk serve different purposes and our role as teachers is to use talk purposefully to accomplish the goals we have for our students.

Even within the broad class of talk called discussion, different talk serves different purposes. In this book, we provide a menu of approaches to discussion about text that teachers can use to foster high-level thinking and comprehension. Some of the approaches are more suited to instructional goals that emphasize responding to literature on an expressive level; others are more suited to goals of acquiring information from a text; and still others are more suited to goals of adopting a critical-analytic stance toward the text. As we will see, different ways of organizing and conducting discussion promote different types of talk, and that talk encourages different ways of thinking about or orientations toward the text. Of course, this is not an all or nothing affair; while a particular approach to discussion might privilege one goal or stance, other goals or stances can still be operating, albeit a bit below the surface. Nonetheless, to use talk effectively, we ask you to consider how your instructional goals align with those of different discussion approaches and how the approaches can be used to support the needs of your students. When talk and learning goals align in the classroom, something very magical happens.

But I Have Standards!

But you have standards, you say? Yes, as teachers we are required to ensure that our students meet certain standards, whether they be the Common Core State Standards (National Governors Association Center for Best Practices, and The Council of Chief State School Officers 2010), individual state standards, or other standards. Thankfully, discussions that promote quality talk about text help meet many of the standards typically found in the English language arts. Most standards express expectations for students to be able to converse and collaborate with each other. Most lay out expectations for students to respond to literature, to build knowledge from informational text, and to think critically about text. For example, let's look at the Common Core State Standards in the United States. In Figure 1.1, we show a sample of the English Language Arts standards for different grade levels.

Figure 1.1 Sample of the Common Core ELA Standards

Conversation and Collaboration	Standard
Prepare for and participate effectively in a range of conversations and collaborations with diverse partners, building on others' ideas and expressing their own clearly and persuasively.	Anchor standard, speaking and listening, K–12
Follow agreed-upon rules for discussions (e.g., listening to others and taking turns speaking about the topics and texts under discussion).	Speaking and listening, K
Continue a conversation through multiple exchanges.	Speaking and listening, K
Response to Literature	**Standard**
Determine a theme of a story, drama, or poem from details in the text, including how characters in a story or drama respond to challenges or how the speaker in a poem reflects upon a topic; summarize the text.	Reading standard for literature, grade 5
Identify words and phrases in stories or poems that suggest feelings or appeal to the senses.	Reading standard for literature, grade 1
Knowledge Building	**Standard**
Determine the main idea of a text; recount the key details and explain how they support the main idea.	Reading standard for informational text, grade 3
Ask and answer such questions as *who, what, where, when, why,* and *how* to demonstrate understanding of key details in a text.	Reading standard for informational text, grade 2
Critical Thinking	**Standard**
Read closely to determine what the text says explicitly and to make logical inferences from it; cite specific textual evidence when writing or speaking to support conclusions drawn from the text.	Anchor standard, reading, K–12
Delineate a speaker's argument and specific claims, distinguishing claims that are supported by reasons and evidence from claims that are not.	Speaking and listening standard, grade 6
Evaluate a speaker's point of view, reasoning, and use of evidence and rhetoric.	Anchor standard, speaking and listening K–12

Classroom discussions are obviously a perfect fit for helping students to develop skills of conversation and collaboration. But discussions that promote quality talk about text are also well suited to fostering students' abilities in other areas of the standards—responding to literature, building knowledge, and thinking critically. We will see that, depending on which approach we use, classroom discussions address these standards to varying degrees—again, different talk for different purposes.

A nice thing about talk is that it makes students' thinking visible. So, from listening to what they say, we can "see" what and how they are thinking and whether they are meeting expectations. And because talk is a building block, or scaffold, for students' thinking, quality talk gives us a ready tool for supporting students' high-level thinking and comprehension. When we know what quality talk sounds like and how to promote it, we have the tools to capitalize on the power of talk in the English language arts classroom.

But I'm Teaching Online!

While putting the finishing touches to this book in the spring of 2020, the coronavirus pandemic hit with a vengeance and we found ourselves teaching online and using web-based platforms (e.g., Zoom, Google Meet) to hold discussions about text. In our online classes with preservice teachers, and in conversations with our K–12 colleagues, we explored the ideas in this book and we learned about some of the pitfalls and promises of engaging students in quality talk in a synchronous web-based environment. In the final section of this book, we share some tips for having discussions with your students in a virtual environment.

Although online teaching and learning presents challenges of inequitable access to computers or high-speed Internet, disruption to the rhythm of face-to-face schooling, and fewer opportunities for social interaction among students, discussions with quality talk are highly adaptable to the online environment. In fact, discussion involving quality talk offers one of the few ways to enrich our students' learning outside of the classroom and to approximate face-to-face learning in an online space. The key words here are *adaptable* and *approximate*—the goal of online education should not be to replicate what we do face-to-face in the classroom; adjustments have to be made to offer a productive learning experience (Brewer and Brewer 2015). The suggestions we offer later in this book are to help you adapt discussion and quality talk for online teaching and learning in web-based platforms.

Where to from Here?

Our goal in writing this book is to provide teachers, literacy leaders, teacher educators, and others with a repertoire of approaches for conducting classroom discussions about text. In doing so, we introduce the discourse features of quality talk—features that reflect and help foster high-level thinking and comprehension. These features not only help us think about the strengths and weaknesses of the different discussion approaches, they also give us clues as to what is going on in the talk. By highlighting the discourse of the different approaches, we hope to help you build an "ear for talk"—a phrase we use throughout this book to refer to the skill of listening for and identifying different kinds of talk during discussion. By developing an ear for talk, we can become more sensitive to what is going on in a discussion—so we know when quality talk is happening and when it is not—and more adept at stepping into the discussion to support students' thinking.

This book is organized into five sections.

- In this first section, we orient you toward talk and classroom discussion. In this chapter, we hope we have convinced you of the importance of talk. In the next chapter, we introduce the discourse features of quality talk. We also introduce the Talk Assessment Tool for Teachers (TATT), an assessment rubric designed to help you assess the quality of talk. In the following chapter, we provide an overview of nine research-based discussion approaches and give you ways of thinking about their similarities and differences. Among these approaches, we hope you will see some familiar faces, as well as some that are not so familiar.

- The next three sections form the core of the book. Each section is devoted to discussion approaches that foreground a particular stance toward the text: talk to emphasize personal response, talk to emphasize knowledge building, or talk to emphasize argumentation. Within each section, we first introduce the discussion approaches. Then follow three chapters, each devoted to a particular approach and sharing a common structure: we provide a graphic summary of the approach; describe what the talk sounds like in terms of quality talk; give a frank, critical appraisal of the research evidence; and describe how to put the approach into practice (how to plan the discussion, the teacher's role, and what it looks like in action). We also describe the origins of the approach and provide a brief list of resources to learn more about it. We conclude each section by asking how we know students are engaged in the kinds of talk we want. Here we try to capture what you should hear in the talk and show how the talk in the three discussion approaches might be scored on the TATT.

- In the last section, we include a chapter describing how to get started with discussions that promote quality talk in your classroom. We also have a chapter providing answers to questions that teachers frequently ask when trying to implement text-based discussions in their classrooms.

This book is organized in such a way that you can dip in and out of the chapters as your time and interest allow. Our hope is that, by reading different parts as you see fit, you will be able to determine which discussion approaches are most aligned with your goals and the needs of your students at any given time so you can make informed decisions about the most appropriate approach to use.

2

Building an Ear for Talk: What Is Quality Talk About Text?

Quality talk is a set of theory- and evidence-based features of language that characterize the discourse of instruction, which is the language in use between teachers and students. In this chapter, we present the features of quality talk in discussions about text. When teachers and students know and use quality talk, they have powerful tools for discussions, and they can talk about text in ways that promote high-level thinking and comprehension (e.g., analyzing and interpreting text). What do we mean when we say a "feature" of language? A question is a common feature of language that we hear in discussions. When students respond to a question, we say the response is another feature of the discourse. A follow-up question would be another, and more specific, feature of the discourse.

"Quality talk" is a label we use to refer to an array of features of discourse in discussions about text that reflect high-level thinking and comprehension. The features of quality talk are based on theory and research, so hearing them in discussions is fundamental to identifying discussions that are productive and reflective of high-level thinking and comprehension. The better the quality of the talk, the better the discussion—so knowing, using, and encouraging the features of quality talk makes it more likely that your discussions will lead to the outcomes you and your students want to achieve.

In the excerpt below, a small group of fifth-grade students discuss *The Giver* (Lowry 1993). Some of the features of quality talk are called out and labeled. Think back to your last discussion with a group of students, and recall if you heard one or more of the highlighted features of quality talk.

Dante: You mean they don't divorce because they want a perfect society?

> Dante asks an authentic question. Note his use of the reasoning word *because*, which indicates generalization and analysis.

Jack: Sure.

Dante: And they don't want hatred.

Mia: Yeah, I think they want a utopia.

> Mia uses the reasoning words *I think*, which indicates position taking.

Alicia: I think it's because they went to sameness and they have to have everything the same, like if they didn't do everything the same way they think people would make the wrong choices and something bad would happen like they do in our society.

> Alicia offers an elaborated explanation. Note the reasoning words *I think*, which indicate position taking, *because*, which indicates generalization and analysis, and *if* and *would*, which indicate speculation.

Reninger (2007)

Authentic questions, or genuine questions that do not have a single right answer, are a singular feature of quality talk. For example, in the excerpt above, the first question is authentic because it's genuine and there is no one right answer. Dante seeks to clarify a previous student's response, and his question is authentic because he doesn't know the answer. The students also use other features of quality talk, such as key words and responses that indicate generalization, analysis, and speculation, and an elaborated explanation.

One of the biggest challenges in facilitating productive discussions, as in the excerpt shared, is knowing when to step in or out of the discussion and finding the balance between stepping in too frequently and sitting back too much. When you know, or have "built an ear" for, the features of quality talk that characterize productive discussions, you have an easier time stepping in and out of the discussion because you have the tools to facilitate in purposeful ways. *Building an ear for talk* is a phrase we use to encourage teachers to listen for the presence or absence of quality-talk features in their discussions. For example, let's say, during a discussion, you hear short and simple, two- or three-word responses. In noticing the short responses and knowing that elaborated explanations are an important feature of quality talk, you can step in and prompt the student to pro-vide longer, more elaborated answers. You might ask a follow-up question that prompts a chain of reasons to support a position about the text (e.g., "How do you know that?" or "Why do you think that?" or "Does the text say that?"). Knowing what quality talk sounds like is helpful for knowing when to step in and use a facilitation move to promote high-level thinking or when to step back and let the students explore ideas and ask questions on their own. Of course, there are other issues you might consider, for example: "Is it right to step in to clarify a miscon-ception?" or "Right now, will stepping in hurt the momentum?" But quality talk is a compass that helps guide your facilitation decisions and gives instructional teeth to your discussions about text, regardless of the approach to the discussion that you use (e.g., Book Club, Socratic Seminar).

Quality talk comprises many features, so we group them into three broad categories: *asking purposeful questions, prompting high-level responses*, and *engaging in reasoning*. The features of quality talk and ways of facilitating them are summa-rized in Figures 2.1, 2.2., and 2.3. The excerpts from transcripts and the callouts showing features of quality talk illustrate what teachers need to listen for as they build an ear for talk.

Asking Purposeful Questions

In the excerpt below, the teacher and a student ask purposeful questions. The discussion takes place in a fourth-grade reading group that's reading *A Lion to Guard Us* (Bulla 1989), a historical fiction chapter book about a pair of orphans in colonial America.

1. **Lucas:** Yeah, he picked them up and threw them out.

    Lucas shares a literal detail from the story but his comment reflects a lack of high-level thinking.

2. **Mrs. Ross:** But why?

    Mrs. Ross hears Lucas' basic response and steps in to ask a procedurally strong, follow-up question that elicits analysis of the text. Her question is an authentic question and demonstrates uptake.

3. **Matthew:** And then he—

4. **Lucas:** Because he's, he's because he said (paraphrasing the text), "how dare you make blah, blah [cannot hear], and then she fainted."

    Note the reasoning word *because*, which indicates analysis here.

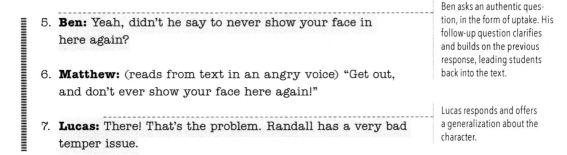

5. **Ben:** Yeah, didn't he say to never show your face in here again?

> Ben asks an authentic question, in the form of uptake. His follow-up question clarifies and builds on the previous response, leading students back into the text.

6. **Matthew:** (reads from text in an angry voice) "Get out, and don't ever show your face here again!"

7. **Lucas:** There! That's the problem. Randall has a very bad temper issue.

> Lucas responds and offers a generalization about the character.

Reninger (2007)

We love this excerpt because it highlights the use of authentic questions and uptake, and it shows how deeper levels of comprehension emerge in students' discourse when teachers and students ask purposeful questions (see Figure 2.1). *Uptake* is a follow-up question that builds on a student's response, "taking up" a little piece of what a student said previously into the question (turns 2 and 5). The teacher shows that she has an "ear for talk," using uptake at the right moment, perhaps noticing Lucas' literal detail in turn 1. Her question, "But why?," prompts the group to consider the text evidence that supports Lucas' original position that the main character, Randall, threw the orphans out of the house. "But why?" is also an authentic question because it's genuine and lacks a single "right" answer.

Authentic questions and uptake almost always create opportunities for high-level responses, because students will typically respond to these questions with connections to other texts, other discussions, or their own lives. Students also

Figure 2.1 Asking Purposeful Questions

Quality Talk Features	Description	Facilitation Example
Authentic question	A genuine question for which the person asking the question does not know the answer or is genuinely interested in knowing how others will answer. There is no prespecified answer. Almost all student questions are authentic.	Model asking authentic questions, such as "Is that right?" "Should the character do that?" "Is it ever okay to . . . ?"
Uptake	A follow-up question that asks about something someone else said previously (it incorporates something they said). Uptake is often marked by the use of pronouns.	Prompt uptake by asking, for example, "Is that always true?" "Do you have an example of that?"

routinely respond to these questions with analysis, generalization, or speculation about the text. Although not present in this short excerpt, sometimes students will reason about the text together (called "exploratory talk"), arguing ideas in a back-and-forth way as they explore an answer to an authentic question. Nevertheless, in this excerpt, the last couple of lines are exciting for high-level comprehension. Ben uses uptake in turn 5, and Lucas responds with generalization about the text in turn 7. The last line shows Lucas' high-level inference and integration of the text details with his prior knowledge, offering a generalization about the main character, Randall. Without the purposeful questions, it's quite likely Lucas' level of comprehension would have remained where it had started—with a literal, "right there" answer from the text. The discourse and features of quality talk scaffolded his, and others', high-level comprehension.

Prompting High-Level Responses

In the excerpt that follows, a small group of fifth-grade students discuss *Deadly Hits* (Tarshis 2012), a short article that highlights the issue of serious injuries to the brain that occur in youth sports. The article centers on the true story of a middle school student, Zack, who was on the school's football team and sustained a life-changing concussion during a game. The authentic question that ignited the discussion was "Who was most responsible for Zack's injuries?" Notice the way the students respond to the authentic question with high-level responses, reflecting generalization, analysis, and speculation (see Figure 2.2).

1. **Teacher:** So, if you think about Zack. Zack got this concussion in this game. Who was the one who was most responsible for his concussion?

   The teacher asks an authentic question.

2. **Students:** (overlapping speech) The player that hit him.

3. **Teacher:** Go ahead, Anthony.

4. **Anthony:** The player that hit him.

   The teacher uses uptake, a follow-up question that incorporates part of a previous student response in the question.

5. **Teacher:** And why do you think the player that hit him is the most responsible?

6. **Anthony:** 'Cause he knocked him out and he had a really bad concussion, so—

   Anthony's response indicates analysis where he builds an idea from different parts of the text (the tackle and the concussion).

7. **Students:** (interrupt, overlapping speech)

8. **Avery:** Well, it started building up when he got back on.

9. **Teacher:** Say that again, Avery.

10. **Avery:** It started to act up when he got back on the field, when he kept on going, when he, it said that his, like um, his brain was kind of like jostling around and that's what makes a concussion. And that's when he got back on the field.

11. **Jake:** It was kind of Zack who could have prevented it because since he hurt his head and if he just would have said, "I don't want to go back on the field," then this all would not have happened to him. Or it could be like some NFL players how like they like get hit in the head and said they get *"blurred vision, throbbing temples, and they can hardly walk"* (reading from the text) and they still go back on the field like to make themselves look tough. I think they set a bad example and make Zack want to be like that, and then he ended up almost dying.

Avery offers an alternative idea, showing analysis and generalization in her response, identifying a piece of text evidence (*jostling* is a detail about concussions and the brain from the text), connecting it to the events of the narrative, and linking the details to her overall understanding of what contributes to a concussion.

Jakes offers a response that indicates analysis (*because*) and speculation (*would*, *could*). This is also an example of an elaborated explanation, or a claim supported with more than one reason (claim: NFL is responsible + reasons: NFL players admit to being injured and going back to the game and this sets a bad example that may have influenced Zack's decision to return to the game). We say more about elaborated explanations in the next section.

Jake makes an explicit reference to the text as evidence to support his claim that NFL players might set a bad example for younger athletes.

Figure 2.2 How to Prompt High-level Responses

Quality Talk Features	Facilitation Questions	Facilitation Examples
Generalization	Students tie ideas together, or build up ideas, to reach a general conception or principle from the particulars.	"What's the author saying here?" "What's it all about?"
Analysis	Students break ideas apart to figure out how they are connected.	"Why is that?" "How do you know?"
Speculation	Students consider alternative possibilities or predict what might happen in certain circumstances.	"What might happen?" "What if . . . ?"
Intertextual response	Students make a connection between the text and other texts, such as literature, art, or media (i.e., text-to-text connection).	Does that come from something you've read or seen on the computer?" "Can you connect that to something you've read before?"
Shared knowledge response	Students make a connection between the current topic of discussion and previous discussions they have had or previous knowledge they have shared.	"How does this remind you of something we already discussed/ learned?"
Affective response	Students make a connection between the text and their feelings or their own lives (i.e., text-to-self connection).	"How does that make you feel?"

The authentic question at the beginning of the discussion was sufficient to prompt reasoned speculation (note the key words *could* and *would* in turn 11) and generalization and analysis (note the key words *because, I think,* in other turns). In fact, almost every student turn in the short excerpt shows students responding to the text in high-level ways. The excerpt also demonstrates how a teacher uses uptake to prompt the high-level responses. Anthony offers an unsubstantiated claim and a simple response in turn 4, and the teacher steps in with *uptake*, asking *why* he thinks the opposing player is responsible for Zack's injury. The result is Anthony's reasoning in the form of *analysis*. Uptake almost always works the way we see in these three lines: a simple response, followed by the teacher's well-timed question in the form of uptake, and then students' deeper thinking and reasoning. When teachers use an "ear for talk" to guide when to step in and when to step back, which the teacher does here because she's quiet for several turns, the result is almost always better thinking, high-level responses, and connected talk (i.e., students talking directly to each other and not "through" the teacher).

We like the way students connected with each other in this short excerpt, showing they listened carefully and built on each other's ideas. In turn 11, Jake affirms Avery's earlier position and adds clarifying language to it. In turn 10, Avery challenges Anthony's thinking, noting the player who hit Zack wasn't responsible, since Zack went back on the field after the hit ("it started building up when he got back on"), and Jake, in essence, is agreeing and clarifying the position, demonstrating *analysis* and *speculation*. Here's our paraphrase of that turn: "Yeah, Avery. I agree that it wasn't the player who hit him. If Zack just would have said 'I'm injured and don't want to play,' he'd be okay today." This kind of listening and collaboration is vital if we want students to engage in high-level thinking. If Jake had jumped in with his own argument straight away, which was NFL players might be responsible for Zack's injuries, the others in the group might have missed Avery's subtle position about Zack returning to the game with the head injury as the more plausible explanation for his concussion. Jake listens carefully and builds onto Avery's turn before forging ahead with his own thinking. This helps everyone follow the line of inquiry that develops in the discussion.

In a short amount of time (eleven turns and about two minutes of dialogue), students hear and think about three reasonable answers (the player who hit Zack, Zack himself, and NFL culture) to the authentic question that kick-started the discussion, and the teacher asks two questions that generate high-level responses in the form of analysis, generalization, and speculation.

We can only imagine what might follow in the discussion, such as asking another well-timed question like, "How does the discussion or the text make you feel?" that might elicit an *affective response*, or a question like, "Has anyone watched NFL games where you see players going back to play after an injury? Does this happen?" that might elicit an *intertextual response*. Alternatively, the teacher could prompt a *shared knowledge response* with a question like, "How do our partner conversations about concussions in soccer that we had yesterday add to this conversation? Are there reasons you discussed yesterday we can add to the discussion today?" This excerpt demonstrates what happens when teachers ask purposeful questions and students respond in high-level ways. Through the questioning that prompts high-level responses, the talk becomes a conduit for learning how to comprehend and interpret the text.

Engaging in Reasoning

In the next excerpt, a small group of fifth-grade students and the teacher are discussing *Return of the Mammoth* (O'Neill 2012). The excerpt demonstrates students engaging in reasoning with quality talk. The text is quite short, but packed with details that prompt readers' thinking about the pros and cons of cloning.

1. **Teacher:** Should the mammoth be cloned?

   The teacher asks an authentic question.

2. **Braden:** No, it should not be. 'Cause they might go extinct again and if they go extinct again then another mission has failed.

   There are several key words here that show analysis ('*cause/because*) and speculation (*might, if*) about what might happen if they clone again.

3. **Matthew:** I agree with you because it said in this one (referring to the text) that I was reading this morning (looks back at the text and turns pages). It said, um, well it said somewhere that like pretty much why um mammoths went extinct was because of "overhunting, humans, and climate." And one of my things that I said was, what if that happens again? What if the same thing happened?

   Matthew gives an elaborated explanation; he takes a position that the mammoth should not be cloned and offers several reasons, including text evidence, to support his position. In quality talk, text evidence is an explicit reference to the language of the text. Note that Matthew uses the key words, *I agree*, which shows position taking.

4. **Rosalee:** Well, I think it would just, maybe while the mammoth lives um they can like research its habitats and like what it, how it acts and maybe they can find out what made it become extinct so they can prevent that from happening again.

   Rosalee challenges the previous responses ("Well . . ."). A challenge to an idea is necessary for exploratory talk, which is a combination of several features in talk occurring in one chunk of dialogue. These features are: sharing alternative ideas, asking questions, giving reasons, and challenging each other's thinking. Together, the features indicate co-reasoning.

   So is a key word that often indicates reasoning.

5. **Morgan:** I agree with Braden and Matthew, um, because like their habitat no longer exists, so where will they live? And most and one of my things was, will it be able to survive? If not, they're just wasting their money.

> Morgan challenges Rosalee's argument for cloning (how would you study the mammoth and habitat if there isn't a habitat to live in?). A challenge is a necessary feature of exploratory talk.

6. **Students:** (overlapping speech) Yeah, yeah.

7. **Braden:** Yeah, and plus I agree with you (looking at Morgan) because like if I would think if they clone them and they like came like back as mammoths, they would have to live somewhere cold because they lived in the Ice Age. Like they would have to be in Siberia, Russia where they found the bodies because well, like if they put them in other cold places, because I was thinking if they put them in Antarctica then like the polar bears can barely survive there. Also because like when it starts heating up, it's like how would they survive if other animals also can't survive (uncertain hearing) and already adapted.

> Braden uses an elaborated explanation to build onto Morgan's position. The claim is "the habitat issue is a reason not to clone" followed by a step-by-step "guide" to his thinking. It would be too hard to find somewhere cold for the new cloned mammoths and some cold parts of the world are heating up and the polar bears are struggling to survive, so how would the mammoth survive?

The excerpt illustrates what it sounds like when students reason about the text together. When students reason, you often hear text evidence to support a claim, elaborated explanations, key words that signal reasoning, and exploratory talk (see Figure 2.3). Almost every turn in the excerpt includes at least one key word (e.g., *because, I agree, why, so, if*), which, when used in appropriate contexts, serve as indicators of reasoning and high-level responses. But what makes the excerpt so interesting is its illustration of *exploratory talk*, signified by a back-and-forth inquiry about an issue or an idea of a text, in this case cloning, and several specific features of talk.

Let's track the features of *exploratory talk*. At the beginning of the excerpt, Braden and Matthew argue the mammoth shouldn't be cloned, offering slightly different reasons to support their claim. The different reasons are important since one of the features of exploratory talk is students sharing *alternative ideas, reasons, or points of view*. In exploratory talk, you'll also hear students *asking questions*, such as Morgan's use of *uptake* in turn 5. Notice how Rosalee prompts additional reasoning from Morgan and Braden, at the end, with a *challenge* to the

Figure 2.3 Engaging in Reasoning

Quality Talk Feature	Description	Facilitation Example
Elaborated explanation	Students explain their thinking in a detailed form or with a step-by-step description of how they arrived at a conclusion. They make their thinking visible with a lengthy description of the reasons or how they arrived at a solution to a problem. Elaborated explanations typically involve key words (e.g., *I think, because, so*).	"Can you say more about that?" "Does everyone agree?" "Is that true?" "How do you know that?"
Key words • *I think/thought* • *I agree/disagree* • *Because* • *Why* • *How* • *If* • *So* • *Should* • *Could/couldn't/could've* • *Would/wouldn't/would've* • *Maybe/might* • *As if/like* • *But*	These are words that, when used in appropriate contexts, indicate student reasoning.	
Text evidence	Students make a direct reference to the text to bolster an argument, support a position, or clarify ideas.	"Where in the text does it say that?" "Did the author write that?"
Exploratory talk	Students collectively explore a topic and reason together (chewing on an idea), over at least several turns without the teacher stepping in. They share ideas, give reasons to support their ideas, challenge each other's thinking, ask each other questions, and share alternatives. Exploratory talk typically involves clusters of key words.	"Some people might say . . . [counterargument]."

"cloning is bad" proposition with the claim, cloning would be good for studying the mammoth's habitat. A challenge to a position or argument is essential for exploratory talk. Without Rosalee's challenge, it's doubtful Morgan would have asked a question in the form of uptake that prompted Braden's elaborated explanation in the last turn of the excerpt. Together, Braden and Morgan argue against Rosalee's "habitat" proposition. Braden's elaborated explanation is quite good, too, if you consider the lengthy and detailed thinking that he makes visible for his classmates.

The excerpt is a beautiful illustration of what happens when students appropriate the quality talk features indicative of reasoning. The teacher asks an authentic question and steps back; he doesn't need to step back in because quality talk is already happening. The teacher uses his ear for the talk to step back and let students do the thinking. In the excerpt, students think in high-level ways, explain their thinking in elaborated forms, work together as co-inquirers, reason collectively, ask each other questions, and offer a critical analysis of the text and the issue of cloning. The single, purposeful question the teacher asked in turn 1 did all of that, showing the relationship between planning and asking purposeful questions and how students respond with reasoning and high-level responses. If you haven't already reflected on the questions you typically ask during discussions, it would be good to do so here as you think about the level of reasoning you typically hear in your students' talk. Consider phrasing your questions so they are authentic. Likewise, build on what students say with uptake. The result of asking purposeful questions will be more reasoning from your students.

Talk Assessment Tool for Teachers

In closing this chapter, we introduce the Talk Assessment Tool for Teachers or TATT (see the Appendix). We developed the TATT to promote reflection on the quality of talk in a discussion about text and to help teachers "build an ear" for talk. We designed the tool to be used in pairs, although a teacher could use the tool for self-reflection just as well. In the pair scenario, a teacher and a literacy coach or a critical colleague view a video recorded discussion and assess the quality of the talk either individually or together (Wilkinson, Reninger, and Soter 2010). After completing the TATT, the teacher and colleague reflect on and discuss the quality of the talk to deepen their knowledge of discourse and to consider any corresponding facilitation moves to promote quality talk. Very often, after scoring a discussion with the TATT, teachers have ideas for how they can make their next discussions better. Some might see a need to emphasize a particular ground rule (e.g., yield to others), whereas others might see something specific in the discourse that they want to work on, such as prompting high-level responses in the form of intertextual and affective connections, or stepping back when students really start "chewing" on an idea on their own and begin an episode of exploratory talk.

The TATT empowers teachers with knowledge of the kind of discourse that reflects high-level thinking and comprehension. When you know whether students are talking in ways that reflect high-level thinking and comprehension (or not!), you have accomplished the first step in becoming a better facilitator of discussions. Gaining a deep understanding of discourse and sharpening related facilitation moves means students will be more likely to talk in ways that support the thinking skills they need to interpret text and meet curriculum standards.

In the following three sections of this book, we use a shorthand version of the TATT to illustrate the features of quality talk you are likely to hear when students are engaged in different types of talk: talk to emphasize personal response, talk to emphasize knowledge building, and talk to emphasize argumentation (see the "How Do I Know Students Are Engaged in . . . ?" pages at the conclusion of the each of the next three sections). You can use these as a guide to help you gauge whether or not students are engaged in the type of talk you intend; if some of the features are missing, then you know you need to scaffold students' talk to better reflect the stance towards the text you are hoping to achieve.

3

Research-Based Models of Discussion for Quality Talk

With apologies to Judy Garland and *The Wizard of Oz*, we were tempted to title this chapter "Book Clubs and Literature Circles and Grand Conversations! Oh my!" As teachers of literacy, we are blessed with a plethora of approaches to conducting discussions about texts (and for some, they might be just as intimidating as lions and tigers and bears were to Dorothy). To these, we could add numerous other approaches—Instructional Conversations, Point-Counterpoint, Socratic Seminar, Conversational Discussion Groups, Paideia Seminar, Questioning the Author, Junior Great Books Shared Inquiry, Idea Circles—the list goes on. Almost every week, it seems a professional book or article comes across our desk proclaiming a new approach to conducting classroom discussion.

Does it make a difference which approach to discussion we adopt? Can I have just one "go to" approach? What is involved in setting up the discussion? How do I organize my classroom? What do we need to think about when using one of the approaches? What sort of text do I use for discussion? Is one type of discussion more effective for students' literacy learning than another? These are the types of questions we seek to answer in this chapter and throughout this book.

In this chapter, we help you make sense of the myriad approaches to conducting classroom discussion about text. We identify the major research-based approaches to conducting text-based discussion and give you ways of thinking about them—their key features—to help you understand their similarities and differences, strengths and weaknesses. As you will see, some approaches are more suitable than others depending on what you hope to achieve for your students. Each of the features of discussion constitutes a question you can ask when deciding which approach to use. Our goal is to enable you to choose the approach to discussion that best meets your needs and those of your students.

Multiple Pathways to Quality Talk About Text

Almost twenty years ago, we and our colleagues asked ourselves these same questions. To answer them, we began by identifying the major approaches to conducting text-based discussion. We conducted an exhaustive search of the research literature on classroom discussion, talked with colleagues, and watched numerous videos of students engaged in discussions. We set two criteria for an approach to be considered a major approach.

- First, the approach must have an established place in educational research or practice based on a record of peer-reviewed, empirical studies conducted since 1970. Research published in articles that have undergone peer review have to meet certain standards, so this helped establish the credibility of the studies.

- Second, the approach must have a reasonably well-defined format—in other words, it should look much the same from one classroom to another. There are some approaches that have the same name (e.g., literature discussion groups, book clubs) but would be hard to recognize in the classroom. If we could not pin down what the approach should look like in a classroom, then it would be very hard for us to characterize it for others or to say anything meaningful about its impact on students' literacy learning.

Using these criteria, we identified the nine major approaches featured in this book: Grand Conversations, Book Club (uppercase), Literature Circles, Instructional Conversations, Questioning the Author, Junior Great Books Shared Inquiry, Collaborative Reasoning, Paideia Seminar, and Philosophy for Children. We summarize them briefly in Figure 3.1.

Figure 3.1 Nine Major Approaches to Conducting Text-Based Discussion

Grand Conversations (Peterson and Eeds 2007): Students and the teacher discuss authentic literary texts, often focusing on literary elements. The process involves daily read-alouds by the teacher, extensive reading alone by students, and dialogue that is sparked by a question designed to elicit students' reactions to the text.

Book Club (Raphael and McMahon 1994): Students engage in a program of literature study involving four contexts for literacy learning and instruction: reading, writing, community share, and small-group book clubs. In the small-group discussions (the core component for discussion), students read and discuss the same book with a small group of classmates and then share information with the whole class during community share.

Literature Circles (Daniels 2002; Short and Pierce 1990): Students meet regularly to discuss their reading in small, temporary, typically student-led groups composed of students who have chosen to read the same text. Students prepare for discussions by completing reading logs or another response activity, and often assume different roles in the discussion.

Instructional Conversations (Goldenberg 1992–1993): Discussion is centered around a central idea or theme in the text. The teacher asks questions that may have multiple correct answers, and "weaves" students' responses together so that each contribution builds on the next. Instructional Conversations are often used with English language learners to facilitate language production and development.

Questioning the Author (Beck and McKeown 2006): Readers are taught to see the author as fallible and to interrogate the author's writing. While reading the text as a whole class, either literary or informational, the teacher poses questions, referred to as queries, to encourage the students to grapple with the language and the meaning of the text.

Junior Great Books Shared Inquiry (Great Books Foundation 1987): Students read a text and meet with the teacher to discuss broad, interpretive questions about the selection. To prepare for the discussion, the students read the text twice and annotate the text with a specific focus. Students' notes are used during the discussion.

Collaborative Reasoning (Anderson et al. 1998): Students read a text that raises a "big question" around an issue that could be resolved in a variety of ways. Discussion centers on the big question and students engage in critical thinking and reading, citing reasons and evidence from the text and elsewhere to support their answers.

Paideia Seminar (Billings and Fitzgerald 2002): The teacher facilitates discussion of a "text," broadly defined, by asking questions to enrich students' understanding of the ideas and values inspired by the text and to foster critical thinking. Discussions are typically conducted in the context of pre-seminar and post-seminar activities.

Philosophy for Children (Gregory 2008): Students read philosophical texts that depict fictional children engaged in philosophical dialogue. The teacher initiates discussion by asking students to generate contestable, open-ended questions regarding the central philosophical issue from the text. One or more of these questions becomes the impetus for discussion.

(Adapted from Wilkinson et al. 2020)

In our judgment, all nine approaches are worthy of consideration. They are supported by a substantial body of research (discussed in later sections of this book) and have a strong record of use in classrooms. What's more, they have the potential to engage students in quality talk about text and to enhance students' literacy development. Although they are similar in many respects, they involve different ways of organizing the discussion and have different strengths when it comes to addressing English language arts standards.

Of course, there are other approaches to text-based discussion besides those featured in this book. We would be remiss if we did not mention Conversational Discussion Groups (O'Flahavan 1989), Dialogical-Thinking Reading Lessons (Commeyras 1993), Idea Circles (Guthrie and McCann 1996), and Point-Counterpoint (Rogers 1990). These approaches do not satisfy our criteria, though they do have important qualities that may prove useful in your classroom. We would also be remiss if we did not mention Accountable Talk (Michaels, O'Connor, and Resnick 2008; Michaels, O'Connor, Hall, and Resnick 2002). Accountable Talk is an important and widely used approach to conducting academically productive talk in a variety of curriculum areas (e.g., math, language arts, social studies). Although applicable for promoting reading comprehension (Wolf, Crosson, and Resnick 2005), Accountable Talk is not included because it is a broad-based approach that is not specific to literacy or the language arts (see Resnick 1999; Resnick and Hall 1998). A useful resource for teachers on Accountable Talk can be found in Resnick, Asterhan, and Clarke (2018; available from http://www.iaoed.org).

Ways to Think About Discussion

Having identified the major research-based approaches to conducting classroom discussions about text, we asked ourselves a series of questions about them. The answers to these questions helped us understand the similarities and differences between the approaches. These are questions you can ask yourself about any discussion approach you are planning to use.

Question Regarding Stance

First and foremost, we asked ourselves about the stance or orientation toward the text: "What stance toward the text does the approach emphasize?" Here the word *stance* refers to the reader's orientation toward the text and reflects the purpose for reading—what the teacher and students hope to get out of it. When individual readers read a text, they can adopt multiple stances, but one stance usually stands out as primary. The same is true of classroom discussions; when students engage with the text, there may be multiple stances evident in the talk, though one stance tends to predominate.

We have Louise Rosenblatt (1904–2005), an English professor and literary theorist, to thank for identifying two different types of stance toward text, *efferent* and *aesthetic*. If a reader adopts an efferent stance toward the text, their focus is on "the ideas, information, directions, conclusions to be retained, used, or acted on *after* the reading event" (Rosenblatt 1978, 27, italics added). Discussions that give prominence to an efferent stance privilege reading to acquire and retrieve information—reading to learn, if you like. By contrast, if a reader adopts an aesthetic stance, their focus is on the lived-through experience of the text *during* reading—the "associations, feelings, attitudes, and ideas" (25) that the words in the text arouse. Discussions that give prominence to an aesthetic stance privilege the reader's personal response, their spontaneous connections to all aspects of the textual experience.

Arguably, not all discussions that privilege personal response achieve what Rosenblatt called an aesthetic stance (Soter et al. 2010). Reading with an aesthetic stance has a connoisseurship-like quality. Much like a wine connoisseur savors the qualities of a fine wine, the aesthetic reader savors the literary qualities of the text and appreciates how those qualities influence their personal response (e.g., "I loved the way the author used those words to conjure up an image of the unworn baby shoes. I felt so sad when I thought about what must have happened"). But some discussions, especially among younger readers, often evoke a response that is less reflective about the text and more emotional (e.g., "I wouldn't like that!"). To capture these less reflective, emotional reactions, we prefer to use the term *expressive* (Jakobson 1987) when describing students' response or stance.

However, Rosenblatt's two stances get us only so far. There is another important stance toward text that readers can adopt, a critical-analytic stance. If a reader adopts a critical-analytic stance, their focus is a more critical reading of the text in search of the underlying arguments, assumptions, worldviews, or beliefs (Wade, Thompson, and Watkins 1994). Discussions that give prominence to a critical-analytic stance engage the reader's querying mind, prompting them to ask questions, to go "below the surface" and interrogate the text.

It is tempting to think that the stance a reader adopts is determined by the text. To be sure, the text plays a role in the stance a reader takes—some types of text (e.g., literary, informational, poetry) reward one type of reading more than the others. But other factors come into play to determine stance as well: the situation, the background and experience of the reader, and the goals for reading (Rosenblatt 2013). In fact, one might say that any text can be read from a different stance. To illustrate, in Figure 3.2 we show how a reader might read "Humpty

Figure 3.2 Different Stances a Reader Might Adopt in Response to "Humpty Dumpty"

Stance	Reader's Focus	Example Response
Efferent	Acquiring and retrieving information from the text	"Oh, I see. Humpty fell off a wall, and the king's men tried to put him back together, but they couldn't."
Expressive/aesthetic	Spontaneously connecting to various aspects of the textual experience	"Ouch! That must have hurt. I wonder if Humpty Dumpty cried? I would have." "The language is light and whimsical, yet what happened is really quite sad. It's odd."
Critical-analytic	Interrogating the text in search of the underlying arguments, assumptions, worldviews, or beliefs	"Who was Humpty Dumpty, and why did the King care about him?"

(Adapted from Lightner and Wilkinson 2017, 437)

Dumpty" from the perspective of any one of the three stances. So, beyond the text, what is important is the overall purpose for reading and the orientation toward the text that you want students to adopt.

Questions About Control

Next, we asked questions that considered how much control the teacher had over the discussion (who chooses the text, decides on the topic, etc.):

- *Who chooses the text for discussion?* In most cases, the teacher chooses the text to be discussed. But for some discussions (e.g., Literature Circles), the teacher might preselect books, perhaps all on the same theme (e.g., immigration or new life), and each group would choose a different book. Giving students more choice over the text helps support their motivation to read.

- *Who controls the topic for discussion?* The teacher can control the topic by asking questions that guide the discussion. On the other hand, students can control the topic when they are free to follow their own interests or themes and to introduce new topics. A third possibility is that both teacher and students control the topic where the teacher guides the direction of the discussion but allows students to explore topics in their own way.

- *Who controls turns for speaking?* When the teacher calls on students to speak, then the teacher controls the turn taking. But sometimes, students have the freedom to decide who gets to talk and when—what we call an "open participation structure" (of course, in peer-led discussions, students have complete control over turn taking). In some discussions, teachers and students share responsibility for turn taking.

- *Who has interpretive authority?* If, during a discussion, the teacher accepts only those answers that they believe to be right, then the teacher holds the interpretive authority (remember the I-R-E pattern we talked about in Chapter 1). However, if students are the ones who evaluate each other's statements and construct meaning without guidance from the teacher, then the students have interpretive authority. Students and teachers can also share interpretive authority.

Question Regarding Author's Intention

Next, we asked "How much emphasis is placed on the intention of the author?"—an important aspect of close reading and analyzing literature. In some discussions, there is a heavy emphasis on discerning the author's intentions. For example, a teacher might ask, "Why do you think the author described the house in that way?" "What do you think the author was trying to do by using the phrase *dark and gloomy?*" "What do you think he is trying to tell you here?" If these types of questions are asked frequently, we would say the emphasis on author intent is high; if these types of questions are asked sometimes or not at all, we would say the emphasis on author intent is medium or low, respectively. These types of questions are often used during close reading to encourage students to attend to the language used by the author, and to make inferences as to why the author might have chosen to construct the text in a certain way (recognizing, of course, that an author's intentions are not always conscious).

Questions About Organizational Features

Finally, we looked at basic organizational features of the discussion and asked these questions:

- What type of text is used (literary, informational, poetry, mixed)?
- Is the discussion conducted with the whole class or with a small group of students?

- Are students in the discussion grouped homogeneously or heterogeneously in terms of their reading ability?

- Is the discussion led by the teacher or by students?

- Do students read the text before or during the discussion?

Putting It All Together

In Figure 3.3, we see how the nine approaches stack up in terms of the answers to these questions. It is important to remember that we have characterized the approaches here and elsewhere in the book according to how they are *typically* conducted in classrooms. There can, of course, be some variations—for example, in the type of text used or in the composition of the group. Note that in Figure 3.3, Book Club refers to the small-group discussions in this approach, not to the whole-class community share (see Chapter 5).

We can see that the approaches are most similar in terms of five features. All except two approaches are teacher led. As we will learn later, Literature Circles can be either teacher or student led. All are conducted with groups or classes that are mixed or heterogeneous in student ability. All except Questioning the Author and, usually, Instructional Conversations, have students read the texts before meeting for discussion. All are typically used with literary texts, though Questioning the Author and Paideia Seminar are often used with informational texts. And all except Questioning the Author have a low to medium focus on the intention of the author (in Questioning the Author, talking about what the author intended is part of the rationale for the approach). For the most part, talking about author intent is incidental to these discussions.

We can see that the approaches vary somewhat in terms of the size of the discussion group (small-group versus whole-class). Questioning the Author, Junior Great Books Shared Inquiry, Paideia Seminar, and Philosophy for Children typically use whole-class discussion (or, at least, discussions with large groups of about ten to fourteen students); whereas the other approaches typically involve small groups. Whole-class discussion provides an ideal and efficient arrangement for modeling and scaffolding the sort of talk you would like students to use. Of course, in whole-class discussion, the teacher has to carefully control turn taking—who gets to speak and when—or encourage the students to carefully monitor and control their own turn taking. This tends to slow down the discussion (which has its advantages when dealing with a large number of

Figure 3.3 Comparing Discussion Approaches by Features

FEATURE	APPROACH								
	GC	BC[1]	LC	IC	QtA	JGB-SI	CR	PS	P4C
Efferent stance?	medium	medium	medium	high	high	high	medium	medium	medium
Expressive/aesthetic stance?	high	high	high	low	low	low	medium	medium	medium
Critical-analytic stance?	medium	medium	low	medium	medium	medium	high	high	high
Who chooses the text?	teacher	teacher	students	teacher	teacher	teacher	teacher	teacher	teacher
Who controls the topic?	students	students	students	teacher	teacher	teacher	teacher	teacher	students & teacher
Who controls turns?	students & teacher	students	students	students & teacher	teacher	students & teacher	students	students & teacher	students & teacher
Who has interpretive authority?	students & teacher	students	students	teacher	teacher	teacher	students	students	students
Authorial intention?	medium	medium	low	low	high	medium	low	medium	low
What type of text?	literary	literary	literary	literary	literary & informational	literary	literary	literary & informational	literary
Whole-class or small-group?	small-group	small-group	small-group	small-group	whole-class	whole-class[2]	small-group	whole-class	whole-class
Grouping by ability?	mixed	mixed	mixed	mixed	mixed	mixed	mixed	mixed	mixed
Teacher- or student-led?	teacher	students	students/teacher	teacher	teacher	teacher	teacher	teacher	teacher
Text read before or during?	before	before	before	during	during	before	before	before	before

Notes: [1] Features refer to discussions that take place during the small-group book club, not whole-class community share. [2] Shared Inquiry is often conducted with large groups of ten to twenty students. (Adapted from Wilkinson et al. 2020).

students or when you want a deliberative focus on the kind of talk you want). Small-group discussion provides more opportunities for students to speak and exchange points of view.

Where the approaches differ most is in the degree of control over the discussion exerted by the teacher versus the students, and in the stance toward the text. When we refer to degree of control, we are thinking about who chooses the text, who controls the topic of discussion, who controls the turns, and who has interpretive authority. In Grand Conversations, Book Club, and Literature Circles, students have most control over discussions. As you would expect, in most cases, these are peer-led discussions. By contrast, in Instructional Conversations, Questioning the Author, and Junior Great Books Shared Inquiry, teachers have most control over discussions. Occupying the middle ground are Collaborative Reasoning, Paideia Seminar, and Philosophy for Children. In these approaches, the teacher chooses the text and either controls or shares control of the topic, but the students have considerable control over turns and interpretive authority. In Paideia Seminar and Philosophy for Children, the teacher exhibits some control over turns because of the need to manage students' speaking rights in whole-class discussions.

As for stance, Grand Conversations, Book Club, and Literature Circles give prominence to an expressive or aesthetic stance. Instructional Conversations, Questioning the Author, and Shared Inquiry give prominence to an efferent stance. And Collaborative Reasoning, Paideia Seminar, and Philosophy for Children give prominence to a critical-analytic stance. As we will see in Chapter 9, the talk in Shared Inquiry shows some similarities with talk in the three critical-analytic approaches, so Shared Inquiry can also be used to foster critical thinking. Nonetheless, the focus of this approach is on deepening students' understanding of the text.

You might have noticed a pattern emerging here: who has control over the discussion and the stance toward the text are connected. Discussions in which students have the greatest control tend to be those that give prominence to an expressive or aesthetic stance toward the text (Grand Conversations, Book Club, Literature Circles). Conversely, discussions in which teachers have the greatest control tend to be those that give prominence to an efferent stance (Instructional Conversations, Questioning the Author, Shared Inquiry). Discussions in which teachers and students share control tend to be those that give prominence to a critical-analytic stance (Collaborative Reasoning, Paideia Seminar, Philosophy for Children).

Deciding Which Approach to Use

The takeaway from this chapter, and indeed the book as a whole, is that we have available to us a menu of well-researched approaches for conducting text-based discussion, and we need to choose thoughtfully. Some approaches are better suited to instructional goals that emphasize acquiring information from a text, whereas others are better suited to goals that require students to respond to literature on an aesthetic or expressive level. Still others are better suited to goals of adopting a critical-analytic stance toward the text.

Deciding which discussion approach to choose might seem daunting but it's not really. When choosing an approach, think about:

- your instructional goals and the standards you need to address.

- your students' needs. Would they feel more comfortable in a whole-class or small-group discussion? How much support will they need from you during the discussion to help address your goals and the standards?

- the discussion approach that aligns best with your goals, standards, and the needs of your students.

Good discussions do not have to adhere strictly to one particular approach. You might find that, in your classroom and with your particular students, the most productive discussions result from using some variation on a known approach or from some combination of approaches described in this book.

Beyond any one approach, the important thing to keep in mind is that the way you set up and orchestrate a discussion matters. The stance you and your students adopt, how much control you exercise over the discussion, the focus on the author, and basic organizational features all make a difference. In the following three sections of this book, we will see that the different ways of organizing and conducting discussion promote different types of talk, and that talk promotes different ways of thinking about and responding to text.

SECTION II

Talk About Text to Emphasize Personal Response

f you wanted students to talk about literary text in much the same way people do outside of school, in book clubs and other social gatherings, what would you do? You would probably use one of the three approaches to classroom discussion described in this section: Grand Conversations, Book Club, and Literature Circles. In these discussions, students have the opportunity to share their thoughts about a story—to make rich, personal connections to their own lives, experiences, and feelings, and perhaps even to savor the literary elements (e.g., character, mood, style) that arouse these connections. The goal of these approaches is for students to enjoy (and learn to enjoy!) good literature, to respond to it in personal, creative, even critical ways, and to engage deeply with it. When students are responding to literary text on a personal, emotional level (e.g., "I felt sad when I read that he died." "I had a friend just like that."), we say they are responding to the text on an "expressive" (Jakobson 1987) level; when they are able to appreciate the literary qualities that influence their personal responses (e.g., "I liked the way the author had her *stagger*. I could just picture it in my head."), we say they are responding on an "aesthetic" (Rosenblatt 1978) level. All the approaches described in this section help students respond to text on an emotional or expressive level; Grand Conversations is also especially suited to helping students respond on an aesthetic level.

As you might expect, students have considerable control over these discussions. In most cases, the students are in charge of the discussions and decide what to talk about, who gets to speak, and when. They also get to decide how to interpret the text (i.e., they have interpretive authority). In Literature Circles, students even choose the text, albeit from a selection provided by the teacher. In Grand Conversations, teachers have a little more control because they lead the discussion and choose the text.

In all three approaches, the students read the text before the discussion and then meet in small groups. Literary texts are typically the subject of discussion although, increasingly, informational texts are used in Literature Circles.

Why do these approaches to classroom discussion work as they do? One explanation comes from Rosenblatt's (1978) reader-response theory. The idea behind this theory is that a reader's personal response to a text enables the reader to make deeper connections to it. In other words, by allowing students to make and share their personal responses to the text, we provide a vehicle for them to engage in higher-level thinking and more sophisticated interpretation of the text. According to this theory, a reader's prior knowledge and experience plays a vital role in shaping the way the reader responds to and understands the text, and each reader will create a somewhat different interpretation.

Another, related, explanation comes from Vygotsky's (1978) theory of the role of language in thinking. When students engage in talk about the text, they are not only sharing their ways of thinking about it, they are also building knowledge and understanding together that goes beyond what each has brought to the discussion (remember "interthinking" from Chapter 1). In other words, the students' talk serves as a scaffold to foster higher-level thinking about the text. Ultimately, the theory goes, by listening to others and thinking together, students walk away from the discussion with an enhanced understanding and appreciation of the text.

4

Grand Conversations

GRAND CONVERSATIONS

Research Support

- Foster deep, personal connections to a story
- Engage students in high-level thinking about a story
- Help students develop literary insights
- Can engage children as young as first grade, and children of varied abilities, in rich conversations about literature

Learning How

Have faith in children's interpretive abilities.

Engage in your own literature study; learn how elements of story and authors' use of them contribute to the meaning.

Goals

To foster students' aesthetic response to literature (i.e., to experience the text as literature, promote deep personal connections, and develop literary insights)

Typical Features

- Literary text
- Small-group discussion
- Heterogeneous group
- Teacher led
- Teacher chooses text
- Students read text before coming to discussion
- Students have control of topic
- Students and teacher share control of turn taking
- Students and teacher share interpretive authority
- Moderate focus on author intent

Typical Teacher Questions

What do you think?

What did you notice?

What did you like?

What did you not like?

How did this make you feel?

What is this (really) about?

What does it mean that . . .?

What do we know about . . . ?

Why do you think . . . ?

What does that tell us (about) . . . ?

Typical Student Comments

I was thinking about . . .

I thought about that too.

When I read that, it made me feel . . .

Maybe . . .

This reminds me of . . .

Teacher's Role

- Act as a regular participant in the conversation.
- Act as a guide by asking interpretive questions to facilitate students' interpretation.
- Act as a "literary curator," drawing attention to, and sometimes labeling, story elements as the opportunities arise in the conversation (called "shooting literary arrows" at teachable moments).

What the Talk Sounds Like

In the following Grand Conversation, a teacher and a small group of third-grade students are discussing *Sarah, Plain and Tall* by Patricia MacLachlan (1985). The story is about a farmer in the Midwest during the late nineteenth century who is a widower and father of two young children. He finds it hard to run the farm and the household without a wife, so he puts an advertisement in an East Coast newspaper for a wife, and Sarah, from Maine, is the woman who answers the ad. In this excerpt, the teacher and the students are discussing Sarah's recent arrival and her reaction to her first Midwest storm. Figure 4.1 lists the features of quality talk in the excerpt.

Kara: Sarah is very frightened and Caleb was. It was a scary moment.

Teacher: Why do you think Sarah might be more upset than Jacob during the storm? What do we know about the characters?

Chris: Because she is a girl and she might get more scared.

Teacher: So you think a girl could get more scared? That's one idea.

Michelle: Maybe she wasn't used to that kind of storm.

Teacher: Did she ever mention that kind of storm where she's from? That's another idea.

Talia: Well, Sarah was very brave when she went out to the storm.

Chris: She is real brave at the part where the buzzards are around the lamb that was dead. She tried to go in and scare them all off. If they get really mad, they could tear you all up.

Michelle: When Jacob said, "I've got to fix the roof." She said, "No, *we've* got to," because she didn't want to feel too left out and too girlish to stay inside and to take care of the kids and stuff. She wanted to try to get some action and do other things sort of dangerous. She could have fallen from the roof.

(Eeds and Peterson 1995, 20)

Figure 4.1 Examples of Quality Talk

Features	Examples	Why They Are Productive
Reasoning words	*would, could, maybe, might, if, I think, because, how, why* Michelle: *Maybe* she wasn't used to that kind of storm.	Reasoning words signal students' high-level thinking and reasoning. Speculation, generalization, and analysis are cognitive functions evidenced when students use reasoning words.
Elaborated explanation	Michelle: When Jacob said "I've got to fix the roof." She said, "No, *we've* got to," because she didn't want to feel too left out and too girlish to stay inside and to take care of the kids and stuff. She wanted to get some action and do other things sort of dangerous. She could have fallen from the roof.	When students offer a chain of linked reasons, they are elaborating their explanations about a position and thinking in high-level ways. Elaborations foster cognitive restructuring and rehearsal on the part of the student giving the explanation. Students benefit from hearing this "visible thinking" as a model for their own elaborated thinking.
Exploratory talk	The students explore whether Sarah is afraid of the storm from Chris' first turn to the end of the excerpt (although typically the teacher is not part of exploratory talk). Notice Talia's challenge to the idea that Sarah was afraid because she was a woman ("Well, Sarah was very brave when she went out to the storm"). A challenge is an essential feature of exploratory talk.	Exploratory talk makes deeper thinking visible, promotes alternative points of view, elicits inquiry, and enables students to sort out ideas collaboratively.
Authentic question	Teacher: Why do you think Sarah might be more upset than Jacob during the storm?	Authentic questions create space for students' talk and high-level thinking about text. This authentic question is also an example of uptake, and it prompts elaborations, use of reasoning words, and exploratory talk.

In Grand Conversations, students hold the floor the majority of the time, though they share control of turn taking and interpretive authority with the teacher. Most of the teacher questions are authentic, demonstrate uptake, and tend to promote students' high-level thinking. There are elaborated explanations, often long ones, and occasional episodes of exploratory talk. Students use reasoning words quite a lot, especially reasoning words that suggest speculation (*would, could, maybe, might, if*), taking a position (*I think*), and analysis and generalization (*because, how, why*). Students also tend to refer to the text when the elements of the story, such as plot or character, are the focus of the discussion.

What is not prominent in Grand Conversations are the kinds of responses that reflect connections to other discussions (shared-knowledge responses) or other texts (intertextual responses). We sometimes see and hear connections made to personal experiences (affective responses) because teachers often ask questions such as "What did you like?" or "What did you think?" during an initial discussion and before a deeper study of the story takes place. Students co-construct their interpretations of the story with a modicum of structure and emphasis on the literary features provided by the teachers. Overall, Grand Conversations promote reasoning and high-level thinking about text.

THE STORY BEHIND GRAND CONVERSATIONS

If you were to walk into an elementary school classroom in the 1970s or even early 1980s, rarely would you find real discussions of authentic literature. Students would be reading excerpts or adaptations of literature in a basal series and the teacher would probably be asking the comprehension questions prescribed in the basal reading program. He would call on students to respond, evaluate their answers against those in the teacher's manual, and guide students toward a predetermined interpretation of the story. When listening to recordings of literature discussions occurring in classrooms at the time, Bryant Fillion (1981), a teacher educator, described them as being more like "inquisitions" (40) than real discussions.

In the late 1980s, Ralph Peterson and Maryann Eeds, professors at Arizona State University, sought to revolutionize literature discussions. They wanted to make them more like the genuine conversations that adults have about literature, so they introduced what they called Grand Conversations. They credit the name to Jim Higgins, who used the term in a speech he gave to teachers in 1985 while visiting Arizona State University. In describing how literature was used in American classrooms, echoing Fillion, Higgins said something to the effect that "what you most often get are gentle inquisitions, when what you really want are Grand Conversations" (Eeds and Wells 1989, 4). The fundamental beliefs underlying Peterson and Eeds' vision of Grand Conversations were as follows:

- Story is an important way of understanding the world.
- Interpretation involves a transaction between the reader and the text.

- Children are born meaning makers.
- Learning is a social process.

   Maryann Eeds and Deborah Wells, a doctoral student at Arizona State University, published the first empirical study of Grand Conversations in 1989. In this study they explored the viability of conducting Grand Conversations with fifth and sixth graders. Since then, other educators have explored their use with different populations of students and with slight variations on the approach envisioned by Eeds and Peterson.

   Today, the phrase *Grand Conversations* has become a banner for almost any response-centered discussion about literature, including literature circles, book clubs, and literature study groups. However, like Eeds and Peterson (1997), we believe that certain key features of a Grand Conversation distinguish it from these other approaches: the role of the teacher in furthering students' dialogue, a focus on story elements as a means of helping students achieve deep understanding of literature, and a fundamental belief in the interpretive abilities of children. We use the phrase *Grand Conversations* in this sense of the term.

Research Support

The research support for Grand Conversations is more limited than that of other approaches included in this book. By our count, there have been six published articles and one doctoral dissertation reporting studies of Grand Conversations (though, with two of the studies, we find ourselves questioning whether the discussions fully represent Peterson and Eeds' vision). Most studies provide descriptive, naturalistic accounts of what happens when students engage in the discussions. The researchers typically transcribe audio recordings of the discussions and categorize students' contributions to gauge the quality of their responses, sometimes supplementing these data with information from teacher journals and field notes.

   Eeds and Wells (1989) conducted the initial, seminal study of Grand Conversations. They audio taped four literature study groups of fifth- and sixth-grade students, led by preservice teachers. Each group met twice a week for four to five weeks and read a different novel (Natalie Babbitt's *Tuck Everlasting*, Betsy Byars' *After the Goat Man*, Louise Fitzhugh's *Harriet the Spy*, and Meredith Pierce's *The Dark Angel*). The researchers encouraged the preservice teachers to refrain from asking comprehension questions and to let meaning emerge from the conversations, although they could step in at teachable moments to talk about literary elements. Eeds and Wells analyzed transcripts of the discussions and grouped students' utterances into categories. What they found was revealing! Even with teachers taking something of a back seat, students demonstrated comprehension of the stories much as they would in traditional discussions. But what was even more interesting was that students went beyond simply sharing ideas about what happened in the novels—they responded to the texts in an aesthetic, or "literary way" (26). They made personal connections inspired by the novels; they actively interpreted what they were reading—hypothesizing, interpreting, and verifying—and they offered critiques of the literature (e.g., commenting on the author's purpose and choice of language). Eeds and Wells' discovery, at the time, was that students as young as ten years old could engage in rich discussions of literary works when given the freedom and support to do so.

Researchers have since found that even younger students can respond to literature in an aesthetic way. McGee (1992) extended Eeds and Wells' (1989) study by conducting Grand Conversations with first graders and examining their responses to stories that had been read aloud to them. McGee also had teachers ask an interpretive question that prompted students to explore the significance of the stories. Her results showed that students offered similar types of responses to those made by Eeds and Wells' fourth and fifth graders.

Sheila Wells (2012), in her doctoral dissertation, conducted Grand Conversations with fourth- and fifth-grade students with disabilities and living in poverty. Using literature describing characters facing problems similar to those of her students, she reported that Grand Conversations led to an increase in students' motivation to read and that students were able to make rich aesthetic connections to the texts. Other researchers have also shown that Grand Conversations can be used to good effect with fourth graders, including those who are at risk in learning to read (Hart, Escobar, and Jacobson 2001; McCutchen, Laird, and Graves 1993).

Researchers have also examined the roles of teachers in Grand Conversations. Eeds and Wells (1991) examined data from third-grade and fifth-grade discussion groups to offer guidelines for teachers. They showed that teachers have an important role to play as a "literary curator"; in this role, teachers identify teachable moments where they can step into the discussion to promote awareness of literary elements that help students gain a deeper understanding of the story. McGee, Courtney, and Lomax (1994), in a follow-up to their earlier study, analyzed the roles of first-grade teachers in Grand Conversations. While painting a broader picture of the teachers' roles, they noted that teachers sometimes found it difficult to adopt the role of literary curator because they were not always able to recognize when students' responses reflected literary elements.

What we learn from this research is that young children of varied abilities can engage in rich conversations about literature. They not only can share ideas about what happened and demonstrate understanding of the text, they also can make personal connections to the text, engage in high-level thinking, and evaluate the text as literature. Because the researchers did not go beyond looking at students' discourse, we do not know whether the rich conversations lead to enhanced comprehension as measured by tests given to students, nor how the results might compare to those from other approaches discussed in this book. Nonetheless, the depth of understanding and literary insight shown in students' talk is extraordinary. Grand Conversations deserve a place in a teacher's discussion repertoire.

GRAND CONVERSATIONS in Practice

Planning for Grand Conversations

QUICK GUIDE

1. Begin with the goal that your students will intensively study a story.

2. Plan how to involve the family at home in the study of the story. Ask and consider: "Should I send the text selection home for family reading?" "Do I simply inform the family of the text?" "Should students report their thinking about the story to a family member or a friend?"

3. Select a literary text with layers of interest to readers (e.g., strong themes, interesting plot, compelling characters, dramatic tensions, inspiring places).

4. Read the selection with an eye toward your own personal response (e.g., interests, connections) and toward thinking about what is intriguing, beguiling, or puzzling. Note where you slow down and reread because you want to do so!

5. Reflect on the structure of the story, noticing how the author captures the reader's attention, and highlight these places. You'll be ready to place these ideas into a discussion when you take on the role of literary curator.

Grand Conversations is an approach to discussion that is part of a broader literature study program and literacy block in the classroom. The literature study program comprises four areas of planning for the teacher: read-alouds with the whole class, working with families, extensive reading, and intensive reading with Grand Conversations (see Figure 4.2).

During intensive reading, students read, study, and prepare for the discussion or Grand Conversation with a small group of classmates and the teacher. Usually, the teacher selects the text for a group, but sometimes students might sign up to read a particular text of their interest from ones the teacher has introduced. Either way, students read the text or selection of the text twice in preparation for the Grand Conversation. Initially, they make notes about their thinking and personal connections and responses as they read (e.g., *This made me think of . . .* or *I like this part because . . .*), but the main point of the first reading is to read for enjoyment and the pleasure of the literary experience.

After this first reading, the teacher meets with the small group to check in, asking the students if they are making progress or having any difficulties. A short, preliminary discussion takes place where the teacher prompts with questions such as "What do you think so far?" "What do you like or not like?" "How does this story make you feel?" This approach to facilitating the initial discussion is straightforward, reflecting the hundreds, maybe thousands of times we have asked children these kinds of questions to get them talking about their reading. Students in the small group engage in a short dialogue with the teacher, while the other students in the class are busy with their independent reading and preparation for a Grand Conversation.

What happens next is a little trickier, but manageable if you keep a focus on the elements of a story (mood, tension, character, theme, etc.). The goal is to facilitate a second discussion, the Grand Conversation, to help the students build on their personal connections and responses from the first discussion and

Figure 4.2 Four Areas of Planning for Classroom-Based Literature Study and Grand Conversations

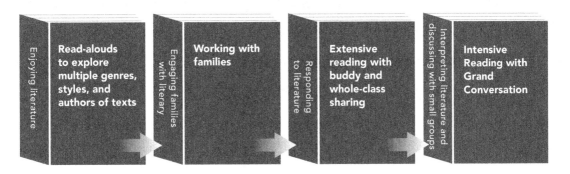

to interpret the text, answering big questions, such as "What is the character's biggest problem?" The teacher assigns students to reread a section of the text more deeply and analytically for the purpose of interpreting the story. To support this process, teachers show students how to mark the text (with sticky notes or annotations) at the places where they "slow down and think." At this point, the students have a section or chapter of the story to study and ponder, and they reread with new, targeted attention as they prepare for the Grand Conversation.

This is how it works. Imagine that a group of third graders is reading *Charlotte's Web* by E. B. White (1952) and that the students, during the first discussion, express intrigue with the introduction of Charlotte's character (Chapter 5) as a cruel, but at the same time, a sweet and clever, new friend to Wilbur. By the end of the chapter, Wilbur is a little worried about befriending such a terrifying creature. Building from the students' interest, the teacher designs the "study," or focus, for the Grand Conversation around the issue or concern. The teacher will assign students to reread the chapter and look carefully at the ways the author softens Charlotte's image while also making her fearsome. At the Grand Conversation, the teachers poses a big interpretive question to begin the Grand Conversation, asking, for instance, "What does it mean that Wilbur is worried about being friends with Charlotte?" or "Should Wilbur be so worried about becoming friends with Charlotte?"

Teacher's Role in Grand Conversations

Teachers use follow-up questions and step into the Grand Conversation to share genuine ideas, questions, and other comments to promote the study of literature and to offer literary insights. The role of the teacher is to listen carefully for places to step in, acting out the facilitation in four ways: to focus attention on ideas and story elements that are rich with meaning, to prompt elaboration and extended thinking about a story element, to ask follow-up questions, and to reply to students with genuine comments. See Figure 4.3.

Approach in Action: Language Arts, Grade 5

The following small-group Grand Conversation took place in a fifth-grade classroom. The teacher and students were discussing *The Secret Garden* by Frances Hodgson Burnett (1911), which is a story about Mary, a sad, lonely, and privileged child of a wealthy family, whose disposition is disagreeable until she begins to change through friendship and the pride that comes with bringing a dying garden back to life.

Figure 4.3 Teacher Participation in Grand Conversation

Teacher Steps in to . . .	What It Does for Learning	Example
Ask a follow-up question to focus attention on ideas and details of the story that are rich with meaning and reflect story elements.	Stepping in to focus on a "meaty idea" elicits the kind of thinking that goes beyond a personal opinion or response, keeping the conversation on the details and evidence from the story.	"But what is this really about, when Wilbur thinks to himself, 'I've got a new friend . . . but what a gamble friendship is'?"
Prompt to elaborate an idea ("Let's think more about that").	Putting the brakes on the conversation to extend it through rereading or reflecting heightens students' perceptive powers needed for critical interpretation. These prompts also draw out additional prior knowledge from students.	"What else do we know about that?" "Let's focus on this more. Were there other characters that acted this way?"
Ask follow-up questions about story elements at "literary teachable moments."	Using a follow-up question to point out story elements, such as character, place, or mood, emphasizes the literary insights students must have in order to enjoy literature. Many curriculum standards relate to story elements.	"Since we're talking about Mary (character) and changing, let's talk about Mary and the garden (place). What do we know about this?"
Participate as a member of the group.	The teacher's participation fosters collaboration, showing that the talk is co-constructed among all the participants, including the teacher. It removes the teacher from being the authority in the discussion. It also shows students that making interpretations is a transaction between the text, one's own thinking, and the thinking of others in discussion.	"I'm thinking, as you say that, about Wilbur." "I wonder why the author described Charlotte as cruel, clever, and sweet?"

Here the teacher gently prompts students to contemplate the regrowth of the garden as a metaphor for Mary's transformation.

Teacher: Since we're talking about Mary and changing, can we talk about Mary and the garden?

> Here the teacher asks a follow-up question to direct attention to an element of literature (character) and the central metaphor of the book.

Randy: It started to grow.

Teacher: The garden did?

> The teachers uses uptake.

Randy: Yeah. It was like magic. It just started to blossom and stuff. The way she took care of it and stuff.

Shawna: I like the way they described how it wasn't dead, but it was wickering or something.

> Shawna shows her appreciation for the author's use of language.

Randy: I think . . . I think . . .

> Here the students grapple with the language and meaning. They build on each other's ideas to reach an understanding of the text. It is not quite exploratory talk because there is no disagreement; it is more cumulative.

Shawna: When you break them (vines) in half they weren't dead. They were all dried out, but there were still some roots getting ready to grow—wickered or something like that.

Randy: Wickered? I think that means still alive.

Shawna: On the outside it was all dried out but when you break them in half it's still good and they grow as soon as the right time and season comes.

Randy: Like it's green! Like when you pick a fruit it looks ripe on the outside and you end up biting it and on the inside and it's all green.

Shawna: Nasty!

Teacher: Except this is the other way around, though, because she's saying it looks bad on the outside but it's good on the inside.

> Notice how the teacher tries to clarify the meaning to help convey the metaphor but also responds as a participant.

Randy: Yeah, yeah.

Teacher: I'm thinking about people when you say that.

Shawna: (looking askance) You break people in half? (both children laugh)

Randy: No, like they're still alive and they look dead, they'd bury them and they'd end up buried alive or something.

Teacher: Hmmm.

Shawna: You see that on a lot of soap operas.

Randy: Only now they have different things to tell to see your heartbeat, and if it goes then you're dead.

Teacher: I'm thinking, as you say that, about the characters in the book.

Shawna: (a pause—then a look of dawning) It seems like Martha, I mean Mary . . . she was like real mean and nasty on the outside, but then later on in the story she taught Colin how to walk.

Randy: And her outside . . . her inside came to the outside. Like she was mean on the outside but inside she was nice. And then after a while her inside came out.

Shawna: All of the good came out. That's when she taught Colin to walk and started taking care of plants.

Teacher: (writing a list of insights about character on chart paper) I want to hold onto this . . . Were there other characters changing?

Here the teacher gently prompts students to think about the parallels between the garden and Mary. Notice, again, how she contributes as a participant.

Because the student did not yet see the connection between the garden and Mary, she prompts them again, only this time more specifically.

Here the students start to understand the metaphor.

Students co-construct an interpretation.

Students explore the metaphor further.

(Peterson and Eeds 2007, 84–85)

This excerpt illustrates several features of a Grand Conversation, the major one of which is the deliberate focus on the main character, Mary, and her transformation as a result of the interaction with the place of the story, the garden. The teacher facilitates a discussion about character in several ways: she asks an authentic question, restates the idea of character, and participates in genuine ways, keeping the ideas focused on Mary's changes. Peterson and Eeds (2007) refer to this targeted and sustained focus on a story element as "shooting literary arrows" for students. For example, the teacher's genuine comment, "I'm thinking, as you say that, about the characters in the book," sets the stage for the students' awareness of the metaphor of the garden for Mary's life. Randy and Shawna consider the idea of Mary's change, using their prior knowledge to make sense of this transformation. The reasoning words in their talk, *I think, but,* and *if,* and some of Shawna's responses reflecting analysis and generalization, suggest that the students are reasoning about the story and thinking in high-level ways as they co-construct an interpretation of what's happening in this section of the book.

A Grand Conversation is a way of using dialogue to interpret literature and contemplate its meaning in order to understand the world, and it is through this process that we come to value literature as an art form and to enjoy reading. If we want students to acquire a disposition to read for joy and pleasure, Grand Conversation is an approach to take on and try. In an age in which we can gain access to information in split seconds, our thoughts rush by in split seconds, too, leaving little time for contemplation, curiosity, or imagination—a few of the sources of reading for enjoyment. We may need discussion approaches like Grand Conversations in our repertoire now more than ever. Just as the secret garden helped Mary find something happier for herself in life, Grand Conversations have the potential to bring a sense of joy for reading to life.

READ MORE

Eeds, Maryann, and Ralph Peterson. 1991. "Teacher as Curator: Learning to Talk About Literature." *The Reading Teacher* 45 (2): 118–126.

———. 1997. "Literature Studies Revisited: Some Thoughts on Talking with Children about Books." *The New Advocate* 10 (1): 49–59.

Eeds, Maryann., and Deborah Wells. 1991. "Talking, Thinking and Cooperative Learning: Lessons Learned from Listening to Children Talk About Books." *Social Education* 55 (2): 134–137.

Peterson, Ralph, and Maryann Eeds. 2007. *Grand Conversations: Literature Groups in Action.* New York: Scholastic.

5

Book Club

BOOK CLUB

Research Support

- Supports students in the elementary grades in learning to talk about and respond to literature in high-level ways
- May provide valuable learning opportunities for English language learners and students with special needs

Learning How

Examine resources listed at the end of this chapter. Read the Book Club curriculum guides for primary and middle school. Study the theme-based units and daily lesson plans in these guides.

Goals

To foster students' enjoyment of, and response to, high-quality literature (i.e., to respond to literature in personal, creative, and critical ways)

Typical Features (Book Club Discussions)

- Literary text
- Small-group discussion
- Heterogeneous group
- Student led
- Teacher chooses text
- Students read text before coming to discussion
- Students have control of topic
- Students control turn taking
- Students have interpretive authority
- Moderate focus on author intent

Typical Student Questions

What do you think?

How would you feel?

Why did they . . . ?

How could they . . . ?

Would you . . . ?

What do you mean?

What if . . . ?

Typical Student Comments

I was thinking about . . .

It doesn't make sense.

Let's think more about . . .

It made me feel . . .

I wrote about that too.

I think (thought) . . .

Teacher's Role

- Provide instruction, modeling, and scaffolding in what to talk about and how to talk so students can engage in book clubs.
- Help students learn a variety of ways to respond to text.
- Monitor and informally assess students' participation in book clubs.
- Provide instruction in comprehension strategies, language conventions, and literary elements as needed.

What the Talk Sounds Like

In the following excerpt of a book club discussion, a small group of fifth-grade students discuss *Tuck Everlasting* (Babbit 1975), a classic novel that is often read in the middle grades. The central theme, "immortality," is intriguing for an age group that enjoys thinking about hypothetical situations. *If you could drink water from a spring that would allow you to live forever, would you?* The students had responded in writing to the novel in their reading logs before the discussion. During the discussion, the group digs into the actions of Winnie, the main character, and considers when she might drink the water that will give her eternal life. In the story, Winnie befriends the Tucks, a family who drank the water and will live forever.

Camille: My best part in the book, of the story, of the whole thing I think is when they got romantic. And when she, I think we did read the, what's it called?

Crystal: Epilogue?

Camille: Epilogue. I think she will drink the water before she is 17.

Crystal: When she is 17?

Camille: Before.

Crystal: When she's 17 because they are gonna like take all the water when she is 17. She drinks the water. She'll probably go and marry him or something.

Camille: She's gonna do it *before* she said she was 17 though. That's what I think.

Crystal: But—Winnie is going to go into the woods, and I think that Winnie is gonna to go into the woods and drink the water cuz she thinks it won't work. She thinks they're just a bunch of crazy people, but they're her friends still. I said she thinks they're just a bunch of crazy people. I bet cha' she'll go in and check it when they leave. Fifteen? Thirteen? Fifteen? Something like that?

Joshua: Yeah.

Crystal: Not old enough to drink or nothing like that.

Latrice: I think she will take it when she is 17 because Tuck told her to do so.

(McMahon 1996, 241–242)

In the Book Club program, the small-group discussions (which we refer to using lowercase "book clubs") are student-led, meaning that students manage all aspects of the conversation without the teacher being present. Students control turn taking, topics, and questions, and they make decisions about how to interpret the story. Almost always, student questions are *authentic* and demonstrate *uptake*; by their nature, student questions are almost always genuine and provoke sincere responses, as in Crystal's question ("When she is 17?") and Camille's responses ("Before," "She's gonna do it *before* she said she was 17 though. That's what I

Figure 5.1 Examples of Quality Talk

Features	Examples	Why They Are Productive
Reasoning words	Latrice: I **think** she will take it when she is 17 **because** Tuck told her to do so.	Reasoning words signal students' high-level thinking and reasoning. Speculation, generalization, and analysis are cognitive functions evidenced when students use reasoning words.
Exploratory talk	Crystal, Camille and the other children go back and forth about when Winnie will drink the water, subtly challenging each other's ideas, and (at least sometimes) giving reasons: Crystal: "When she is 17?" Camille: "Before." Crystal: "When she's 17 because they are gonna like take all the water when she is 17. . . ." Camille: "She's gonna do it before she said she was 17 though. That's what I think." Crystal: "But—Winnie is going to go into the woods, and I think . . ."	Exploratory talk makes deeper thinking visible, promotes alternative points of view, elicits inquiry and reasoning, and enables students to sort out ideas collaboratively.
Authentic question	Crystal: When she is 17?	Authentic questions create space for additional ideas and high-level thinking about text. This authentic question elicits high-level thinking, evidenced with the reasoning words 'I think' and 'because' in later turns.

think."). Crystal's question is also an example of *uptake*, because the wording of her question "takes up" a bit of Camille's response from the previous turn. Questions that demonstrate uptake tend to deepen students' thinking and strengthen the reasoning in a discussion, as we see when Camille evokes a detail from the text as a reason to support her position. Both authentic questions and uptake in book clubs tend to generate *high-level responses*, as with Crystal's long response toward the end, when she challenges Camille's position about the main character.

The excerpt also shows some elements of *exploratory talk*. Exploratory talk is what it sounds like when students "chew on" an idea. In a back-and-forth way, students share their thinking, uncertain ideas, alternative points of view, and questions that push the limits of the group's thinking. The uncertainty of what is right, true, or absolute leads students to ask questions, return to the text, defend their positions with reasons, present alternative views, and challenge each other's thinking. Hence, exploratory talk is co-reasoning, and it is a defining feature of some of our best classroom discussions. Camille's challenge to the "age 17" position, with an ever so brief reference to the text ("she said"), is an essential feature of exploratory talk, and the challenge likely gets Crystal to come around and see it the other way. Winnie will indeed drink the water *before* she's 17. Crystal changes her position, and gives a lengthy explanation of why Winnie will drink the water before she's 17 (i.e., Winnie doesn't believe the Tucks).

Because there is a lot of exploratory talk in book clubs, students use *reasoning words* frequently, especially reasoning words that suggest speculation, although in this short excerpt, Crystal speculates just a little, when she says "probably" and "I bet cha'. . . ." Latrice, Crystal, and Camille take positions on the issue (*I think*) and engage in analysis (*because, but*) in their responses.

During book clubs, students also tend to refer to the text quite a lot, especially when they use their reading logs that accompany the discussions to talk about elements of the story, such as plot or character. Here, they don't refer directly to the text, but if they did it would sound like, "In the text, it said . . . ." When students refer explicitly to the text, reading a part of it in their response, we call this feature *text evidence* in quality talk; however, in the excerpt, all the students' ideas relate to the text and what happened in the story.

What is less often overheard in book clubs are the kinds of responses that reflect long chains of reasons (elaborated explanations) and connections to other discussions (shared knowledge responses). We might hear quite a few personal responses to the text where students share their feelings and make connections to their life experiences (affective responses). Camille's first statement, "My best part . . ." is an affective response. We sometimes hear students make connections to other texts (intertextual responses), especially when the students are reading thematically related texts. When several texts, or even a pair of texts, are thematically linked, making connections to other texts is a natural feature of the talk.

THE STORY BEHIND BOOK CLUB

The development of Book Club coincided with the movement from the mid-1980s to the late 1990s toward a literature-based approach to reading instruction, as an alternative to the more traditional skill-based approach in basal reading programs. Like Peterson and Eeds (with their Grand Conversations), Taffy Raphael, a professor at Michigan State University, was searching for a way to engage students in meaningful conversation about literature that would be similar to the conversations people have about books outside of school. Unlike Grand Conversations, however, the discussions she envisioned would be led by students who would be guided in how to comprehend and respond to text.

Much of the program was developed under the aegis of the Book Club Project, a three-year (1989–1992) collaboration between university- and school-based teachers and researchers. From 1989 through 1990, Raphael and a doctoral student, Susan McMahon, conducted a pilot study in two fourth-grade classrooms in a university community school. There they explored the use of small, student-led book clubs with high-quality children's literature. As a result of the pilot study, Raphael and McMahon conceptualized the framework for the Book Club program. The challenge confronting them was how to promote students' personal, aesthetic response to literature while providing instruction in comprehension and interpretation. Their solution was a framework that included four contexts for literacy learning and instruction: reading, writing, small-group book clubs, and whole-class "community share" (a term they borrowed from scholarship on process writing). From 1990 through 1992, they partnered with Laura Pardo and Deborah Woodman, two upper-elementary-grade teachers, who helped them flesh out the design of the program and ways to implement it.

The next several years saw various extensions to the program. The founders of Book Club, together with former classroom teachers who had returned to university as doctoral students, extended the program to students from first through ninth grades, students with learning difficulties, and students for whom English was a second language. They also explored the role of assessments and connections to different subject areas.

Most recently, Taffy Raphael, Susan Florio-Ruane, and colleagues in the Teachers Learning Collaborative have modified Book Club to provide a focus on teaching word-level reading skills and strategies while still engaging students in meaningful discussions of text. Again working in collaboration with teachers, they developed Book Club *Plus* for the primary grades. This program combines Book Club with a literacy block that includes guided reading and independent work.

Research Support

Taffy Raphael, Susan McMahon, and others have conducted at least fifteen studies of Book Club. Almost all of them are qualitative case studies of individual students or a group of students; many of them draw on data collected from Linda Pardo's and Deborah Woodman's classrooms. Studies include students in kindergarten through seventh grade, with students in fifth grade being the most highly represented. As with Grand Conversations, the studies provide descriptive, naturalistic accounts of how students participate in Book Club. The researchers typically transcribed discussions, collected samples of students' writing in their reading logs and think sheets, and kept field notes. Most of the studies focused on the small-group, student-led book clubs; a few focused on whole-class community share.

In the initial studies, McMahon and colleagues (McMahon 1992, 1994; McMahon, Pardo, and Raphael 1991; Raphael and Goatley 1994) explored how Book Club influenced students' talk and their responses to literature. At issue in much of the research was identifying the right balance between providing instruction in reading and promoting personal response to literature. Findings suggested that students were indeed able to manage their talk and engage in high-level thinking about text without the teacher participating in the discussion—provided that the appropriate supports were put in place. The beauty of Book Club is that what happens in reading, writing, and whole-class community share, and the instruction the teacher provides, work together to support talk and response in the small, peer-led book clubs; particularly important are the instruction, modeling, and scaffolding the teacher provides in community share. Findings also showed how peers as well as teachers can serve as "more knowledgeable others" to help students make meaning from the text.

In one series of studies, researchers examined how students from culturally and linguistically diverse backgrounds participated in Book Club. Brock and colleagues (Brock and Raphael 1994; Brock et al. 1998; Raphael and Brock 1993) followed the experiences of multilingual learners as they participated alongside their English-speaking peers. In two studies, they traced the experience of a Vietnamese girl, Mei, from when she came to the United States in third grade, participated in Book Club in the fourth and fifth grades, and returned to regular instruction in the sixth grade. The research showed how Mei learned to use academic language to discuss text and even assumed a leadership role in the discussions. Similarly, Kong and Pearson (2003) described the process by which multilingual learners in a fourth- and fifth-grade class of culturally and linguistically diverse students learned to participate in Book Club. Over the school year, the students demonstrated increasing levels of sophistication in their response to literature in the small-group, peer-led discussions. At the end of the year, they showed larger than expected gains in both word recognition and awareness of reading strategies.

In another series of studies, Goatley and colleagues examined how students with specific learning needs participated in Book Club. Goatley and Raphael (1992) studied how a group of five upper-elementary-grade students in a special-education resource room learned to talk about text. Over several months, with much modeling and scaffolding by the teacher, students slowly learned to interact with each other and grew in their understanding of what and how to share during book club discussions and their written responses. Goatley (1996) also conducted a case study of Stark, a student identified as learning disabled, as he learned to participate in Book Club in a fifth-grade regular education class. Over the year, Stark learned to interact with others and contribute to the book club discussions. In both studies, students learned how to go beyond literal interpretations and grapple with multiple interpretations of a text.

Still other studies have explored how Book Club can be used with other populations. Hill and Van Horn (1995) studied how Book Club could be adapted for youth in a juvenile detention center. Kendall (2006) implemented a modified version of Book Club with her kindergarten students.

So what do we learn from this research? We learn:

- Book Club supports elementary school students in learning how to manage their talk and interact in small, peer-led groups and to respond to literature in high-level ways. The four-part structure of reading, writing, small-group book clubs, and whole-class community share is key to providing this support.

- Book Club may provide valuable learning opportunities for English language learners in classrooms where English is the primary means of instruction. Book Club provides an environment where multilingual learners can experiment with language in meaningful ways and can be guided by their teacher and peers.

- Students with specific learning needs can participate in Book Club and make progress in language and literacy.

The caveat to keep in mind, of course, is that these findings all come from case studies. We would love to see some experimental studies comparing Book Club with regular instruction. As Raphael and her colleagues acknowledge, we do not know whether results of the case studies can be extended to all teachers and students who might use Book Club. Nor do we know if there is a direct causal link between students' participation in Book Club and their growth in comprehension or other language and literacy outcomes. In the absence of experimental studies, we think it reasonable to assume that the frequent opportunities to engage in meaningful discussions about literature and to receive instructional support afforded by Book Club should pay rich dividends for students' language and literacy learning.

BOOK CLUB in Practice

Planning for Book Club

QUICK GUIDE

1. **Select books**. Since students will typically choose their books, you should first identify a common theme, author (e.g., Gary Paulsen novels), genre, or topic of study and gather three or four narrative texts of interest to your students (e.g., engaging plot, relevant themes). Text selections determine the groups, so, for example, if you gather three texts, there will be at least three book club groups. Select texts of interest, and modify the reading format if the students need more support with the selection (e.g., reading in pairs, audio reading). Alternatively, select books at students' independent reading levels.

2. **Make groups.** Use a Google form or other survey tool to keep the initial reading choices private; this way, students choose their interest over a friend's interest. Have students make their top two choices and form heterogeneous groups of four to five students, based on reading levels and personalities. Alternatively, if you're new to Book Club, you might choose one book (or have students vote on one book) and form groups.

3. **Support the discussion.** Plan short lessons for community share to support book club discussions—for example, lessons on what to share and how to share it—and

plan to end book club discussions with a whole-class reflection on the talk and topics of conversation.

4. **Support and implement a reading log routine.** Plan and manage a reading log routine to facilitate students' response to reading, setting up several writing prompts for each theme (e.g., in a Google Drive folder or a special notebook), teaching the prompts through modeling, and giving students choices in which prompts to write about.

5. **Manage a structure.** Manage and organize the flow of the Book Club activities, holding community share and book clubs in a rotation of one or two instructional periods over the course of the week. Alternatively, and if you integrate book clubs into another literacy model, hold short book club meetings (ten minutes) several times during the week, following an independent reading time period and holding community share lessons once or twice per week (Figure 5.2).

Book club is an approach to discussion that is part of a broader literature study program and literacy block in the classroom, which is referred to as Book Club (uppercase). Book Club comprises four contexts for literacy learning and instruction: reading, writing, community share, and book club (see Figure 5.2). When planning for Book Club, you need to think about these four contexts.

The instruction that takes place during Book Club relates to and supports what happens in each of the four contexts of the program, so lessons about having a good discussion (to support the small-group discussions) are just as important as more typical comprehension-strategy lessons (to support

Figure 5.2 The Book Club Program's Four Contexts for Literacy Learning

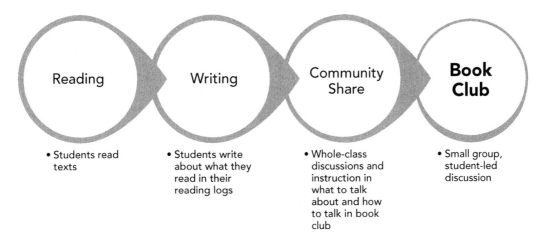

Reading
- Students read texts

Writing
- Students write about what they read in their reading logs

Community Share
- Whole-class discussions and instruction in what to talk about and how to talk in book club

Book Club
- Small group, student-led discussion

independent reading). For some teachers, Book Club is the primary language arts program in the classroom, but it doesn't have to be. Other teachers condense the model, incorporating independent reading and book club discussions into the larger literacy block and with other instructional models.

The Book Club program empowers students to read, write, and talk about text with lots of choice in what to read, write, and talk about. The underlying premise is that students have ownership of the learning process and enjoy reading. The real wisdom of Book Club, however, is that students talk a lot about their reading and writing. This happens in the whole-class, community-share discussions and small-group, student-led book clubs. These discussion contexts provide an authentic purpose for reading and writing, and motivate students to invest in deeper, more deliberate thinking about text. Vygotsky theorized that learners "grow into the intellectual life of those around them" (Vygotsky 1978, 88) through social interaction; so, in considering social interaction in this way, discussions should be the heart and soul of any language arts teaching. Eventually, the thinking and language of the social space (i.e., the discussions) become the internalized way of thinking of the individual. Enrich and improve the language of discussion, and you enrich and improve students' thinking about text.

Community share is a roughly ten- to fifteen- minute, whole-class discussion period that occurs shortly before and, for a few additional minutes, as a follow-up to the small-group, student-led book clubs. The goals of community share are to prepare students for book clubs and to reinforce the ways of holding productive discussions. Teachers sometimes conduct a short mini-lesson to support response to reading; other times they prime the pump for student participation in book clubs with a read-aloud of a related text; or they conduct a mini-lesson, modeling how to engage in productive talk. Spending time on teaching students how to talk and troubleshoot some of the challenges of group discussions (e.g., a dominating or an uncommunicative participant, off-topic dialogue) is a smart design feature for building capacity for learning during discussions.

Once the expectations are set and the pump has been primed, students convene in their small groups to have their book club discussions for about twenty to thirty minutes. The teacher circulates about the room and may jump into a discussion to support the group or conduct informal assessments if needed, but the idea is to monitor the groups without becoming an active part of the groups. After book clubs, the teacher reconvenes the class for community share and conducts another short, whole-class discussion (three to five minutes) to reflect on the talk and the content of the conversation. The teacher might ask, "Which log response(s) did you talk about today?" "Did anyone ask a thick question?" or, more generally, "Was the discussion good for your learning today?" "Did your discussion help you think about the story more . . . how so?" These kinds of questions support learning how to talk in book clubs through reflection on the elements of talk that support learning through dialogue.

Both discussion activities, the small-group book clubs and community share, comprise one fifty- to sixty-minute instructional period or several shorter instructional periods (e.g., book club meetings of ten to fifteen minutes two days during the week with two shorter community-share sessions). During the other days and instructional periods of the literacy block, teachers hold reading and writing workshops and teach literacy lessons, and students read or write independently or in pairs and respond in their reading logs.

Teacher's Role in Book Club Discussions

Borrowing a metaphor from Kong and Pearson (2003), teachers must organize instruction from behind the scenes in Book Club. This teaching style is much like that of a football coach at a large university game, who wears the headset and watches carefully every player from the upper decks of the stadium in order to call the next play. This coach isn't on the field but manages the game. Since book clubs are student led, teachers are like those coaches in the upper deck. From the upper deck or from behind the scenes, teachers deliver short lessons in community share to scaffold sustainable, student-driven book club conversations. These lessons fall into two broad categories, *what to talk about* at book club and *how to talk* in book clubs (Figure 5.4). The short lessons follow the gradual release of responsibility model of instruction (Pearson and Gallagher 1983) and include a series of steps, as summarized in Figure 5.3.

Figure 5.3 Sequence of Steps in a Community-Share Minilesson

The Teacher:
1. Motivates interest in learning and setting a purpose and goal.
2. Models a tool or strategy for thinking, talking, or writing with a direct explanation and a think-aloud.
3. Prompts students through guided practice to use the tool collaboratively, with the teacher and/or a partner.
4. Releases more responsibility to students, guiding the practice and prompting students to use the tool again, either independently or in pairs.
5. Closes the short lesson with the whole class doing a "status check," a debrief, and a reflection on the strategy, making sure the tool is clear and ready to try in the group or individually.

Figure 5.4 Suggested Lessons for Community Share in Preparation for Book Clubs

What to Talk About		
Lesson Title	Example Lesson	What It Does for Learning
Writing better log responses: Write for a "know-nothing audience"	Say: Today I want to show you what it means to write a response for a "know-nothing audience." **[direct explanation:]** Writing for a know-nothing audience means I have to use many details to make my thinking clear. **[modeling:]** Listen to my thinking as I respond to this section of the story in my writing with a know-nothing audience in mind. (teacher reads and writes out loud in front of the class, thinking aloud why he or she uses details in the response). **[guided practice:]** Let's read and write together, trying to write for a know-nothing audience.	Writing in reading logs supports comprehension of the text and reader response. A "know-nothing" audience elicits details in writing. Prompts assist students' transactions with the text, eliciting a reaction that gives the group in the book club or the teacher something to build on and elaborate. Meaning lies in both the transaction and in the elaboration.
Go beyond literal interpretations—making inferences about your reading	Say: Today I want to show you how I answer thick questions by connecting ideas in the text with my thinking. **[direct explanation:]** Inferences need long answers. It's hard to say my inference in one or two words; I need to explain my thinking with chains of reasons. **[modeling:]** Listen to my thinking as I read this section, ask myself a thick question, and try to answer with a chain of reasons to show my thinking.	The goal of any discussion is to use talk as a tool for interpreting text, so modeling how to answer questions with long chains of reasons supports interpretations or inferences across texts, prior knowledge, and contexts.
Write and ask thick questions vs. thin questions in order to think about the text in better ways	Say: **[direct explanation:]** *Thick questions* are questions that will help us have a long conversation because we need many different ideas to answer them. We need to really explore a thick question. **[modeling:]** I'm going to read this section of the story again and show you thick and thin questions about it, so we can talk about what makes these thick questions.	Sustaining good conversation requires asking good questions, so making students aware of the quality of questions supports the use of interpretive questions (*how, why* questions), and these typically lead to inferences and high-level thinking in the form of speculation, generalization, analysis, and exploratory talk.
How to Talk		
Lesson Title	Example Lesson	What It Does for Learning
Follow ground rules for participation	Say: Today, in our book clubs, we are going to focus on these ground rules for our talk—asking thick questions, listening with our whole bodies so we can connect to what someone says, giving reasons, challenging ideas, and connecting our log responses to each other and the story. Let's choose just one ground rule to really make sure we do well, and we will talk about it after book club. Which one? (students throw out ideas)	When students use ground rules, they have a common understanding of their roles and purpose in discussion; this supports quality talk, in particular, high-level thinking, elaborated thinking and responses, and the co-construction of ideas through exploratory talk.

continues

continued

How to Talk		
Lesson Title	Example Lesson	What It Does for Learning
"Listen with all your might!" Bid for the floor and articulate your ideas	Conduct a mini-lesson in the form of a simulation or a "fishbowl modeling" demonstration, where the teacher shows students how to jump into a conversation to connect to what others say. Teach kids the language of bidding for the floor, (e.g., *I have an idea; Well, I think I can connect; I agree; I disagree*) and yielding to others to give space for their ideas.	Teaching kids how to listen "with everything they have" is essential for quality talk. The only way students grow ideas is through building on and connecting to the ideas shared in the conversation. They can only do this through considering seriously—and listening to—what others have to say.
Ask follow-up questions to challenge each other's thinking and to clarify	Conduct a fishbowl modeling activity where a small group of students (with or without the teacher) models asking follow-up questions on the "inside" of a large circle of desks in your class. Students sitting on the outside of the circle observe the small group and record notes about the follow-up questions. Following a very short period of modeling, debrief with a whole-group discussion to focus students on the purpose and outcomes of asking follow-up questions.	Follow-up questions in the form of uptake are ideal for quality talk. Teaching how to challenge an idea, clarify a muddy point, or call for evidence is critical for eliciting high-level thinking and reasoning during discussions.

Approach in Action: Language Arts, Grade 5

This small-group book club discussion took place in a fifth-grade inclusion class-room. The class had been studying World War II in language arts and social studies lessons. The students were discussing *Faithful Elephants* by Yukio Tsuchiya (1988), a historical fiction text that recounts the true events of euthanizing elephants and other large zoo animals in cities that were bombed during World War II. One of the other book club groups was reading about the bombing of Hiroshima. In this excerpt, the students are discussing the ethical aspects of war.

Bart: I wrote about the survival, too, and I wrote about the Japanese. I was speaking about Japanese people and their culture. That's what I was really thinking about. But I wrote—

Chris: (interrupts) (unclear)

Bart: I know, but I was thinking, if they can't bomb Americans—

Bart is incorporating a reading log response into the discussion. This is the beginning of an episode of exploratory talk– notice the subsequent reasons, alternative ideas, and disagreements.

Chris: It's war though. They bombed us and we bombed 'em back.

A challenge to Bart's thinking

Bart: I know, but still.

Chris: (unclear)

Lissa: Yeah, but the Americans had the war.

Bart: Yeah, but if Japan bombs a part we don't have the right to go back and bomb them. Two wrongs don't make a right.

The earlier challenge likely elicits the reasoning here. This is high-level thinking (generalization).

Chris: Japan bombed Pearl Harbor.

Bart: I know, but still—

Chris: But Americans had to bomb them back.

Bart: It doesn't make sense to go back and bomb them. That's like President Bush. He makes a mistake, like really uhm, if they make a move on us, we have a war. Two wrongs don't make a right. That's wrong. I would say run me over, if they do something . . .

A connection between the topic of the conversation and prior knowledge about the first Gulf War. An example of giving reasons during exploratory talk.

Martisse: Bomb them back.

Lissa: No!

Bart: No! Just leave, leave it.

(McMahon 1992, 29)

This excerpt illustrates features of both book club discussions and quality talk. In terms of quality talk, the students engage in exploratory talk (e.g., challenging ideas, giving reasons, sharing thinking and alternatives) to wrestle with the idea of when and whether it's ever okay to go to war. Chris' challenge to Bart's pacifist stance kick-starts exploratory talk, which is why teaching kids *to* challenge and *how to* challenge is so important. Without challenges, it's hard to give reasons that build a deeper understanding and to explore and inquire about ideas.

In terms of Book Club, Bart shares his log entry and the students decide to take up his ideas. Prior to the small group book club discussion, the students read and wrote about their responses to the story in their reading logs, so Bart's first turn in the excerpt, a reference to his writing, generates the talk. Students need to grapple with an idea from a classmate's log before sharing another log entry; that is, students should stay with one idea in the conversation instead of sharing all their log responses in round-robin fashion. This is illustrated in the subsequent turns as all four students in the discussion group take turns at wrestling with the ideas of going to war.

Enacting the four components of Book Club is nothing short of instructional brilliance because the outcome is a culture that empowers students to be self-directed in their own learning, and this is a powerful catalyst for student agency as well as high-level thinking and quality talk about text. The key to the achievement is conducting the community-share discussions. The learning in book club requires a persistent focus on *how to talk* and *what to talk about*, or teaching the norms of participation that draw attention to the co-construction of knowledge and the elements of language that reflect and generate high-level thinking. Student-led book clubs are magical when all the pieces are in place. We could use a little more magic in learning as we try to balance the need to adhere to standards and testing schedules with a need to make sure that students are empowered to learn and enjoy what they do at school.

READ MORE

McMahon, Susan I., and Taffy E, Raphael (with Virginia J. Goatley and Laura S. Pardo), eds. 1997. *The Book Club Connection: Literacy Learning and Classroom Talk*. New York: Teachers College Press.

Raphael, Taffy E., Susan Florio-Ruane, Marianne George, Nina Hasty, and Kathy Highfield. 2004. *Book Club Plus!: A Literacy Framework for the Primary Grades*. Lawrence, MA: Small Planet Communications.

Raphael, Taffy E., Marcella Kehus, and Karen Damphousse. 2001. *Book Club for Middle School*. Lawrence, MA: Small Planet Communications.

Raphael, Taffy E., Laura S. Pardo, and Kathy Highfield. 2002. *Book Club: A Literature-Based Curriculum*. 2nd ed. Lawrence, MA: Small Planet Communications.

Literature Circles

<table>
<tr><td colspan="3" style="text-align:center">LITERATURE CIRCLES</td></tr>
</table>

LITERATURE CIRCLES

Research Support

- Help students become actively engaged in reading, discussions, and writing in response to literature
- Support students in making rich personal connections to text
- May foster students' high-level thinking about text
- Improve students' reading engagement, attitudes, and motivation

Learning How

Examine resources listed at the end of this chapter. Try it! Listen and observe carefully how students respond in their groups.

Goals

To foster students' enjoyment of, engagement with, and personal response to literature

Typical Features

- Literary text
- Small-group discussion
- Heterogeneous group
- Student or teacher led
- Students choose text
- Students read text before coming to discussion
- Students have control of topic
- Students control turn taking
- Students have interpretive authority
- Little focus on author intent

Typical Student Questions

Do you think . . . ?

Why did they . . . ?

How . . . ?

Would you . . . ?

What . . . ?

Typical Student Comments

I think (thought) . . .

I don't think . . .

It made me feel . . .

I wrote about that too.

I wonder . . .

Maybe . . .

It's like . . .

That reminds me of . . .

Teacher's Role

- Organize student-led groups by choosing the books; giving book talks from which students make choices; and managing time for students' reading, written responses, and discussion.
- Provide focus lessons in how to engage in rich discussions, modeling ways that students can respond to and talk about text.
- Monitor and informally assess students' participation in Literature Circles.

What the Talk Sounds Like

In the following excerpt from a Literature Circle discussion, a group of four third-grade students are discussing *Helen Keller,* a biography by Margaret Davidson (1969). The students had recently read and discussed *Hannah* by Gloria Whelan (1991), an historical fiction story about a young girl who was blind—a story their teacher had introduced to the class to help students make the transition from fiction to biographies. The group chose to read *Helen Keller* from a range of biographies about people who had been blind at an early age (Louis Braille, Helen Keller, Anne Sullivan). The biography of Helen Keller relates how, under the tutelage of Anne Sullivan, Helen learned to draw on her strengths and her passion for learning and go on to graduate from college. The students are discussing the story on their own, without the teacher.

Nancy: How do you think Helen would be if she hadn't learned anything yet?

Tom: I think she would still be cranky, and mad, and throw stuff.

Richard: She would be so wild, and they would probably have to send her away to somewhere they could keep her locked up so she wouldn't destroy anything.

Nancy: But remember—they said they didn't want to do that.

Tom: Mrs. Keller said that she didn't want Helen to go away to school; she wanted Helen to stay at home.

Nancy: I think that she would be wild and that her mom and dad would get another teacher. But I don't think they'd find another teacher like the first one she had.

Tami: Whenever I read this, it reminds me about . . . Did anyone see that movie about Helen Keller, with that little girl in it?

Tom: Yes!

Tami: This book always reminds me of that movie.

Tom: Yeah, with that little girl kicking and screaming. I can also make a connection to another book we read about a girl who was blind, but not deaf . . .

Nancy: *Hannah* [Whelan 1991].

Tom: Yeah. Every time I read a chapter in this book, I remember about Hannah and try to make out things that are similar and stuff that's different.

Richard: There's much more that's different.

Nancy: Why is that?

Richard: Because it's so much easier to learn if you're only blind, than being blind and deaf.

(Stien and Beed 2004, 515)

Literature Circles are student or teacher led, though student-led discussions, as in this excerpt, are most common. Students typically choose their texts from a selection introduced by the teacher, and small groups are formed based on their choices. During the discussion, the students control the topic and turn taking, and they make decisions about how to interpret the story.

When you listen to the talk in Literature Circles, you almost always hear students asking authentic questions and questions showing uptake, which means that their questions are genuine and build on the responses and thinking of other students. Their authentic questions and uptake tend to generate quite high-level thinking in the form of generalization, analysis, and speculation. In the excerpt, when Nancy asks her hypothetical—and authentic—question, "How do you think Helen would be if she hadn't learned anything yet?", we hear the students engaging in a lot of speculation (notice their use of *would, if, probably*). Similarly, when Nancy asks Richard why he thought the Hellen Keller and Hannah books are different, Richard responds, "Because it's so much easier to learn if you're only blind, than being blind and deaf." Here Richard is analyzing the two texts and making a generalization (and presumably speculating) about what it is like being impaired in both sight and sound.

As far as reasoning is concerned, in Literature Circles, you will sometimes hear exploratory talk where students are "chewing" on ideas together but, more often, you will hear "cumulative talk." This is a kind of talk where students build on each other's ideas and share their perspectives but do not really challenge the ideas or engage in explicit negotiation of meaning as in exploratory talk. In the excerpt, notice how the students share their ideas about what Helen Keller's life might have been like if she hadn't learned to talk and read but without any real

▎**Figure 6.1** Examples of Quality Talk

Features	Examples	Why They Are Productive
Authentic question	Nancy: "How do you think Helen would be if she hadn't learned anything yet?"	Authentic questions create space for students' ideas and high-level thinking about text. This authentic question elicits high-level thinking in the turns that follow, with students engaging in generalization, analysis, and speculation based on their background knowledge.
Uptake	Nancy: "Why is that?"	Uptake involves a question that incorporates what someone else said previously, and is often marked by a pronoun (e.g., *that*). Uptake valorizes and builds on a previous student's response, and enables their comment to shape the discussion.
Intertextual response	Tom: "I can also make a connection to another book we read about a girl who was blind, but not deaf . . ." Nancy: *Hannah* [Whelan 1991].	Intertextual responses make connections between the text and other texts and media (i.e., text-to-text). They involve making connections to prior knowledge they have built from previous readings or viewing experiences, and enrich students' understanding.
Key words	*I think, I don't think, would, if, why, because*	Key words are words that, when used in certain ways, indicate reasoning. They indicate students are taking positions, speculating, and analyzing.

disagreement, challenge, or argument. Their explanations for their thinking are not very elaborated, and they tend to agree with almost everything that is said with an ostensibly calm sensitivity that suggests friendly support and affirmation. There is an instance where Nancy problematizes Richard's idea ("But remember—they said they didn't want to do that") and Tom offers some evidence to support her assertion ("Mrs. Keller said that she didn't want Helen to go away to school; she wanted Helen to stay at home") but, for the most part, students simply add on to each other to create a shared understanding. Although the talk tends not to show a commitment to exploring different positions and negotiating meaning—features of exploratory talk—cumulative talk can be productive, as it is this excerpt.

In Literature Circles, students also tend to make extra textual connections. Quite often you will hear students make affective responses, where they share their feelings about the text and make connections to their lives. Although students in the previous excerpt used their imaginations to discuss what Helen Keller's life would have been like if she had not received an education, their affective responses are not as obvious as they might be. To illustrate what they sound like, imagine a student in the previous discussion adding how she thinks she would feel if she were Helen Keller. She might say something like, "I love to read. If that happened to me, I would have been so happy I could read!" In this way, students make connections between the text and their own lives and feelings. They show they are highly emotionally engaged with the text and are interpreting it through the lens of their own lives.

In Literature Circles, you may also hear intertextual responses where students make connections to other texts or media. In the earlier excerpt, Tami and Tom are reminded of the movie they saw about Helen Keller, and the students also make a comparison between the biography about her and the historical fiction text, *Hannah*, that they read and discussed as a class. On occasion, you may also hear students making connections to previous discussions they have had or knowledge they have built together (shared-knowledge responses). The intertextual responses in the Helen Keller excerpt also make connections to the shared knowledge students had built as a class.

Research Support

Research on Literature Circles is abundant. There are more studies of Literature Circles than there are of any of the other discussion approaches described in this book. Literature Circles have been studied with students in kindergarten through grade 12 (though most of the studies have been conducted with fourth, fifth, and sixth graders). They have been studied with English language learners, struggling readers, high-achieving readers, and students identified as having learning disabilities. Reports of empirical studies of Literature Circles have appeared in more than thirty-five journal articles, book chapters, and research reports, in more than ninety-five master's theses, and in thirty doctoral dissertations (and counting!). Conducting research on Literature Circles seems to have become something of a cottage industry for students pursuing graduate degrees.

Most of the studies are case studies describing teachers' implementation of Literature Circles and students' participation in the discussions. Many are teacher action-research projects or studies examining growth in students' literacy before and after the introduction of Literature Circles. Quite a few are experimental studies comparing the effects of Literature Circles with those of other types of literacy instruction (e.g., sustained silent reading, the directed reading activity). Most studies focus on the student-led version of Literature Circles popularized by Harvey Daniels (2002).

Making sense of research on Literature Circles is tricky. Researchers often use different names for the discussion groups and frequently confuse Literature Circles with Grand Conversations and the small-group discussions in Book Club. We have to look carefully to make sure the core features of Literature Circles are present. What's more, researchers sometimes combine Literature Circles with other instructional elements, such as strategy instruction, making it hard to tease out the contribution of the discussions themselves.

What are we to make of this abundance of research? From the case studies, we learn that **students in Literature Circles become actively engaged in reading, discussion, and writing in response to literature; they make rich personal connections to the texts they read; and they may exhibit high-level thinking.** Some studies suggest that students' talk is more focused and productive in teacher-led versions of Literature Circles than in student-led versions (e.g., Allen, Möller, and Stroup 2003). Some note that overreliance on role sheets "may restrict students' participation and get in the way of thoughtful, genuine discussion among readers" (Peterson and Belizaire 2006, 43; Lloyd 2006). Some caution that issues of gender and power may surface in student-led Literature Circles and disrupt the dialogue (e.g., Evans, Alvermann, and Anders 1998).

THE STORY BEHIND LITERATURE CIRCLES

It was the summer of 1982. Karen Smith, a fifth-grade teacher in Arizona, was setting up her classroom for the upcoming school year when a colleague dropped off a box containing multiple copies of paperback novels she no longer needed. Thinking they could be used for independent reading, Karen put the box aside at the back of her room. Several months into the year, her students found the box, chose books to read, and started meeting regularly in small groups to talk about their reading. Karen, then a graduate student at the Arizona State University, was so impressed with students' responses to the books that she invited colleagues and professors to observe and offer suggestions. Among these were Ralph Peterson, who showed her how to participate in the groups without taking control (and would later go on to develop Grand Conversations), and Jerry Harste, a professor visiting from Indiana University. Karen called her groups "literature studies."

In 1984, Kathy Short, a doctoral student at Indiana University, was conducting her dissertation study in collaboration with a first-grade teacher, Gloria Kaufman. Both were looking for a way to deepen first graders' response to literature. Kathy talked with Karen Smith about her literature studies—having heard about them from her advisor, Jerry Harste. Kathy and Gloria decided to combine the idea with their notion of "author circles," where students bring drafts of their writing to think about with others, and developed a teacher-led approach to book discussion called "Literature Circles."

Meanwhile, in Chicago in 1981, Becky Abraham Searle was teaching a multiage class of fourth, fifth, and sixth graders and looking for a way to challenge her older, high-achieving readers. She decided to organize them into peer-led discussion groups and assign them books to read. But the discussions were not as rich as she would have liked. Knowing about cooperative learning and ways of managing group work, she introduced role sheets (discussion director, literary luminary, vocabulary enricher, process checker) to help structure the discussions. These role sheets did indeed lead to richer discussions, though, after a few discussions, she replaced them with response logs.

From these beginnings in the early 1980s, Literature Circles have been taken up and adapted by thousands of teachers throughout the world. Like Grand Conversations and Book Club, they represent teachers' efforts to emulate the conversations adults have about literature. Harvey Daniels, a teacher–educator at National Louis University, working in collaboration with teachers in Chicago, is credited with popularizing the peer-led version of Literature Circles and, to his chagrin, the use (some might say "overuse") of role sheets. Today, Literature Circles are found in a variety of learning contexts and are even used with comprehension strategy instruction, content area instruction, nonfiction texts, and online discussions.

From the action-research projects and studies examining growth in students' literacy before and after the introduction of Literature Circles, we learn that **students do indeed experience growth in comprehension and other literacy outcomes. Students also show improvements in reading attitudes and motivation.** For example, Daniels (2002) cited research he and his colleagues conducted between 1995 and 1998 to support the language arts instruction in several struggling Chicago schools. They helped teachers learn how to implement Literature Circles as part of a reading-writing workshop. Daniels reported that there were large gains in the percentage of students meeting or exceeding state goals on the Illinois Goals Assessment Program in reading and writing, relative to the citywide average. Of course, in studies like these it is hard to know what contribution the Literature Circles alone made to students' growth, as many factors might be responsible for the improvements. In Daniels and colleagues' school improvement effort, teachers were "convinced their Literature Circles were working" (Daniels 2002, 8).

From the experimental studies comparing the effects of Literature Circles with those of other types of literacy instruction, we learn a little more about the effects of the discussions. These studies confirm that **students show improvements in motivation, engagement, and attitudes toward reading as a result of participating in Literature Circles.**

But what about the effects of Literature Circles on students' comprehension when compared with other instruction? The best evidence we have on this comes from two experimental studies. Marshall (2006) compared the effects of participation in Literature Circles versus a directed reading activity on students' comprehension of texts discussed. Eighty-six eighth-grade students participated in each type of instruction for four weeks. Marshall found no overall differences in effects of the two types of instruction, but she did find that Literature Circles showed benefits for the better readers. In the other experiment, McElvain (2005, 2010) compared the effects of what she called Transactional Literature Circles (TLCs) with that of business-as-usual instruction on the reading comprehension of seventy-five English language learners in fourth, fifth, and sixth grades. After a year, the TLC students outperformed students in the comparison group on standardized tests of English reading comprehension. Teachers and students also reported increases in the TLC students' reading engagement and motivation.

These two experimental studies probably offer the best evidence we have that Literature Circles improve students' comprehension. That said, because the studies were complex and there was a lot going on in the classrooms, the results are not as "clean" as we would like. For a practice that has been so widely adopted and studied, we would love to see more evidence of the benefits of Literature Circles for students' comprehension. Nonetheless, there is abundant evidence that Literature Circles foster students' motivation, engagement, and positive attitudes toward reading and help students make rich, personal connections to text. They can be an important addition to a comprehensive literacy program.

LITERATURE CIRCLES in Practice

Planning for Literature Circles

QUICK GUIDE

1. **Select book titles and give book talks.** Identify a common theme (e.g., survival), author, genre, or topic of study and gather several literary or informational texts. Text selections determine the groups—three different texts means that there will be at least three Literature Circle groups. Give book talks to initiate the choices.

2. **Plan the response activities.** A common feature of Literature Circles is the use of role sheets to help focus students' independent reading and to help structure their responses to the reading and Literature Circle discussions. Teachers also use reading logs with prompts, sticky notes, short writing/drawing tasks, and other technology-inspired mechanisms such as Voice Thread or video logs, to promote responses to the reading.

3. **Make groups.** Have students choose their top three or four book choices and make heterogeneous groups of five or six students, based on the choices, personalities, or reading levels. If you're new to Literature Circles, you might choose one book (or have students vote on one book) or start with a short story and form groups on your own. Over time, you could release the responsibility of grouping entirely to students.

4. **Support independent reading and preparation for Literature Circles.** Plan short focus lessons to support response and Literature Circle discussions (e.g., using role sheets) and conduct read-alouds to deliberately model Literature Circle behaviors and routines. Take notes during the discussions to identify topics of future focus lessons. Modify the reading if some students need more support reading their selection (e.g., reading in pairs).

5. **Manage a structure.** Manage and organize the flow of Literature Circle activities, providing in-class, independent reading and preparation time, organizing a "read by" deadline (or have groups make their own deadlines), and giving time for a roughly thirty-minute Literature Circle discussion at least once per week.

Students read independently and respond each day, either in class or as homework, preparing for their Literature Circle discussions (Figure 6.2). The students conduct their discussions in small groups while you monitor and observe. The cycle of preparing for and conducting discussions repeats until the book is finished. You might use a project assignment to have groups or individuals prepare a final reflection (see Figure 6.3 for ideas), and this is typically assessed formally. For some teachers, when books and projects are finished, the class moves on to another language

Figure 6.2 Sample Schedule for Literature Circles Routines in Elementary and Middle Schools with Block Scheduling

Monday 10:00-10:30	Tuesday 10:00-10:30	Wednesday 10:00-10:30	Thursday 10:00-10:30	Friday 10:00-10:30
Goal setting: determine read-by deadline Independent reading and response	Independent reading and response	Focus lesson Groups meet for short Literature Circle discussions	Independent reading and response	Literature Circle discussions

Figure 6.3 Project Ideas to End a Book Read in Literature Circles

Choice Menu of Group Projects
- Screencast design and production
- Video book advertisement for next year
- Multimedia display for promoting the book
- Reader's theater design and production
- Process drama activity, such as tableau

Choice Menu of Individual Creative Responses
- Become a character pen pal: write four letters to a character or four letters between two characters as if they are writing to each other.
- Rewrite the text as a graphic novel/picture book.
- Write an extended inquiry report related to the setting of the story, the author, or another aspect of the text.
- Design a wallpaper display for the main character's cell phone.
- Create a multigenre writing project.

arts unit, such as a writing workshop unit; for others, the cycle repeats and new books are selected. The idea is to make Literature Circles part of your literacy teaching practices, which, depending on the grade level, might also include small-group reading instruction, read-alouds, shared reading, writing, and word study.

The central ideas behind Literature Circles are student agency in independent reading and a real-life, genuine purpose for reading (i.e., a book-club-type discussion about text). These are balanced by the teacher's management of the structure for student-led discussions. Another key idea behind Literature Circles is personal response to reading, which is the practice of connecting one's own personal stories, feelings, and lives to the ideas in the text. Through these key elements, Literature Circles motivate readers and help promote comprehension.

Response to reading is the heart of the learning in Literature Circles. Louise Rosenblatt, a literacy educator and English professor, popularized the premise that readers have transactions with the text, taking the author's ideas and making personal connections in an "exchange" that leads to comprehension. The tool that supports these transactions is structured response to reading. Rosenblatt argued that readers first have to make personal responses to text before graduating to deeper analyses of the text. Literature Circles embody this theory, ensuring personal responses are made while reading, either using the traditional Literature Circle roles (Figure 6.4) (Daniels 2002) or another way (e.g., a reading log routine—see Figure 6.5).

Figure 6.4 Literature Circle Roles (Daniels 2002)

Basic Roles

connector—prepares connections to self, other texts, and other events in the world

questioner—prepares thick questions

passage master—prepares ideas that seem important or memorable (based on a quotation, paragraph, section, etc.)

illustrator—prepares a visual rendering of a section of the text

Optional Alternatives or Additions

summarizer—prepares summaries

researcher—investigates and prepares additional information about something in the text

vocabulary enricher—identifies several tier 2 words or other words that are new and prepares descriptions

Figure 6.5 Response to Reading Activities (low preparation to high)

> **Sticky notes:** Students record thinking on sticky notes and mark pages in the reading.
>
> **Response logs:** Teachers provide prompts; students write in response.
>
> **Double entry or buddy journals:** Students write their thinking and the teacher or a classmate writes a short reply.
>
> **Role sheets:** Students follow a graphic organizer that defines a different role for each student in the group (e.g., connector, time keeper). Students participate in the discussion as their role is described, but they may also make other contributions.

Teacher's Role in Literature Circles

Because Literature Circles are often student led, the teacher's role is to create a classroom context that supports discussion. Students need to know what they're doing, why they're doing it, and how they go about it on their own, so the teacher plans short focus lessons to teach the process for engaging in rich discussions. The other instructional practice is to use an intentional modeling technique with targeted talk moves to demonstrate the way in which participants in a discussion talk to each other and engage with the ideas of the story.

Early proponents of Literature Circles suggested teachers should use "kid-watching," or monitoring and noticing student needs in order to identify topics for high-need focus lessons. Today, we would say that teachers engage in informal and formative assessment during Literature Circles, making anecdotal notes about the students' performance based on the criteria that define quality Literature Circles. To make notes about the quality of students' thinking, create a checklist using criteria such as the following:

☐ Students refer to the text during discussions.

☐ Students ask questions.

☐ Students elaborate ideas with long responses.

☐ At least a couple of times, students challenge or disagree.

☐ Students share the responses in a conversational way (no round robin sharing of the log entries!).

To make notes about the context for, and norms of, productive discussions, add to the checklist these kinds of criteria:

☐ Conversation is shared (with no dominating and few interruptions).

☐ Body language is positive and supportive (e.g., making eye contact).

☐ Students appear on task and focused on the text.

If you have already been using Literature Circles, your assessments might show that a couple of students dominate the group or maybe some groups demonstrate lackluster interactions with a heavy reliance on the role sheets. Certainly, focus lessons will help, but an advanced teaching practice that will elevate student talk, perhaps even more than a focus lesson, is the use of intentional modeling of the kind of talk you want students to use in discussions. We like to think of this intentional modeling as a "snowball" technique. Here's the idea: if, in *your* talk, you routinely ask clarifying questions during read-alouds (e.g., "So, are you saying that Augie's parents were unfair?"), the form of the clarifying question will get picked up or snowball into student questioning in other lessons and contexts. Literature Circle experts propose teachers use this technique during read-aloud routines, using the kinds of talk that facilitate dialogue, explore ideas, and make connections. These very specific and academic ways of talking will grow or snowball across your class when you talk in these ways. See Figure 6.6 for focus lessons and "snowball" modeling ideas.

Figure 6.6 Suggested Teaching Practices to Support Literature Circles

Focus Lessons: Response Activities in Logs or Journals		
Lesson Title	Example Lesson	What It Does for Learning
"Taking it back to the book"	Say: **[goal:]** Today I want to show you what it means to write a response that "takes it back to the book." **[direct explanation:]** Taking it back to the book means I have to write a connection that links to (goes back to) something in the text—a detail, evidence, a picture and so on. It helps Literature Circles because we want our talk to stay focused on the book. **[think aloud:]** Listen to my thinking as I make a connection to this section of the story in my note making—as I take it back to the book (teacher reads and writes out loud in front of the class, thinking aloud why he or she links a personal connection to a quotation, and notes the quotation and page reference). **[guided practice:]** Let's read and write together, trying to make a new note that "goes back to" the book.	Writing connections as they relate to the text is a kind of personal response that supports readers' thinking about their prior knowledge as they read. "Taking it back to the book" helps students link their ideas about reading and the text with their prior knowledge (personal connections).
"Save the last word for me"	Say: **[goal:]** Today I want to show you how I choose a quotation to write about; this is called "save the last word for me." **[direct explanation:]** It is best to choose a quotation that you like a lot because it makes you think a lot. What you write is your thinking about the quotation. Maybe it's a personal story, a question, or another connection. At your Literature Circle, these are the ideas that will help keep the conversation going. **[think aloud:]** Listen to my thinking as I read this section, ask myself whether the author wrote something I like, and write about the quotation with my thinking.	Identifying quotations or language the author uses that we like is what good readers do all the time; they reflect on the ideas that resonate. "Save the last word for me" prompts learners to pause while reading and reflect on the language of the text.
Focus Lessons: Procedures of Discussion		
Lesson Title	Example Lesson	What It Does for Learning
Follow ground rules for participation	Say: Today, in our Literature Circles, we are going to focus on these ground rules for our talk—asking "thick" questions, listening with our whole bodies, giving reasons, challenging ideas, and connecting our role sheet responses to each other and the story. Let's choose just one ground rule to really make sure we do well, and we will talk about it after Literature Circles. Which one? (students make suggestions).	When students use ground rules, they have a common understanding of their roles and purpose in discussion; this supports collaboration, quality talk, and the co-construction and negotiation of ideas through exploratory talk. Talking about ground rules *after* the discussion is essential for learning, building students' capacities to reflect on the kind of talk they use.

continues

continued

Focus Lessons: Procedures of Discussion		
Talk Move	Example Lesson	What It Does for Learning
Using your responses and role sheets in productive ways	Conduct a mini-lesson in the form of a simulation or a "fishbowl modeling" demonstration, where the teacher shows students how to use their role sheets in academic ways, limiting round-robin sharing. Teach kids the language of bidding for the floor with their role and response—for example, *As the "connector," I have an idea that relates to what Emma said; Well, I think I can connect with my drawing; I disagree*—and yielding to others to give space for other classmates' responses.	Teaching kids how to use their role sheets in academic conversations is important in Literature Circles. However, Harvey Daniels who, as noted earlier, was an early adopter of Literature Circles and author of Literature Circle texts, cautions that role sheets should be used only as a temporary support in the early stages. If students rely on role sheets too much, there is the risk that students simply share their responses in isolation from other comments and questions. The only way students grow ideas and negotiate meaning is through building on and connecting to the ideas of others.
Intentional Modeling: What to Model in Your Talk to Support Literature Circles		
Talk Move	Example of Using It	What It Does for Learning
Facilitative move: **Clarify through revoicing** "So, when you say that, do you mean . . . ?"	During read-alouds or other language arts lessons, ask a follow-up question that clarifies. The form of the question begins with the stem, "So, are you saying . . . ."	Clarifying improves and increases connections that are made in discussions.
Exploratory move: **Disagree** "I'm not sure I agree with the reason, but I agree with your idea. . . . Is it true that . . . ?"	In your read-alouds, build on a student response with a statement that challenges. The challenge has a particular form, so start with the stem, "I'm not sure I agree" (and be specific about the part with which you disagree) "with that second reason." An extension of this move is to coach students to agree or disagree by asking, "Does anyone disagree with . . . ? And which part . . .?"	Disagreements are a pathway to negotiating meaning and making interpretations with dialogue. If we want students to make interpretations collectively in discussions, we must show them how to disagree.

Approach in Action: Language Arts, Grade 5

The following small-group Literature Circle discussion took place in a fifth-grade class. The small group had been reading Dawn Nelson's *Dark Isle* (2007), a fantasy that takes place in Scotland. In the excerpt, the students are discussing the main character, Foyce, who is a dark, malicious character. However, a tribunal called the Ancient Crones is known for reforming those who are wicked, and Foyce visits the tribunal.

Fiona: Do you think Foyce got cured and is now a Trueheart?

Fiona poses an authentic question.

Jenny: I don't think so.

Jenny disagrees and Shona presents an alternative view.

Laura: I think so.

Shona: Not now obviously, in like twenty years, or thirty or fifty.

Delaney: OK now, right now. . . can I say, right I think no because I think she was just plain evil that cannot be cured and even when she knew, I think she knows how bad she is, I think she knows how bad she is though she just can't accept like she just says "I'm greedy, I want everything . . ." (reads from text) "hello boy—

Delaney disagrees with Laura and Shona and offers an elaborated explanation with a reference to the text as evidence for her position.

Shona: (interrupts) Well, to be honest I think the same as Delaney, I don't think she could ever be a Trueheart because . . . because I can't imagine her being nice . . . I wrote that her eyes would have to change because she's evil.

Delaney: Yeah her eyes are red.

Jenny: No her . . . eyes are silver.

Laura: No, I think that Foyce that maybe after a hundred years as an Ancient Crone in the end she'll . . . she might not ever be good, completely good, but she'll be better . . . you know. A bit.

This is a response to Delaney's challenge above.

Delaney: Maybe.

Shona: I still think she's evil.

Jenny: I don't think she can because she can't get her horns away.

Jenny is challenging Laura's position that Foyce will become good. The presence of a challenge with a reason is a key feature of exploratory talk.

(Pearson 2010, 6)

This excerpt illustrates features of Literature Circle discussions and quality talk. In terms of quality talk, Fiona asks an authentic question about the main character that kick-starts the dialogue. The question generates high-level thinking because Delaney and Shona express their answers with reasons, using reasoning words, such as *because*. The students negotiate whether the main character in the story can ever be a Trueheart. At the beginning, the girls disagree with each other, saying, "I think so" and "I don't think so." Delaney's comment shows her disagreement with Laura's position and is followed by a chain of reasons, which makes the entire episode an example of exploratory talk. Delaney's turn is also an *elaborated explanation,* or a claim with more than one reason. Laura responds to the challenge with an alternative claim, "Yes, she will be good," and a reason, "time as an Ancient Crone" will make her better. Laura's response, though, is not elaborated because it lacks extended reasoning to support the claim.

In terms of Literature Circles, the discussion is student led, and, in her comment, Shona refers to a response to the reading from an earlier writing response routine. Notice that the integration of the response is "natural," in that Shona refers to the response in the context of the dialogue, and that it doesn't waylay the group into sharing all their responses in round-robin fashion. The students stick with one idea, exploring it in the conversation.

What's never compromised in Literature Circles is the student choice of text for independent reading and the focus on response to reading prior to the discussions. We thrive as readers when we have agency. And Louise Rosenblatt was right about the role of personal response. Don't we first have a personal connection or thought about a character that leads us to more thoughts and deeper analysis? The current focus on analysis, close reading, and using text evidence may be robbing students of the necessary "personal first step" toward analysis. Myriad high-stakes literacy assessments that emphasize analysis and the use of text evidence have likely led to this point, but a commitment to Literature Circles and personal response to text may be the safety line that pulls us all back.

READ MORE

Daniels, Harvey. 2002. *Literature Circles: Voice and Choice in Book Clubs and Reading Groups.* 2nd ed. Portland, ME: Stenhouse.

Daniels, Harvey, and Nancy Steineke. 2004. *Mini-lessons for Literature Circles.* Portsmouth, NH: Heinemann.

Hill, Bonnie Campbell, Nancy J. Johnson, and Katherine L. Schlick Noe, eds. 1995. *Literature Circles and Response.* Norwood, MA: Christopher-Gordon.

Hill, Bonnie Campbell, Katherine L. Schlick Noe, and Janine A. King. 2003. *Literature Circles in Middle School: One Teacher's Journey.* Norwood, MA: Christopher-Gordon.

Samway, Katherine Davies, and Gail Whang. 1996. *Literature Study Circles in a Multicultural Classroom.* York, ME: Stenhouse.

Schlick Noe, K. L., and N. J. Johnson. 1999. *Getting Started with Literature Circles.* Norwood, MA: Christopher-Gordon.

Short, Kathy G., and Gloria Kauffman. 1999. "'So, What Do I Do?' The role of the teacher in Literature Circles." In *Book Talk and Beyond: Children and Teachers Respond to Literature,* edited by Nancy L. Roser and Miriam G. Martinez. Newark, DE: International Reading Association.

Walker, Katie. 2018. "Literature Circles as a Sliding-Glass Door to Social Equity in the Middle-Grades." *National Journal of Middle-Grades Reform* 1 (1): 23–25.

SECTION ▌▌ How Do I Know Students Are Engaged in Personal Response?

When students are engaged in personal response, they talk about the text as if they are solving a puzzle. Their questions are authentic and relate to the text or topic under discussion (e.g., "What does it mean, when it says, 'wickered?'"). They share their thinking and hypothesize about characters (e.g., "I think Mary is like the dead vine."). You might hear them speculating (e.g., "I wonder if . . ."), analyzing how or why something happened (e.g., "I think he did that because . . .") and tying things together to try to make sense of a story (e.g., "It's like a marathon. It ends and starts, it ends and starts."). They often challenge each other's ideas, saying things like: "I disagree . . . I think Mary was like wickered, alive on the inside, but appeared dead on the outside." If they make references to the text, they will usually be about elements of the story (e.g., the character, language) that prompted their thinking.

Figure 6.7 shows how the three approaches described in this section might be scored on the TATT (Talk Assessment Tool for Teachers), if well implemented and practiced. A tell-tale sign that students are engaging in personal response, of course, is that many of their remarks fall into the 'affective response' category. Here students are making connections between the text and their own lives or feelings (i.e., text-to-self connections). For example, you might hear them say:

- When I read that, it made me feel . . .
- That reminds me of when . . .
- In my family, we . . .
- I felt sad when I read that . . .

You might also hear a lot of emotion in students' voices (e.g., "Nasty!," "No way!").

As a general rule, you will hear students engage in exploratory talk much of the time but offer elaborated explanations only some of the time. Because the teacher takes a back seat in these discussions, students have a lot of opportunities to think together and figure out what is happening in a story and why. Some of this talk will be cumulative where students simply agree with each other and build on each other's ideas, and this can be fine. Yet quite a bit will be exploratory

Figure 6.7 Typical Personal-Response Talk

	1 Not Yet	2 Emerging	3 Developing	4 Blooming
Questions				
Authentic	____ None	____ Some	____ Many	✓ Almost all
Uptake	____ None	____ Some	____ Many	✓ Almost all
Analysis/ Generalization	____ None	____ Some	✓ Many	____ Almost all
Speculation	____ None	____ Some	✓ Many	____ Almost all
Textual Connections				
Reference to text	____ Do not use text evidence	✓ Once or twice	____ Some of the time	____ Many times
Extratextual Connections				
Affective response	____ Do not make connections	____ Once or twice	____ Some of the time	✓ Many times
Intertextual response	____ Do not make connections	____ Once or twice	✓ Some of the time	____ Many times
Shared-knowledge response	____ Do not make connections	✓ Once or twice	____ Some of the time	____ Many times
Individual Reasoning				
Elaborated explanations	____ Do not provide reasons or provide only one reason	____ Once or twice	✓ Some of the time	____ Many times
Collective Reasoning				
Exploratory talk	____ Do not collectively explore a topic or reason together	____ Some of the time	✓ Much of the time	____ Almost all of the time

talk where students are more rigorously exploring each other's ideas. But because the teacher plays a fairly minor role, there are fewer opportunities to extend students' thinking and prompt elaborated explanations. Of course, it all depends on how much the teacher is involved. In Grand Conversations, where the teacher is a bit more involved, you will hear fewer episodes of exploratory talk and more elaborated explanations; in student-led Literature Circles and small-group book club discussions, you will hear more exploratory talk and fewer elaborated explanations. Listen carefully! Try to develop an ear for these nuances in students' talk.

To sum up, in discussions that prompt personal response, there is a real sense that students are sorting out the text as if it's a puzzle to be solved. Because students in these approaches usually have a choice about what they read and what they talk about, they have a vested interest in the text and in figuring out what it means. And without the teacher playing much of a role in the discussion, students readily gravitate toward a problem-solving orientation, working together, asking authentic questions, and answering their classmates' questions.

SECTION III

Talk About Text to Emphasize Knowledge Building

In this section, we introduce three approaches to classroom discussion that engage students in what we call "knowledge-building talk": Instructional Conversations, Questioning the Author, and Shared Inquiry. We use the term *knowledge building* because these discussions focus on the text and on reading to acquire information—what Rosenblatt (1978) called an "efferent stance" toward the text. The goal of these approaches is for students to engage deeply with the ideas in the text, especially the complex ideas, and grapple with them to build a coherent understanding of the text. In these discussions, students analyze the text, consider carefully the ideas, and engage in close reading. The Shared Inquiry approach has the added goal of enhancing students' critical thinking abilities and shares some features with the approaches we describe in Section IV. We include it here because its primary focus is fostering students' understanding of complex ideas in challenging text.

You will see that the teacher exerts considerable control over these discussions. The teacher chooses the text, leads the discussion, and maintains control over the topic. She usually controls the turn taking by calling on students and exercises considerable interpretive authority when evaluating their responses. The box below shows the typical format of these discussions.

Why do these three approaches support students' knowledge building? The best explanation comes from a cognitive view of reading. According to this view, while reading, the reader identifies what is important in the text, holds that information in memory, and connects it with what came before in the text and with relevant background knowledge (Kintsch 1998). The reader is actively making sense of incoming information by integrating it with other text information and with prior knowledge to build a coherent mental model of the text. All three approaches are good for helping students to identify what is important in the text and to integrate the important ideas with their relevant background knowledge. In Instructional Conversations, the quality of the language interactions between the teacher and students are also thought to be important for scaffolding students' understanding (Vygotsky 1962, 1978). The rationale behind Shared Inquiry is less clear, though it is thought that engaging students in inquiry and interaction around complex ideas and challenging texts propels their intellectual growth (Adler and van Doren 1972; Dewey 1933).

Typical Format for Knowledge-Building Discussions

Approach	Text	Reading	Grouping
Instructional Conversations	literary	during	small group
Questioning the Author	literary and informational	during	whole class
Shared Inquiry	literary	before	whole class

7

Instructional Conversations

INSTRUCTIONAL CONVERSATIONS

Research Support

- Deepen students' comprehension and thematic understanding
- Appropriate for students in K–12 classes, in various content areas
- Well suited to students from culturally and linguistically diverse backgrounds
- Foster English language learners' comprehension when used with literature logs

Learning How

Consult the teacher-friendly resources listed at the end of this chapter. Plan Instructional Conversations with your colleagues, and together review and analyze videos of your discussions.

Goals

To engage students in meaningful conversation about text to enable them to build knowledge and understanding around important concepts and ideas. To promote more complex language and expression.

Typical Features

- Literary text
- Small-group discussion
- Heterogeneous group
- Teacher led
- Teacher chooses text
- Students read text during discussion
- Teacher controls topic
- Students and teacher share control of turn taking
- Teacher has interpretive authority
- Little focus on author intent

Typical Teacher Questions

Can you tell me more about that?

What does [word] mean?

How do you know?

What makes you think that?

Why do you think that is important?

How does that connect to what you know?

Typical Student Comments

Because . . .

If . . . then . . .

I don't think so.

It says [reading from text]

This reminds me of the time . . .

I think (thought) . . .

Teacher's Role

- Identify a theme in the text and maintain that thematic focus throughout the discussion.
- Be responsive to students' comments, knowing when to step in to enlarge their understanding of ideas and concepts, and when to step back.
- "Weave" together students' comments around the important ideas and concepts and help students to integrate the text information with their background knowledge.

What the Talk Sounds Like

In the following Instructional Conversation, a teacher and a small group of first-grade students with specific learning disabilities are discussing Syd Hoff's *Sammy the Seal* (1959), a story about a seal who leaves the zoo and explores the city.

Teacher: Has he had a good time in the city, away from home?

Eddie: Yea, uh huh.

Sergio: Nooo.

Jamison: He gonna go to that, to the man's house.

Eddie: He gonna go to the zoo.

Teacher: (pointing to the picture) Why would he go to the man's house?

Frank: Because -

Sergio: (interrupts) He's going to go back to the zoo.

Frank: (interrupts) to take a bath.

(several students comment at once)

Eddie: (speaks over other students) back to the zoo.

Teacher: Why would he go back to the zoo?

Eddie: Because it's too hot and it's not that hot at the zoo.

Frank: No, he's going to take a bath.

Eddie: Uh-uh. He's going to the zoo.

Frank: No.

Teacher: He tells us what he wants (pointing to the text). He says (they all read the text), "I am hot. I want to go swimming, said Sammy."

(Echevarria and McDonough 1995, 111)

Instructional Conversations are teacher-led discussions that emphasize the construction of meaning and exploration of different perspectives and interpretations of the text. The teacher chooses the text and topic and writes an authentic or "big" question about a central theme or main idea of the text. Authentic questions, or questions without a single, right answer, are common in Instructional Conversations, but *test questions,* or those that have a single, correct answer, are quite common too. In the example above, the teacher asks, "Has he had a good time in the city, away from home?" Although it sounds like a test question, where the teacher has an answer in mind, it actually functions as an authentic question because the students respond with different positions (e.g., yea, no), and the teacher doesn't correct or redirect the students toward a specific, "right" answer. If the teacher had redirected the students toward a specific answer (e.g., "Yes, that's right"), then the question would indeed have been a test question.

Figure 7.1 Examples of Quality Talk

Features	Examples	Why They Are Productive
Authentic questions	Teacher: Has he had a good time in the city, away from home?	Authentic Questions provide students with multiple "access" points for thinking about the text; they open space for thinking about the text since there are multiple "correct" answers.
Uptake	Teacher: Why would he go to the man's house?	Follow-up questions that build onto a previous comment facilitate an elaboration of ideas previously shared.
High-level thinking questions	Teacher: Why would he go back to the zoo?	These questions elicit high-level thinking in the form of analysis, generalization or speculation. Questions that begin with *why, how,* or *should* tend to generate students' high-level thinking.

When teachers ask authentic questions and step back from the discussion, students talk in connected ways during Instructional Conversations, as Eddie and Frank do in the last several lines of the excerpt. Frequently, authentic questions during Instructional Conversations elicit high-level thinking in the form of analysis and speculation, as happens in the excerpt when the teacher asks, "Why would he go back to the zoo?" Eddie replies with the word *because,* which is the most common reasoning word found in Instructional Conversations, and one that indicates analysis or generalization. Another typical reasoning word found in this approach is *if,* which indicates speculation.

Very common in this approach is the teacher's routine use of *uptake,* or asking follow-up questions to build on the students' responses and to engage ideas that relate to the students' prior knowledge. Follow-up questions that elicit connections to personal experiences, or *affective responses,* are fairly typical during Instructional Conversations, whereas questions that elicit connections to other texts, or *intertextual responses,* and connections to other lessons, or *shared-knowledge responses,* occur rarely. Sometimes uptake will generate *elaborated explanations,* which means that students respond in extended ways, with more than one reason that supports a position. These elaborated explanations can be quite lengthy in Instructional Conversations.

Instructional Conversations offer a more teacher-centered approach than others, which does not necessarily mean the teacher is doing all the work and thinking, but the teacher does step in frequently to model, to connect students' contributions to support cohesiveness, and to elicit prior knowledge to contextualize the text. As an example, in the last line of the excerpt, the teacher points directly to the text, modeling how text evidence can support an interpretation. Since the guidelines for Instructional Conversations encourage the teacher to step in, students almost never demonstrate *exploratory talk,* which is student-to-student talk, where students challenge each other, ask each other questions, give reasons and alternatives or, otherwise, really dig into an idea or topic of the text without interruption from the teacher. The talk of Instructional Conversations is primarily *cumulative,* which means that students connect to each other, as they do in the excerpt, but they do not explore all the facets of an interpretation in any depth.

THE STORY BEHIND
INSTRUCTIONAL CONVERSATIONS

The idea of Instructional Conversations dates back to the 1970s and the work of Roland Tharp and Ronald Gallimore with the Kamehameha Early Education Program (KEEP) in Hawaii. Tharp and Gallimore were seeking an alternative to the traditional recitation form of instruction that would be more culturally appropriate for native Hawaiian children. Working with Kathy Au, a teacher and researcher at KEEP, they developed the Experience-Text-Relationship (ETR) method for teaching reading comprehension (Au 1979), along with a range of other strategies for fostering language, literacy, and thinking. All strategies encouraged children to "weave together" text information and prior knowledge in order to understand what they read. Tharp and Gallimore (1988) characterized these strategies under the generic label "Instructional Conversations."

Although Tharp and Gallimore (1988, 1989) coined the term, it had been used earlier by Green and Wallat (1981). Whereas Green and Wallat described an Instructional Conversation as any instructional talk in a classroom, Tharp and Gallimore viewed it as a specialized form of discourse to scaffold children's understanding within their zone of proximal development.

Claude Goldenberg, a colleague of Tharp and Gallimore, sought to make Instructional Conversations more practical for teachers to implement. In 1988, he began a three-year collaboration with a small group of elementary school teachers in a low-income, language-minority school district in Southern California. The model evolved over weekly meetings as teachers tried Instructional Conversations in their classrooms, shared videos of their lessons, and revised their teaching (Goldenberg, 1992–1993). In addition to the previous work by Au (1979) and Tharp and Gallimore (1988) on fostering reading comprehension among at-risk minority students, Goldenberg drew on research on the role of background knowledge in comprehension and on comprehension instruction. What emerged was a more precise description of Instructional Conversations and the ten elements described later in this chapter.

Although interest in Instructional Conversations has waned in recent years, it continues to receive attention both as a stand-alone model of discussion and as one of the Five Standards of Effective Pedagogy (Tharp et al. 2000). The Five Standards comprise a set of teaching principles for effective instruction particularly for learners from linguistically and culturally diverse backgrounds: teachers and students producing together, developing language and literacy across the curriculum, connecting schools to students' lives, teaching complex thinking, and, of course, Instructional Conversations.

Research Support

Goldenberg and others have conducted many studies of Instructional Conversations using a variety of research methods in a variety of educational settings. These include several small-scale experimental studies to investigate the effects of Instructional Conversations on students' reading comprehension as well as a large number of qualitative studies of what the discourse looks like in Instructional Conversations. What do we know from this body of research?

Instructional Conversations enable students to achieve a deeper, more nuanced understanding of important concepts. For example, Saunders and Goldenberg (2007) found that, after an Instructional Conversation with a text centered on the theme of friendship, students displayed more complex understandings of friendship (e.g., recognizing that friends are sometimes in conflict) in their post-discussion essays than did students who participated in a recitation-style lesson with the text. The students' deeper understandings of the concept could be traced back to their talk in the Instructional Conversations (Saunders, Patthey-Chavez, and Goldenberg 1997). Moreover, these gains in deep understanding were achieved without sacrificing students' literal comprehension of the stories; students who participated in the Instructional Conversation understood the literal details as well if not better than did students in the conventional lesson. This is an important point because the focus of Instructional Conversations is the big ideas or themes in a story rather than the details.

True to its origins, Instructional Conversations can be implemented with students from culturally and linguistically diverse backgrounds and in a variety of educational settings. Instructional Conversations have been used extensively with Spanish-speaking students in transition to English instruction (e.g., Patthey-Chavez and Clare 1996). They have been used in classes ranging from kindergarten (Geisler 1999) to high school (Olezza 1999), and in a variety of content areas including math (Dalton and Sison 1995; Lin 2012), social studies (Villar 1999), and foreign language education (Davin 2013; Takahashi, Austin, and Morimoto 2000; Todhunter 1999). They have also been used, with adaptation, in special education classes (Echevarria 1995; Echevarria and McDonough 1995).

Instructional Conversations help both English language learners (ELLs) and English-proficient students. Saunders and Goldenberg (1999) conducted an experimental study of the effects of Instructional Conversations when used in combination with literature logs where students responded in writing to the literature selection before coming to the discussions. One hundred and sixteen fourth- and fifth-grade ELLs and English-proficient students were involved in the study.

Results showed that both ELLs and English-proficient students who participated in the Instructional Conversations plus literature logs condition scored significantly higher in literal and inferential comprehension of the story than did students in three other conditions (literature logs only, Instructional Conversations only, and a reading plus study control condition). The ELLs in the Instructional Conversations plus literature logs condition also performed significantly higher than students in the other conditions in terms of their ability to explain and exemplify the theme of the story.

Almost all of the research on Instructional Conversations has assessed students' comprehension of the stories discussed; what we need to know more about is whether they yield generalizable gains in students' reading comprehension abilities. Research on the Five Standards of Effective Pedagogy, of which Instructional Conversation is a part, has examined their general effects on standardized tests of reading achievement and, to date, results have been mixed (Doherty and Hilberg 2008). Nonetheless, Instructional Conversation appears to be the most powerful component of the five standards.

INSTRUCTIONAL CONVERSATIONS in Practice

Planning for Instructional Conversations

QUICK GUIDE

1. Identify a small group of students. Whole-group discussion works with the approach, but our recommendation is to use small, heterogenous groups to stimulate diverse perspectives.

2. Choose an appropriate text and identify a broad theme to interpret (e.g., friendship, survival, honesty). Instructional Conversations are typically used with literary text, but they can be used with informational and multimodal texts.

3. Create authentic questions based on your close reading of the text. The authentic question should relate to the central theme or main idea (e.g., Are these characters true friends?)

4. Be ready with follow-up questions that may elicit or connect to prior knowledge. Follow-up questions are the heart of Instructional Conversations. The primary role of the teacher is to notice opportunities to step in with a follow-up question to elicit prior knowledge, connect to other texts, elicit reasons and positions, or model an approach to thinking about text.

Instructional Conversations is an approach to discussion that emphasizes analysis and reflection on the themes and central ideas of texts (e.g., literary text, informational text, subject-specific text such as science). The proponents of Instructional Conversations argue that students don't learn these ways of thinking on their own (e.g., Tharp and Gallimore 1991). Students need assistance in developing these high-level thinking skills and practice with the kind of language that supports the application of high-level thinking to reading. An Instructional Conversation offers students an instructional space to use conversation as a "workshop" for exploring ideas and enlarging their understanding.

During discussion, students hear over and over the ways their classmates analyze and reason about the text. Likewise, the teacher assumes students have high-level thoughts about text, so she listens carefully to grasp the student's intended meaning and assists or responds in ways that strengthen the students' thinking about the text. The teacher often weaves into the students' talk her own follow-up questions to probe students' thinking and to elicit more elaborated responses. Before the discussion even begins, however, the teacher creates an Instructional Conversation plan premised on the idea that students and the teacher assist each other through questioning and sharing of knowledge during the discussion.

When planning an Instructional Conversation, you will need to think about grouping, choosing a text and a thematic focus, and writing an initial big or authentic question to kick-start the dialogue. Figure 7.2 provides a snapshot of these planning features and Figure 7.3 highlights a couple of themes and text selections to help get you started.

In Instructional Conversations, authentic questions are referred to as "unknown-answer questions," which, in this approach, should have a thematic focus. Proponents of Instructional Conversations advocate team planning, using the conversation among your colleagues to generate authentic questions. If team planning is not possible, then read the text you have selected or the section of a longer novel twice, noticing places in the text that point toward a central issue or theme. Key issues and themes are the substance of good authentic questions, and the questions become much easier to write when you have a handle on one of the text's central themes.

In thinking about authentic questions for Instructional Conversations, let's consider the popular children's chapter book, *Charlotte's Web* by E. B. White (1952). The beginning of the story is about Fern, who saves the runt of a litter of

Figure 7.2 Decisions to Make When Planning an Instructional Conversation

Features of Plans	Decisions to Make	Examples
Grouping	Small groups—optimal; 5–8 students; heterogenous or homogeneous Whole group—may be used after students are very comfortable with the approach	Rotate small groups of students through an Instructional Conversation text and discussion, modifying the reading, if needed (e.g., shared reading). If modifying the reading for level, it would be okay to keep heterogenous groups. Instructional Conversations take place during reading, stopping to ask an authentic question and discussing, or after reading.
Text selection	This is typically literary text, but it could be any subject-specific informational text or multimodal text. A strong theme or a thought-provoking main idea are very important features of the text you choose.	Reading the text in class is based on several factors, such as the prior knowledge of your students, the complexity of the text, and the experience of the students with the English language.
Authentic questions	If you're reading a literary text and connecting to a standard, consider one of the central themes that relates to the plot or the character. If you're reading informational text, focus on a central idea that's interesting.	If you want to focus on character traits, a good authentic question might be: "Is [the character] a good person? A good friend?" If reading an informational text about the benefits and drawbacks of zoos, you might ask, "Should we have zoos in our communities?"

Figure 7.3 Examples of Themes and Texts to Try with Instructional Conversation

For Younger Children:
Thematic focus: Being a child and immigrant from a different country and culture

- *My Name is Sangoel by Karen Williams and Khadra Mohammed (2009)*
- *The Name Jar by Yangsook Choi (2001)*
- *Mama's Nightingale: A Story of Immigration and Separation by Edwidge Danticat (2015)*

For Older Children:
Thematic focus: Growing up as a child of immigrants

- *The House on Mango Street by Sandra Cisneros (1984)*
- *Refugee by Alan Gratz (2017)*
- *The Circuit: Stories from a Life of a Migrant Child by Francisco Jiménez (1998)*

pigs from its demise, promising her father that she will take care of the tiny pig-let. Over time, Fern's visits to the barn to take care of Wilbur slow down and stop altogether, and this makes Wilbur feel sad and lonely.

After reading, we can see that the central themes are friendship, depression, and loneliness. Wilbur's sadness and longing for Fern makes us feel and know how profound it is to have a special friend and to lose a special friend (this theme is relevant, too, when we meet Charlotte a little later in the story). Writing an authentic question begins at the point where you have a personal connection or a strong reaction to a central theme of the text.

But you have to keep thinking about the issue before writing a question, asking yourself additional questions before you land on the central point that becomes the thematic focus of the Instructional Conversation. Is the central idea more about the loss of Fern, the loss of a special friend, or Wilbur feeling sorry for himself? Wilbur's life carries on at the barn, and he has other friends, so a way to facilitate deeper consideration of the theme (e.g., rereading and using text evidence) and interpreting the "special friend" theme is to ask a question about why his other friends at the barn aren't enough. For example, we might ask, "Wilbur is with his other friends in the barn, but why is he so sad?" This question is authentic since it would generate several acceptable answers and elicit ideas from students about special friends or best friends, which is a central theme of this part of the story.

Teacher's Role in Instructional Conversations

The teacher's role in an Instructional Conversation is, first, to assume that children have the capacity to produce high-level, analytical, and reflective thoughts about their reading, and, second, to be responsive and ready to assist students by asking follow-up questions. This means the teacher is active and ready to step in to promote elaborations, to extend responses with questions that elicit students' reasons for their opinions, and to cue students to what they are doing well. When listening to an Instructional Conversation, the teacher's facilitation style may seem heavy-handed, but, in actuality, the teacher is deliberately stepping in, based on several instructional decisions and conversational moves to assist students. These decisions and moves comprise ten elements of Instructional Conversations (Figure 7.4).

The ten elements of Instructional Conversations can be organized in a *before-during-after* structure for facilitating Instructional Conversations. *Before* the discussion, the teacher identifies the thematic focus, activates prior knowledge

Figure 7.4 Ten Elements of Instructional Conversations (Goldenberg 1992–1993)

Instructional Decisions

1. *Thematic focus:* The teacher selects a theme or idea to serve as a starting point for focusing the discussion and has a general plan for how the theme will unfold, based on a thorough understanding of the text. This includes a plan for how to chunk the text to permit optimal exploration of the theme.

2. *Activation and use of relevant background knowledge:* The teacher activates or provides background knowledge (schemas) necessary for understanding the text.

3. *Direct teaching:* The teacher provides direct teaching of a skill or concept when necessary.

4. *Promotion of more complex language and expression:* The teacher promotes or elicits more extended language and expression.

5. *Elicitation of bases for statements or positions:* The teacher promotes students' use of text, pictures, and reasoning to support an argument or position.

Conversational Moves

6. *Fewer "known-answer" questions:* Much of the discussion centers on questions and answers for which there might be more than one correct answer.

7. *Responsivity to student contributions:* The teacher is responsive to students' statements and the opportunities they provide.

8. *Connected discourse:* Discussion is characterized by multiple, interactive, connected turns; utterances by teachers and students build upon and extend previous ones (cf. uptake).

9. *Challenging, nonthreatening atmosphere:* The teacher creates a zone of proximal development, where students are challenged but within a positive affective climate.

10. *General participation, including self-selected turns:* The teacher encourages participation of all students and does not hold the exclusive right to determine who talks. Students are encouraged to volunteer or otherwise influence the selection of speaking turns.

before reading the text or the section of text, and creates ground rules to provide a safe environment and to encourage connected discourse (e.g., no raising hands).

During the Instructional Conversation, the teacher's mindset should be responsive, ready to assist but not to take over. Assistance takes the form of asking follow-up questions that are authentic to elicit students' language production or bases for their positions, modeling or direct teaching to clarify the text or an idea of the text, and promoting connected discourse through stepping back and encouraging students to talk to each other (see Figure 7.5 for examples).

After the Instructional Conversation, although the proponents do not explicitly state a need for a follow-up activity, the use of a literature log and writing are beneficial and foster deeper thinking about the text and the thematic focus (Saunders

Figure 7.5 Some Elements of an Instructional Conversation Addressed Through Follow-Up Questions

---

Element 7. Responsivity to student contributions:

Follow the "lead" of students, building onto their ideas and connections.

Example: "So, you are saying . . . ? Why do you think that is important?"

Element 4. Promotion of more complex language and expression:

Restate a student's idea to support academic language expression or to assist in clarifying an analytical or reflective thought.

Example: "I hear you saying that friends are nice. Can you say more about what it means to be nice?"

Prompt extended language production.

Example: "Okay. You said, 'Sammy is hot.' How do you know that?"

Element 5. Elicitation of bases for statements or positions:

Assist students with taking positions and giving reasons to support their positions.

Example: "You said, 'Sammy is hot.' That's an interesting opinion. Can you say more about why you think that? How do you know he feels hot?"

Element 3. Direct teaching:

Model a reading skill in a direct way or teach a concept or word in a direct way.

Example: "I'm not sure we understand this yet, because we're saying very different things, and so we might need to look back. Let's reread."

---

and Goldenberg 1999). Teachers often reflect on the outcomes of the conversation, the quality of the thematic focus, and the utility of the authentic questions.

Approach in Action: Language Arts, Grade 4

The following excerpt of an Instructional Conversation comes from a discussion with a group of students learning English in the fourth grade. The thematic focus the teacher had selected was friendship. The students had written essays about friendship and read short stories about friendship. The teacher had also activated background knowledge about friendship before beginning the discussion with a big question.

Teacher: Do we sometimes get mad at our friends?

Students: (overlap) Yes.

Cal: Yes, course.

Teacher: When do we get mad at our friends? Why do you say "course" like "of course?" What happens when you get mad at your friends?

Cal: They get mad at you.

Teacher: Okay. They get mad at you.

Ming: They do something that you don't like.

Teacher: Okay, tell me a little more about that.

Ming: They do something that you don't like or they don't talk to you or not share or not be a good friend.

The teachers uses uptake or a follow-up to the previous response to extend the language production and to elicit a basis for the position, "friends get mad at each other." This is also an authentic question.

Here the teacher promotes more complex language production with a prompt, which is important for English language learners.

The prompt to elicit more complex language from the previous line works! Ming elaborates her position, "[We] get mad at friends when they do something that you don't like," with several additional examples.

(Saunders and Goldenberg 2007, 242)

This short excerpt of discussion characterizes Instructional Conversations and quality talk. In terms of quality talk, the teacher asks an authentic question in the form of uptake to extend students' language production when she asks, "When do we get mad at our friends?" This kind of question is a typical facilitation move during Instructional Conversations since the approach pushes the teacher to listen carefully, to be responsive to what students say, and to make decisions to step in and assist students with expressing their thinking in stronger ways.

For students who are learning English, Instructional Conversations may be an especially important tool for using and producing academic language. Ming and many other students who are learning English may benefit from the teacher stepping into a discussion to give them time and opportunity to elaborate their thinking and to produce academic discourse. The last line of the excerpt is nearly an example of an elaborated explanation—and from a student who is not yet proficient in English—where, if we assume Ming is taking the position that friends get mad at each other when they do hurtful things, she offers several reasons to support her position.

Language doesn't help us learn unless we use the language. Instructional Conversations is about teaching through dialogue, and the early developers of the approach, Roland Tharp, Claude Goldenberg, William Saunders, and others, had hoped teachers would draw on their experiences as caregivers when they were teaching. Caregivers often listen to their own or other children and assist them with dialogue, clarifying, elaborating their ideas, and promoting more complete expressions and exchanges of ideas.

At some point in American education, teachers learned to ask a question that had a *single* right answer, thus changing forever the natural interaction pattern between an adult and a child. Paradoxically, they were the same adults who would go home at the end of the day and have real conversations with their children.

The developers of Instructional Conversations have a simple wish for schools, teachers, and children: a return to *conversation*, or the authentic and natural way children acquire thinking and language skills with the assistance of caregivers as they interact and talk. They posited that if teachers just used more of what they did with their own children at home while they were at school, children would improve their abilities to form, express, and exchange ideas. In the process, students would develop high-level reflective and analytical skills no matter the text or topic. Instructional Conversations would create classrooms that reflect who we really are and how we actually learn through using language.

READ MORE

Benner, Susan. 2010. "Dialogue and Instructional Conversation as an Instructional Strategy," 95–110. In *Promising Practices for Elementary Teacher: Make No Excuses!* Thousand Oaks, CA: Corwin.

Goldenberg, Claude. 1992–1993. "Instructional Conversations: Promoting Comprehension Through Discussion." *The Reading Teacher* 46 (4): 316–326.

Saunders, William, and Claude Goldenberg. 2007. "The Effects of an Instructional Conversation on Transition Students' Concepts of Friendship and Story Comprehension." In *Talking Texts: How Speech and Writing Interact in School Learning*, edited by Rosalind Horowitz, 221–252. Mahwah, NJ: Lawrence Erlbaum.

Yamauchi, Lois A., Seongah Im, and Nanette S. Schonleber. 2012. "Adapting Strategies of Effective Instruction for Culturally Diverse Preschoolers." *Journal of Early Childhood Teacher Education* 33: 54–72.

Questioning the Author

<table>
<tr><td colspan="3" align="center">

QUESTIONING THE AUTHOR

</td></tr>
<tr>
<td valign="top">

Research Support

- Improves quality of classroom discourse
- Increases student engagement with text
- Enhances student comprehension of texts read and discussed
- May support growth in students' general comprehension abilities

Learning How

To learn how to use queries and make other instructional moves during QtA discussion, consult the teacher-friendly resources at the end of this chapter. Beck and McKeown's (2006) book is a great place to start.

</td>
<td valign="top">

Goals

To help students engage with text, think deeply about the important ideas, and build understanding

Typical Features

- Literary and informational text
- Whole-class discussion
- Heterogeneous group
- Teacher led
- Teacher chooses text
- Students read text during discussion
- Teacher controls topic
- Teacher controls turn taking
- Teacher has interpretive authority
- Strong focus on author intent

</td>
<td valign="top">

Typical Teacher Questions

What is the author trying to say here?

What is the author's message?

How does this connect with what we already read?

Does the author tell us why?

How is the author trying to make you feel about the character?

Typical Student Comments

He means that . . .

I think that the author . . .

I think she's saying . . .

Why do they . . . ?

That probably connects . . .

</td>
</tr>
<tr>
<td colspan="3" valign="top">

Teacher's Role

- Identify places in the text where you plan to stop reading and pose a query to begin discussion.
- Take an active role in directing the discussion.
- Ask initial and follow-up queries to help students connect text ideas and integrate them with their background knowledge.
- Share your own reactions to the text to make visible your own struggles to make sense of the information.

</td>
</tr>
</table>

What the Talk Sounds Like

In the following Questioning the Author discussion, students in a fourth-grade social studies class are discussing a section from their social studies textbook that describes early Polynesian settlements on the Hawaiian Islands.

Justine: (reading first sentence from text) *When the Polynesians settled on the Hawaiian Islands, they began to raise plants that they brought with them.*

Teacher: What does the author mean by just this one sentence?

Antonio: He means that they brought some of the food that they had there with them.

Teacher: Um–hmm, we decided that yesterday. But what does the author mean by they began "to raise" the plants they brought with them, Temika?

Temika: Like the plants and stuff, they began to plant them.

Teacher: They began to plant them, why?

Temika: For their food!

Teacher: Right! They can plant the things that they brought, then they're going to have their own crops in Hawaii. OK, good.

Alvis: Why do they need to plant things when they already brought things over?

Teacher: Who can answer Alvis' question? He said, they already had food, why did they have to plant the food? Roberta?

Roberta: Maybe because, like back then in the Hawaiian Islands (pause) probably, you couldn't drive to the store, like they do now.

Teacher: OK, so Roberta's saying they couldn't get in their car and drive to the stores, but Alvis still has a point. Why not just eat the food they brought?

Alvis: They could run out.

Teacher: Oh, I think you just answered your own question. Alvis, say what you just said.

Alvis: 'Cause they'll run out of food.

Teacher: OK. That makes sense now. Let's read the rest of the paragraph. (students read to end of the paragraph)

Teacher: What's the author telling us in the rest of this paragraph?

Antonio: Well, they're naming some of the things that they ate.

Roberta: The author's telling us plants or food, like the taro, the bananas. And they're telling us how they cooked it, and where they found it.

Teacher: Yes, they pounded it on a board to make a paste called poi.

(Beck et al. 1997, 28–29)

In Questioning the Author, the teacher controls the text, topic, and often the students' turns. The first thing you might notice in the excerpt is how actively involved the teacher is in the discussion. Most of the exchanges follow a teacher–student–teacher pattern, and the teacher talks as much as the students, asks most of the questions, and calls on some of the students to respond. These features of a discussion are common in Questioning the Author as are the bursts of discussion that take place *during* reading. The teacher typically chooses points where the reading stops and plans questions to generate dialogue, engage thinking, and construct meaning about a small section of the text.

Figure 8.1 Examples of Quality Talk

Features	Examples	Why They are Productive
Authentic questions	Alvis: Why do they need to plant things when they already brought things over?	Authentic questions are "unknown answer" questions, or questions with multiple possible answers. They encourage participation and engagement, high-level thinking, and divergent and creative thinking.
Uptake	Teacher: He said, they already had food, why did they have to plant the food?	Follow-up questions that build onto a previous turn create space for elaboration, connections, clarifications, and other questions.
Reasoning words	*why, because, could*	These words signal reasoning, such as analysis, generalization, and speculation.

In Questioning the Author, the teacher asks almost all of the questions, some of which are *authentic questions*, or genuine questions with multiple possible answers, and many of which are *test questions* or those that have either a single, correct answer or a preferred answer. When teachers evaluate the students' answers after they respond, we identify the question as a *test question*. For example, near the middle of the excerpt, the teacher asks, "They began to plant them, why?" The student responds, and the teacher replies, "Right!" The teacher's reply signals an evaluation of the student response, suggesting that there is only one correct answer (remember the I-R-E pattern from Chapter 1). We tend to see more test questions in Questioning the Author than in the other approaches perhaps because students respond to questions about short segments of text that are related to the author's purpose, such as "What does the author mean by this sentence?" Occasionally in Questioning the Author, students will pose authentic questions, as Alvis does when he asks, "Why do they need to plant things when they already brought things over?"

As a result of the laser-like focus on the language of the text, the teacher uses a moderate number of *uptake* or follow-up questions that build on a student's response. An example of the teacher's use of uptake is toward the middle of the excerpt, when he asks, "Why did they have to plant the food?" This question also generates high-level thinking, since Roberta's response shows a generalization. A moderate number of the teacher's questions in the approach are *high-level thinking questions*.

Because the focus in Questioning the Author is on wrestling with the meaning of specific language in the text, students' responses are very text bound. Students rarely make explicit connections to their own lives or feelings or to other texts they have read, so we seldom see (well, hear) affective responses or intertextual connections. Sometimes, however, the teacher asks shared-knowledge questions that prompt students to make connections to knowledge and understanding that they have built up in previous discussions about the text (e.g., "What did the author tell us yesterday, when we were reading?"); indeed, shared-knowledge questions are more common in Questioning the Author than in any other approach.

In Questioning the Author, there are relatively few, if any, opportunities for *exploratory talk,* or the kind of connected student talk where students discuss the big ideas of a text, giving reasons, challenging ideas, discussing alternatives, and weighing the evidence. Reasoning words (e.g., *because, might, if*) are a feature of exploratory talk, so without exploratory talk, you will hear a limited range of reasoning words. We do, however, hear students frequently using *because, might,* and *if* to indicate analysis, generalization, and speculation, which are, no doubt, a result of the teacher asking students to explain what the author means in a section of the text. In the excerpt, Roberta uses *maybe* and *because* to speculate about a reason that also indicates generalization or tying together an idea from the reading and her prior knowledge, saying, "Maybe because, like back then in the Hawaiian Islands (pause) probably, you couldn't drive to the store, like they do now." On occasion, students will respond with *elaborated explanations,* which are responses that are lengthy and characterized by a chain of reasons, but these are infrequent in this approach.

THE STORY BEHIND QUESTIONING THE AUTHOR

Questioning the Author was developed in the 1990s by Isabel Beck and Margaret McKeown, two professors at the University of Pittsburgh. In the 1980s, Beck and McKeown analyzed the content of social studies textbooks for students in the intermediate grades, and they found that the writing lacked coherence and that authors assumed background knowledge students did not have (Beck, McKeown, and Gromoll 1989). As a result, students found it very difficult to make sense of the texts (McKeown and Beck 1990). Frustrated with the quality of the texts and students' lack of understanding, McKeown and Beck experimented with ways to improve things. Armed with a cognitive perspective on reading that emphasized how readers need to actively connect text ideas and integrate them with their background knowledge, they revised the texts to improve their coherence and include the required background knowledge. Studies showed that these changes helped (e.g., Beck et al. 1991), but many students still attained only a surface-level understanding of the texts. Something more was needed.

As Beck and McKeown were revising the texts to make them more considerate for students, they realized that approaching texts with a "reviser's eye" was just what readers needed to do. And as they worked one-on-one with students, they noticed that asking open-ended questions that focused on what the author meant or was trying to say was particularly effective in promoting students' engagement. Questioning the authority of the author allowed readers to challenge the author's use of language, suggesting that students' difficulties in understanding the text might be due to the author's failure to explain things clearly.

Building on their work with the revised texts, Beck and McKeown's next move was to work collaboratively with teachers to develop Questioning the Author. Working with two fourth-grade teachers in an inner city private school, they first implemented Questioning the Author in 1992–1993 (Beck et al. 1996). Then, in their second year of implementation, 1993–1994, they worked with four fourth-grade teachers (Beck and McKeown 1998). Over the years, they collaborated with more and more teachers in both public and private schools to refine the approach.

Research Support

There is convincing evidence, albeit from a small number of studies, that Questioning the Author produces dramatic improvements in classroom discourse, improves students' engagement with text, and enhances their comprehension of texts read and discussed. It may well support growth in students' general comprehension abilities, but more research is needed to understand fully the extent to which this happens. Let's look at each of these points in a little more detail.

Questioning the Author produces dramatic improvements in the quality of classroom discourse. This observation was evident in the first year of implementation of Questioning the Author (Beck et al. 1996), in the second year (Beck and McKeown 1998), and in subsequent professional development work with teachers (McKeown and Beck 2004). The results of these studies clearly showed that when teachers used Questioning the Author:

- teachers' questions shifted from retrieving information to constructing and extending meaning

- teachers' responses shifted from simply repeating students' comments to refining them in a way that moved the discussion forward

- student-initiated comments and questions increased; indeed, student talk more than doubled.

In another study, McKeown et al. (1995) found that there was a decline in responses where students simply reiterated the text almost verbatim and an increase in responses where they focused on meaning and integration of text ideas with their prior knowledge. Qualitative analyses of the lesson transcripts showed that students were learning to explore and build meaning and to develop ownership of their ideas.

Questioning the Author improves students' engagement with text. In a yearlong study, Almasi, McKeown, and Beck (1996) analyzed qualitative data from two fourth-grade classrooms that were using Questioning the Author. They found that students' engagement increased when the teachers posed queries that implied a challenge to the author's writing (e.g., "Is the author making sense with that sentence?"). They also found that their engagement seemed to increase when the teacher or students asked follow-up questions that challenged the ideas discussed (e.g., "Is it true that the person telling the story is the author?").

Questioning the Author enhances students' comprehension of the texts read and discussed. Sandora, Beck, and McKeown (1999) compared the effects of Questioning the Author and Junior Great Books discussions with sixth- and seventh-grade students reading complex texts. They showed that students in the Questioning the Author class had greater recall and higher scores on answers to interpretive questions about the texts than did those in the Junior Great Books class. In a later study, McKeown, Beck, and Blake (2009) conducted two experiments with fifth-grade students, comparing a scripted version of Questioning the Author with both comprehension strategy instruction and a basal reading condition. They found significant differences between students in the three conditions in favor of Questioning the Author on open-ended and probed recall of the texts discussed.

Questioning the Author may support growth in students' general comprehension abilities. The more interesting question, of course, is whether students who participate in Questioning the Author learn comprehension skills that they can use when they read new texts outside of the discussion. Here the picture gets a bit muddy. Bear with us here.

In the initial studies of Questioning the Author, Beck et al. (1996) and Beck and McKeown (1998) tested students at the end of each year on an individually administered comprehension task using a novel text. Both studies showed Questioning the Author benefited students' abilities to construct meaning and to monitor how well they were comprehending. However, there was no comparison group in the Beck et al. study; students were simply tested at the beginning and end of the year. This means it was difficult to know what caused the improvements. In the later Beck and McKeown study, there was a comparison group that was given business-as-usual instruction, but the number of students in the study was small. What's more, the comprehension task given to students included questions that were very similar to what students heard in Questioning the Author—so it is not surprising that the students did well on the questions. In the McKeown, Beck, and Blake (2009) study, the researchers also tested students' comprehension of texts read outside of the actual discussion, and they had comparison groups. However, the results were mixed; students in the Questioning the Author group performed about as well as those in the strategy instruction and basal reading groups.

Probably the most compelling evidence that Questioning the Author enhances students' general comprehension abilities comes from a carefully conducted study of instructional coaching by Matsumura, Garnier, and Spybrook (2013). The study involved large numbers of schools and students, and results showed significant benefits of Questioning the Author for students' comprehension as measured by a standardized test, at least when the discussions were implemented well. Because this was as much a study of instructional coaching as it was of Questioning the Author, it is hard to disentangle the effects; nonetheless, we find the results encouraging.

QUESTIONING THE AUTHOR in Practice

Planning for Questioning the Author

QUICK GUIDE

1. **Select a text**. The text may be fiction or nonfiction and, ideally, one that requires close, careful reading.

2. **Read the text selection twice to identify places to stop reading and discuss**. Your first reading should focus on the curriculum: what do you want students to take away from the reading? After reading a second time, try to anticipate student difficulty and/or interest with the text: which sentences, word choices, or ideas might be confusing and/or interesting? Find the places where you pause when reading because you have a genuine interest in the idea.

3. **Mark the text, indicating the stopping point.** Use sticky notes or annotations in the margins of text to remind yourself to stop the in-class reading and initiate a burst of Questioning the Author discussion.

4. **Write initial questions.** Initial questions are either authentic or test questions that you ask at a stopping point, and they are worded to help students interrogate the author and the language the author uses. Here are some examples: *What do you think the author is saying here? Why is the author telling us this now? Did the author write that in a clear way? How does this part connect with what the author told us earlier?*

Questioning the Author is an approach to discussion that takes place during reading and emphasizes the collaborative construction of meaning through bursts of short discussions and connected student talk. Teachers choose places in the text to stop reading and pose questions to help students stay active during reading, interrogating the author and the language the author uses. The mindset behind interrogating the author is the belief that the author is fallible, meaning that the author, just like the reader, is a regular person who attempts to write with clarity, but who doesn't always do so or who might not have all the answers. The author, just like readers, makes mistakes. This is a broad concept, referred to as "author fallibility," and it's a core premise of the approach that upends what many students and teachers traditionally believe about the author of the text they are reading.

Author fallibility gives readers a purpose and plan for reading, which is to "revise" or make understandable the language of the text in order to construct meaning. Operationally, this means that readers have to stop during reading to ask questions about the text and the language of the text and that, when discussing a text together, readers must try to connect to each other's ideas through asking each other questions and elaborating on each other's ideas.

The teacher coaches these reading behaviors through organizing in-class reading of text, either small-group or whole-class, identifying stopping points in the text, and planning questions that probe meaning and interrogate the author. Teachers plan Questioning the Author discussions when the instructional goals warrant reading a complex text and when students would benefit from close, analytical reading of the text.

Since Questioning the Author provides a high level of support during reading, texts that are complex and require close reading work well. The approach grew from the realization that a change might need to be made to social studies textbooks, so nonfiction or other technical texts are especially suited to the approach. Examples of good texts to get started with the approach, include, but are not limited to, primary sources, passages from science texts, nonfiction articles, and math word problems. But fiction works, too. If using fiction, you might read longer segments of text before stopping to discuss so as not to disrupt too much of the story.

Teacher's Role in Questioning the Author

In Questioning the Author, the teacher's role is to ask initial and follow-up *queries*, a term the developers of Questioning the Author used to evoke the concept of interrogating or querying the author in order to depose the author's authority. Queries are simply questions, crafted to elicit students' talk and comprehension by way of probing and connecting the language of the text with the students' prior knowledge.

A teacher might ask an initiating query or a big question to kick-start an episode of discussion, stopping during reading and asking, "What is the author trying to say here?" or "What is the author talking about in this section?" These questions put the focus of the discussion on making meaning through analysis of the author's words. Other examples of these kinds of big questions are as follows:

- What is the important message in this section?
- What do you think the author wants us to know?
- What's happening now?

There is no prescriptive next step after asking an initial query, or question, to initiate discussion. The idea is to listen to student responses and make decisions as to whether an idea can be further elaborated, connections can be drawn from past lessons, or clarity is still needed. The teacher asks follow-up questions to assist students in extending their thinking and to make deeper connections between the author's ideas and students' prior knowledge or other lessons. For example, a teacher, using Questioning the Author with a science text and a standard about the seasons, might ask, "Okay, so we are saying a lot about the seasons. How do you think seasons connect to the idea of tilt that the author told us in this section?" Here are some other examples of follow-up questions:

- What does the author mean here?
- That's what the author said, but what does the author mean?
- How does that make sense with what the author told us before?
- Why do you think the author tells us that now?
- Does the author tell us why?

Since Questioning the Author was developed in the context of social studies curriculum, many of the example questions work well with nonfiction texts, but some questions are particularly useful with narrative fiction and literary reading standards. These can be used to focus students' attention on a character's motivation behind an action, a detail of the plot, or the author's use of dialogue and description (e.g., description of the setting). For example:

- Given what the author has already told us about this character, what do you think he's up to?
- How do things look for this character now?
- How is the author trying to make you feel right now about these characters?
- How does the author's description help you see what's happening?
- What language does the author use that helps you see the setting?

The important thing to remember is that these examples are just that—examples. As Beck and McKeown (2006) say, "There's nothing magical about the way they [questions] are worded. The important thing is to understand the purpose" (43). Questions should kick-start a "conversation" with the author about the meaning of the text. They encourage students to engage with the important ideas, and they remind students that the "fallible" author wrote the text and, therefore, needs to be interrogated. Follow-up questions are posed to help students clarify meaning or extend an idea. When asking questions, the idea you want to impart is that good readers know that their responsibility is to question the author, so they must pause when reading to think about the author's language, reread a segment of text to make sure they understand, and evaluate the language for its clarity and quality.

Posing questions at pre-planned stopping points is a significant aspect of Questioning the Author, but, as we know when we sit down and get into a discussion, a lot of things can happen that make us wonder how we should respond and whether we should step in or step back. To help guide the facilitator's role with more depth and detail, Beck and McKeown (2006) recommend using six "teaching moves" during the discussion to promote focused and productive talk about the text. These moves include: *marking, turning back, annotating, revoicing, modeling*, and *recapping* (see Figure 8.2).

Figure 8.2 Six Teaching Moves for Questioning the Author

Teaching Move	Description of the Move	Example
Marking	Putting special emphasis on an idea because it is important	"Notice what Adam said, he said that maybe the man at the door wasn't actually real."
Turning back	Prompting students to refer back to the text to clarify something or to give responsibility back to students to work out the meaning	"Did the author tell us about this?" "But what does that mean?"
Annotating	Restating the main idea of an especially challenging section of text or filling in information where there might be gaps in students' background knowledge	"So it looks like the colonists really struggled when they first arrived. How did they struggle?"
Revoicing	Restating something a student said in a way that foregrounds the important idea for the others in the group, providing clarity.	"So, are you trying to say that the colonists were challenged in Jamestown?"
Modeling	Making public a thought process or reaction to teach students ways of thinking about the text	"That really puzzled me."
Recapping	Taking stock of what students have learned so far and signaling that it is time to move the discussion forward	"So we figured out that the man at the door was really a ghost. Let's see how the characters react to him.".

Approach in Action: Social Studies, Grade 6

In this example of Questioning the Author, the students and teacher are discussing the meaning of the following sentences from their textbook: *There is no sunlight during most of the winter months in Antarctica. However, during the summer months the sun shines 24 hours a day.* During the discussion, the students explore Antarctica's weather patterns. The excerpt shows examples of the Questioning the Author approach and quality talk.

Teacher: Think about this for a minute. There's something else that Amber said a little while back. She said there's something funny about the earth. It's not straight up and down.

> Here the teacher is marking an important idea and revoicing what Amber said. The teacher is deliberately making a key point obvious for students.

Tammy: It's tilted.

> This is an example of uptake. Notice how the teacher weaves the previous response into the follow-up question. This is also reflective of the teacher move, "turning back."

Teacher: It's tilted. Now, how does that connect with what the author has told us here?

Brandy: It doesn't get as much sun in the winter, 'cause the sun has to come up under, but it's tilted the other way in the summertime.

> The reasoning word, 'cause, or because, indicates analysis (pulling ideas apart) or generalization (tying ideas together). In this case, the student is breaking down an idea from the text in order to draw a conclusion. She is engaging in analysis of information from the text.

Thomas: I think he's saying, like Brandy said, it goes around for 24 hours a day and, here goes the sun, the sun shines on Antarctica, slanted, all the way around 24 hours a day.

> Another reasoning word.

> The student responds with an elaborated explanation. The position is, paraphrasing here, "Brandy is right, I know why the sun shines for 24 hours a day." The paraphrased reasons are: "The earth is rotating (reason), and the sun rises every 24 hours" (reason). The earth is tilted, so the sun hits Antarctica (reason).

Shanelle: Um, Um, I think I know what they're saying because when, when the earth is going around and the sun is coming, it's hitting the lower part of Antarctica, is showing, 'cause it's tilting more. So then it has sunshine 24 hours.

Teacher: I think we've worked this out. What Shanelle and Thomas are saying is that because the earth is tilted when it's going around the sun, we got 24 hours of sunlight in the summer.

> The teacher annotates and recaps here to signal that it's time to move forward, perhaps with reading another segment of the text.

(Beck et al. 1997, 40)

Notice how the teacher's moves spark high-level thinking from Brandy, Thomas, and Shanelle. The teacher asks an authentic question, which is also an example of uptake, when she asks, "Now, how does that connect with what the author has told us here?" This is a great place to step in and ask a follow-up question because it clarifies a key idea (i.e., how the Earth is tilted) and pushes students to elaborate their thinking. Arguably, the use of uptake generates space for more student-to-student dialogue.

In those last three student turns, the students use their talk to build knowledge about the earth's tilt and rotation. When Thomas connects to Brandy's comment, elaborating on her idea of the tilt with the word, *slanted,* the other students likely benefit from a clearer understanding of the concept. Shanelle further describes the concept with the phrase *[the sun] is hitting the lower part of Antarctica [because of the tilt].* Thomas' response is pretty close to an elaborated explanation, since he gives a "trail" of ideas to explain the position that Brandy is correct in her thinking. The short excerpt highlights features of quality talk that reflect knowledge building and illustrates a few of the teacher moves of Questioning the Author (e.g., annotating, recapping, revoicing). The teacher asks questions and uses uptake to prompt the return to the text to reread and analyze the language. Simply stated, the excerpt illustrates Questioning the Author and quality talk beautifully, since the students co-construct meaning with their dialogue.

Let's face it! Reading complex texts is a slog sometimes. Have you ever been in the voting booth and you're reading a proposed state or municipal law and your eyes cross a little with the technical legal language? Can you imagine your students, who are much less experienced readers, trying to comprehend a complex document about the Dark Ages in social studies or a difficult passage in a science text about the water cycle?

Isabel Beck and Margaret McKeown and the other researchers and teachers who helped develop Questioning the Author want teachers and their students to know that it takes work to gain meaning from challenging texts. They want readers to engage with texts and to remain active, but they don't want readers to think there's an easy away around the slow, close and careful reading that we sometimes need to employ. That's why the approach is primarily used *during* reading, so teachers and students can coach and model for each other the slow, deliberate process of stopping while reading to check your understanding, to reread, to monitor and to ask, "Wait, is this clear?"

Some things just don't have short cuts and reading difficult texts is one of those things. Questioning the Author is a tool that helps readers make sense of difficult texts, providing a path toward meaning that is enjoyable (you get to talk with your friends), interesting (you get to challenge the author), and productive (you feel successful when you understand something hard).

READ MORE

Beck, Isabel, Margaret McKeown, and Cheryl Sandora. 2020. *Robust Comprehension Instruction with Questioning the Author: 15 Years Smarter.* New York: Guilford.

Beck, Isabel, Margaret McKeown, Rebecca Hamilton, and Linda Kucan. 1998. "Getting at the Meaning: How to Help Students Unpack Difficult Text." *American Educator* 22 (1–2): 66–71, 85.

Beck, Isabel, and Cheryl Sandora. 2015. *Illuminating Comprehension and Close Reading.* New York: Guilford.

McKeown, Margaret, and Isabel Beck. 2004. "Transforming Knowledge into Professional Development Resources: Six Teachers Implement a Model of Teaching for Understanding Text." *The Elementary School Journal* 104 (5): 391–408.

Shared Inquiry

SHARED INQUIRY

Research Support

- Promotes students' use of text evidence to support their opinions
- Fosters critical thinking about text
- Probably increases comprehension of the text discussed
- Probably produces gains in general comprehension abilities

Learning How

Participate in training, on-site consultation, video coaching, or webinars offered by the Great Books Foundation, designed to support implementation of Shared Inquiry with Great Books materials. The Foundation encourages a whole-school approach to professional development.

Goals

To engage students in rigorous discussion of challenging text to help them build a deep understanding and interpretation of the text. To expose students to quality literature.

Typical Features

- Literary text
- Whole-class discussion
- Heterogeneous group
- Teacher led
- Teacher chooses text
- Students read text before discussion
- Teacher controls topic
- Students and teacher share control of turn taking
- Teacher has interpretive authority
- Moderate focus on author intent

Typical Teacher Questions

Why does [character] do that?

Is there something in the story that tells you that?

What makes you think that?

How do you know?

What does that mean?

Where does it say that?

Typical Student Comments

Because on page x, it says . . .

In this part of the story, it's telling . . .

I think it means . . .

I agree (disagree) with [student] . . .

Teacher's Role

- Ask an interpretive question that promotes deep understanding and interpretation of the text.
- Listen carefully for places to step into the discussion to ask follow-up questions that will further students' thinking about the text.
- Encourage students to support their ideas with evidence from the text.
- Maintain focus on the text.

What the Talk Sounds Like

In the following excerpt, students in a fifth-grade class are discussing *Crow Call*, a picture book by Lois Lowry (2009). The story is about a father and daughter who share a day together after the father returns home from the war. The two go hunting together but the daughter, Liz, is uncertain about the hunting activity. The focus question, "Why does Liz go hunting?" is written on the board.

Teacher: Is there someone who would like to start us off?

Mia: I think that maybe that since he just got back from the war, maybe she wants to spend more time with him, so that's why even though the word "hunter" scares her, she still wants to be with her father.

Ty: And when she said, "Daddy," she never gets to say, "Daddy" because he'd been gone for a long time.

Jaden: I agree with you, Ty, because when you go to page 23—

Teacher: Everyone, back to the beginning, 23, (pause) and which part there, Jaden?

Jaden: Right here in the middle. She said that she was practicing his name, and whispering. It says, (reading from text) "I practiced his name to myself, whispering it under my breath."

Kallon: I think that [she practiced his name] because they have not spent much time with each other because he has been in the war a lot. So, she was just practicing the word, "Daddy," because she doesn't usually call anybody "Daddy" because she mostly lives with her mom.

Rosario: I agree with (unclear) and Mia because since she never gone hunting before, maybe it's new for her, so she don't know, like, how it feels.

Teacher: And so why would she go? Weren't you saying she might be nervous if she's never done it before? Why would she go anyway?

Rosario: Maybe because if she wanted . . . she knows that her father was bad maybe she wants to spend more time with him and learns things that he likes to do.

Gabi: I think Liz goes hunting with her father even though the word "hunter" makes her feel uneasy because once she gets to know him, she knows that he's not a bad guy at the end.

(Great Books Foundation 2020 video)

Shared Inquiry is an approach to discussion that is a part of the Junior Great Books program for students in grades K–8 and the Great Books program for students in grades 9–12. The goal of the Shared Inquiry approach is to dig into a complex text, going beyond a literal understanding of the text, usually fiction, and to develop collaboratively a more significant interpretation of the text.

The teacher controls the text and topic of the discussion and students, with the teacher, share turn-taking responsibilities. In the excerpt above, students talk to each other, as Mia, Ty, and Jaden do in the first few lines of the excerpt. The connected student-to-student talk indicates that a conversation has developed without the teacher managing the turn taking. During Shared Inquiry discussions, the students indeed talk to each other and tend to control

Figure 9.1 Some Examples of Quality Talk

Features	Examples	Why They are Productive
Authentic question	Focus question: Why does Liz go hunting?	The focus question for this discussion is a "why" question, and it is authentic, encouraging interpretations of a main character's motivation to take action in the story.
Uptake	Teacher: And so why would she go?	This follow-up question builds onto a previous comment and facilitates an elaboration of ideas previously shared.
Text evidence	Jaden: Right here in the middle. She said that she was practicing his name and whispering. It says (reading from text), "I practiced his name to myself, whispering it under my breath."	Students use text evidence when responding to questions.

the direction of the discussion, but the teacher steps in to maintain a focus on building knowledge and an interpretation of the text. The teacher's question toward the end of the excerpt, "Why would she go?" helps the students return to the focus question and, thus, to press on with making an interpretation of one central idea of the story.

The teacher and the students' questions are mostly authentic, having multiple right answers, such as, "And why would she go?" Questions that demonstrate uptake are also a common feature of Shared Inquiry discussions. Uptake is where a follow-up question builds on the responses of previous comments and, at the same time, promotes elaboration of the ideas in subsequent student responses. For example, in the excerpt, the teacher's question about why Liz decides to go hunting, when she didn't want to go, picks up a part of what Rosario had said earlier in the discussion. After the teacher's use of uptake, Rosario indeed offers a reason to support her thinking, and Gabi elaborates and builds on the response of Rosario to extend the interpretation. Uptake helps the group stay on topic, connect their ideas, and elaborate their thinking.

During Shared Inquiry, the authentic questions tend to generate high-level thinking in the form of speculation, such as Rosario's speculation that Liz goes hunting because it's a novel activity, and analysis, which is illustrated by Kallon's response that Liz feels like her father is a stranger. The reasoning words that signal high-level thinking that you will hear most often are *because,* which suggests analyzing or synthesizing, *if* and *would,* which suggest speculation, and *I think,* which suggests position taking.

Shared Inquiry discussions are characterized by frequent elaborated explanations, which display students' detailed thoughts about how something works or why something is the way it is. They include a position and multiple reasons, such as the use of examples, text evidence, or beliefs to justify a position. In the excerpt, Mia gives an elaborated explanation for why Liz goes hunting, suggesting that she wants to be with her father because the war was long and they didn't see each other for a long time.

The discussions are also characterized by occasional, short episodes of exploratory talk. In the excerpt, the students are so close to engaging in exploratory talk. What's missing? A real challenge to the ideas that the students share with each other. When students use exploratory talk, they share ideas, discuss alternatives, challenge each other's thinking, give reasons for their thinking (e.g., refer to the text for evidence), and, more or less, volley ideas back and forth to answer a big question on their own, without the teacher intervening. The excerpt lacks disagreement or even one, tiny challenge to any of the ideas the students discuss; and challenges, along with the other features mentioned, form a package of discourse features known as exploratory talk. Instead, the excerpt is reflective of cumulative talk, where students sort out an idea in a connected way but fall short of any disagreement that would promote creative and critical thinking. Disagreements matter in discussions. Just think what happens when your thinking is challenged. Almost always, you will keep thinking, trying to find the "right" way or the "right" evidence to make your position stronger or clearer. Challenges and disagreements are the gold standard for ensuring that critical thinking is part of a discussion.

During Shared Inquiry discussions, students rarely connect the text or the discussion to their previous lessons (i.e., shared-knowledge responses) or other texts (i.e., intertextual responses), though students will occasionally ask questions that generate affective responses, where students share the way the text arouses feelings or evokes connections to personal experiences. With a strong focus on interpreting the text, however, you will more often hear students connecting directly to specific sections of the text, as Jaden does in the middle of the excerpt, rereading the text to use as evidence to support a position.

THE STORY BEHIND
JUNIOR GREAT BOOKS SHARED INQUIRY

Junior Great Books began its life as an adult reading and discussion program. Its origins can be traced to two educators and philosophers at the University of Chicago, Mortimer Adler and Robert Hutchins. Both were concerned with the quality of higher education in the United States and the decline of liberal arts education. Their solution was to give people opportunities to read and discuss the works of the greatest writers of the Western intellectual tradition, such as William Shakespeare and Geoffrey Chaucer—the "Great Books."

The first Great Books seminar was taught in 1920 by Professor John Erskine at Columbia University; Mortimer Adler was a student in this first seminar. In 1930, Adler moved to the University of Chicago and took the Great Books seminar with him. It was there that he met Robert Hutchins, then President of the University of Chicago, and they cotaught the Great Books. In 1947 Adler and Hutchins established the nonprofit Great Books Foundation with the mission of encouraging lifelong learning beyond the classroom and providing opportunities for all citizens to participate "in Great Conversations of some of the world's best writing" (Great

Books Foundation 2002). The Foundation formalized the discussion method of Shared Inquiry to help readers explore and interpret complex ideas in the texts.

The Foundation introduced the Junior Great Books program in 1962. Intended for students in grades 5–9, it initially consisted of books from the adult program plus others, such as excerpts from *The Adventures of Huckleberry Finn*. Over time, the range of literature available and the grade levels covered expanded.

For several decades, most educators viewed the program as an enrichment program for gifted students, but calls for activities to engage average and low-progress students slowly gained momentum. In 1992, after years of development and piloting, the Foundation launched the *Junior Great Books Curriculum of Interpretive Reading, Writing, and Discussion* for students in grades K–12. This represented a major expansion of the program and made it easier for schools to incorporate it into their language arts curricula.

Today, Junior Great Books and the Shared Inquiry (JGB-SI) approach is used with thousands of students throughout the United States. The Foundation recently introduced new editions of the program for students in grades K–5, including a digital platform, and, in line with standards requiring students to have more experiences with informational texts, developed materials for Nonfiction Inquiry.

Research Support

Although there are a large number of studies of the Shared Inquiry approach (twenty-four by our count at the time of writing, dating as far back as 1964), the quality of the studies is somewhat mixed. The studies span grades K–12 with the majority having been conducted in grades 3–6. Studies have been conducted with gifted students or high-progress readers and with students from low-income or minority backgrounds. However, only five studies have been published in peer-reviewed journals (studies that survive the test of peer review tend to be of higher quality). Most of the evidence of the effects of Shared Inquiry comes from doctoral dissertations, master's theses, reports of pilot programs conducted in conjunction with the Foundation, and the like.

Does Shared Inquiry benefit students' comprehension of the texts they read and discuss? Probably. Biskin, Hoskisson and Modlin (1976) found that first- and third-grade students who were read stories and asked interpretive and follow-up questions, like those in Shared Inquiry, outperformed students who were asked prediction questions or who did not participate in discussion on literal comprehension of the stories. In another study, Graup (1985) asked sixth-grade students to generate inferential questions about Junior Great Books stories and to formulate answers either in group discussion or individually. When asked to write essays about the stories, students who had discussed the questions in groups demonstrated greater comprehension than did students who had answered them independently. These findings are positive, though we note that the discussions did not follow Shared Inquiry procedures exactly.

There is also some contrary evidence. As we mentioned in our description of Questioning the Author (see Chapter 8), Sandora, Beck, and McKeown (1999) compared the performance of students in a Junior Great Books class with that of students in a Questioning the Author class. They reported that the Junior Great Books students did not perform as well in their recall of the stories or in their answers to interpretive questions.

Does Shared Inquiry produce gains in students' general comprehension abilities beyond those demonstrated on the texts discussed? Again, the answer is probably. There are numerous reports from school districts attesting to gains in students' scores on standardized tests following introduction of Junior Great Books (e.g., Gasser, Smith, and Chapman 1996). Some of these are reported on the Great Books Foundation website ("Measuring the Benefits of Junior Great Books—2006 to 2013"). These are suggestive of the benefits of the program but, in the absence of data from comparison groups or more transparent reporting, it is hard to know how to interpret these findings. There are other factors that might have contributed to gains in students' test scores.

The best evidence that the benefits of Shared Inquiry transfer to students' general comprehension abilities comes from two dissertations. Bird (1984) examined the performance of high-progress, fifth-grade students who participated in the Junior Great Books program in comparison with the performance of similar students who received instruction in their regular program. After three to six months, Bird found that participation in Junior Great Books resulted in significant gains in critical thinking and reading as compared to participation in the regular program only. In another dissertation, Cashman (1977) randomly assigned fourth-, fifth-, and sixth-grade students to experimental and control groups. Students in the experimental group participated in Junior Great Books for five months, meeting once a week for fifty minutes during the day, and also participated in the regular reading program. Students in the control group participated only in the regular reading program, but for an equivalent amount of total reading time. Cashman concluded that Junior Great Books resulted in significant differences favoring the experimental group on tests of students' vocabulary knowledge and verbal reasoning.

What is quite clear from the research is that **students become more rigorous and critical in their thinking about text when engaging in Shared Inquiry.** Numerous studies note that students are more likely to cite evidence from the text to support their opinions during the discussions (Criscuola 1994; Dudley-Marling 2014; Dudley-Marling and Michaels 2012; Feiertag and Chernof 1987; Great Books Foundation 1992; Hait 2011). Indeed, several studies describe students in the discussions constructing or co-constructing sophisticated arguments—making claims, citing text to support the claims, and linking the two with evidentiary warrants (Dudley-Marling and Michaels 2012; Dudley-Marling 2014; Hait 2011). Discourse of this rich nature is more typical of discussions focused on argumentation described in Section IV.

SHARED INQUIRY in Practice

Planning for Shared Inquiry

QUICK GUIDE

1. **Select a text.** Traditionally, the texts used are fiction. Stories should have contestable themes related to a dilemma, such as whether the actions of a character are right or wrong. The Great Books Foundation also offers anthologies of short stories.

2. **Read the text carefully.** Identify central themes, dilemmas, contestable issues, and arguments.

3. **Write a focus question to initiate the Shared Inquiry.** Create a focus question that is authentic and promotes interpretation (e.g., "Why . . . ?").

The primary instructional focus of Shared Inquiry is to facilitate students' deep and rigorous interpretations of text. As you may be aware or have experienced, some discussion approaches are geared toward "following" the interests of students in terms of topics and questions, and this often leads to jumping around from one topic to the next very quickly. The Shared Inquiry approach is the opposite of "jumping around." Shared Inquiry is about "holding a line" of inquiry that leads to rigorous thinking, deep comprehension, and strong interpretations of the text. To this end, the teacher facilitates a focused, deliberate inquiry into a single authentic big question, encouraging students to reason, identify evidence from the text, and justify ideas that support a robust interpretation of the text.

Part of the preparation for Shared Inquiry discussions is the teacher identifying a focus question, or big question, and getting students to engage with the focus question before the discussion. The purpose of the focus question is to elicit rereading, using text evidence to support positions, and giving elaborated explanations. In preparation for Shared Inquiry discussions, students read the text—typically fiction, but it could be informational—two times. Figure 9.2 shows the preparation process that teachers use to organize a Shared Inquiry discussion.

Perhaps the biggest job involved in planning a Shared Inquiry discussion is crafting the focus question (or sometimes two questions in order to have one as a backup). An analogy to help with the concept of crafting focus questions is a basketball coaching scenario. Basketball coaches teach players how to "steal" or "defend" through teaching them how to anticipate. When the players anticipate, they watch a play or a pass develop before it actually takes place. Anticipating where the ball is going makes them that much better at defending, stealing, or breaking up a play. This is true of discussions, too. The idea is to write a focus question and anticipate where the talk is headed when the students discuss the focus question. Anticipating where the discussion may be headed is a way to test and adjust the focus question. Often, teachers ask why a discussion didn't work well, and experience shows that the problems started with the big questions.

Remember that the goal of Shared Inquiry is to collaboratively generate an interpretation of a complex text. The best focus questions, then, are authentic, text focused, interpretive, clear and concise. The four-point checklist for writing good focus questions (Figure 9.3) will help you craft one. Then, double-check the question, anticipating and imagining the student talk that follows it.

Figure 9.2 Preparing for a Shared Inquiry Discussion

The teacher selects a text and scaffolds students' first reading.

The teacher writes and posts a focus question that generates interpretation.

Students read the text or a selection of text a second time, making directed notes about the focus question.

Sometimes students write a short response to the focus question.

Figure 9.3 Four-Point Checklist for Writing Good Focus Questions

Check the Question Is it . . . ?	Example	Non-example	Anticipate!
Authentic and genuine	Why does Liz go hunting with her father?	Does Liz go hunting with her father to get to know him again?	The non-example is too leading; a single student will likely answer it, and the other students will have nothing more to say. Authentic questions are genuine, meaning *you*, as an adult, would like to discuss them. The example question intrigues me, and I anticipate that students will have a lot to say because the author provides clues as to Liz's state of mind in the story.
Text focused	Why do you think Liz goes hunting, when she doesn't like hunting?	Is Liz's father a good dad?	Both questions are authentic (having multiple right answers), but there's only text evidence to use to respond to the first question. In the non-example, we could anticipate that students would likely talk about good parenting, which is *not* part of the story. The non-example will take students too far from interpreting the text.
An interpretive question (e.g., beginning with *Why* or *How*)	How do you think of the relationship between Liz and her father? Why does Liz hesitate to go on the hunting trip with her father?	What is Liz's relationship to her dad?	"Why" and "How" questions typically lead to interpretations of text, if there's a text focus to them. To respond to an interpretive question, a student has to tie ideas from the text together (or from prior knowledge). Interpretation is "making sense" through analyzing the text and pulling different ideas together.
Clear and concise	Why does Liz go hunting?	What is more important to Liz— getting to know her father again or going hunting with him? Maybe something else?	I can anticipate lots of diverse responses to the example question. For the non-example, I can anticipate students' confusion. When students are confused, they usually stay silent.

The checklist for writing good focus questions may seem like a lot of planning for writing a couple of questions to kick-start a Shared Inquiry discussion, but good questions matter for creating a conversation that is centered on the text and generative of an interpretation of that text. With quality focus questions, students will think beyond a basic, literal level of meaning. Students will justify their thinking and, in doing so, think more deeply, often returning to the text to use text evidence, to reread, and to make inferences based on the ideas in the text and their prior knowledge.

Teacher's Role in Shared Inquiry

Teachers use follow-up questions in Shared Inquiry discussions to keep the conversation focused on interpreting the text and to promote rigorous thinking. The

Figure 9.4 Key Moments in Shared Inquiry Discussions When Teachers Step In to Follow-up Questions

Stepping In During Shared Inquiry		
Stepping In to . . .	What It Does for Learning	Example
Clarify with a revoicing move	Stepping in to clarify student talk helps all the students follow the discussion, giving more opportunity for student-to-student connections between ideas.	So when you say, "she doesn't know her father anymore," are you saying she forgot him completely?
Reinforce the use of the text to justify thinking with a "how do you know" question	Putting the text front and center in the discussion, with students rereading, identifying a quotation that supports a claim, and scanning, makes the actions of good readers visible and routine.	How do you know that? Did the author write something that supports what you are saying?
Promote evaluation. When students seem too comfortable with the ideas, get the students to be evaluative and critical with a "truth" question.	The teacher asks students to consider the validity of an idea. When using the word *that* in the follow-up question, the teacher is also using uptake, which serves to elicit more ideas.	Is that always true? How do you know that idea is right?
Solicit new and alternative viewpoints, when you hear a lot of agreement. Even if the talk is cumulative and there is use of text evidence, the teacher needs to solicit alternative interpretations from students.	Alternative ways of thinking lead to challenges and disagreement, and these are essential for critical thinking.	Does everyone agree that Suray is right?

role of the teacher is to listen carefully to the student talk, listening for too much agreement, not enough text evidence or reasons, and ideas that sound a little jumbled or unclear. Proponents of Shared Inquiry suggest stepping in to ask follow-up questions at four kinds of "key moments" in the dialogue. Figure 9.4 shows examples of the key moments and what a teacher can do to step in and support the Shared Inquiry.

Approach in Action: Language Arts, Grade 5

The following whole-class discussion took place during a series of Junior Great Books lessons about *Fire on the Mountain,* an Ethiopian folktale by Jane Kurtz (1998). The folktale is about a rich man, Haptom, who tries to take advantage of a servant, Arha. Haptom promises Arha his freedom if he wins a bet to stay out all night in the cold without fire or food. Arha survives this ordeal by watching the light of a fire that a friend tends on a distant mountain. Nonetheless, Haptom does not initially honor the bet because he claims Arha "had" fire.

Teacher: According to the story, is Haptom Hasei a man of his word?

> This focus question is interpretive and authentic.

Lauren: I don't think that um Haptom is really a man of his word because in the beginning of page 59 it said that he was bored.

> Here, Lauren takes a position with a specific reference to the text, noted with the page number. Note her use of a reasoning word, *because.*

Teacher: Can we all look at that on page 59?

> Sometimes teachers ask "other" questions that function as procedural questions to help organize the students.

Ethan: I think that he is a man of his word 'cause he just made a mistake, he didn't realize that the fire didn't warm him and then he realized his mistake because it said that on um [page] 71 that he was shamed.

> Ethan disagrees with Lauren. Ethan supports his opinion with specific text reference and offers an elaborated explanation of his position.

Teacher: What does that mean, he was shamed?

> Here the teacher uses uptake to clarify Ethan's explanation.

Robert: That he realized his mistake and that he was like (inaudible) was sorry to Arha.

Katie: I don't think he is.

> This is important for exploratory talk because Katie challenges Robert's assertion that Haptom felt remorse. Challenges to positions and ideas or text evidence are essential for exploratory talk.

Eduardo: He said that Arha, that Arha was right. He couldn't feel the fire and, and um I don't think that Haptom really wanted to give him his stuff.

Janine: At the end he was shamed because he was (inaudible) man and he wanted—he knew, he, he was a man of his word because he did give him his stuff after he learned his lesson.

> Janine makes her thinking visible, giving reasons for her claim that Haptom was shamed.

(Great Books Foundation 2002, video)

This excerpt illustrates several features of quality talk and Shared Inquiry. The teacher begins with a genuine, authentic question that is also a strong focus question. In the story, it seems doubtful that Haptom is a man of his word, so the focus question elicits multiple possible answers and different interpretations, depending on how you interpret, or make sense of, the character's actions and motivations. Lauren and Ethan, straight away, refer to the text in their responses. Ethan elaborates his thinking, stating a claim and justifying the claim with a reason from his beliefs or values (making a mistake) and a reason from text evidence ("shamed" on page 71). The teacher uses uptake to help students clarify their thinking and, presumably, to return to the focus question. In the last four turns, Robert, Katie, Eduardo, and Janine engage in exploratory talk. They give reasons for their thinking, paraphrasing the text. Katie challenges Robert's claim that Haptom was shamed and felt remorse for not giving Arha his freedom. Eduardo paraphrases the text in response to Katie, and Janine summarizes an earlier position. The students dig in, "hold the line" of inquiry, and work collaboratively to interpret the text.

This example of Shared Inquiry illustrates the use of talk as a tool to build knowledge. Since the focus of the approach is on the meaty ideas of the text, both students and teachers strive toward the goal of making sense of or interpreting the text together. Whether the teacher is asking a follow-up question with a call for text evidence or the students are elaborating their thinking with several ideas from the text or personal examples related to the text, the search for what it all means is paramount. It's when readers do this figuring out that they become engaged citizens, reasonable thinkers, and better problem solvers.

In a modern era, *what* we know is becoming less important than *how* we know it. We can find information about almost any topic in milliseconds, but thinking and getting better at thinking still happens slowly, over time, and through the process of high-quality dialogue. When the instruction includes a discussion approach, such as Shared Inquiry, students use language in productive ways, hear diverse views, appropriate new ways of thinking about text from better thinkers, and practice civil discourse as the medium for their growth. In a society that continually emphasizes increasingly quick access to new information and a need to sift truth from fake news, we must encourage slow and deliberate instructional approaches because there are no shortcuts to developing high-level, critical thinking and deeper comprehension. Broadening your teaching repertoire and mastering discussion approaches like Shared Inquiry may be more important today than ever.

READ MORE

Dudley-Marling, Curt, and Sarah Michaels. 2012. "Shared Inquiry: Making Students Smart. In *High-Expectation Curricula: Helping All Students Succeed with Powerful Learning*, edited by Curt Dudley-Marling and Sarah Michaels, 99–110. New York: Teachers College Press.

Great Books Foundation. 2014. *Shared Inquiry: Handbook for Discussion Leaders and Participants*. www.greatbooks.org/wp-content/uploads/2014/12/Shared-Inquiry -Handbook.pdf.

SECTION III

How Do I Know Students Are Engaged in Knowledge Building?

We know that students are building knowledge during discussions when they are heavily engaged in making sense of the text, grappling with the meaning to build a coherent understanding. Their talk is very text bound. They will often return to the text and frequently reread it in response to a teacher question to clarify, reason, question, and learn from the discussion. Likewise, students will ask questions that are authentic and inquire about the meaning of a word, a phrase, or a meatier idea or theme of the text (e.g., "What does it mean to be shamed?").

Figure 9.5 shows how the three approaches described in this section might be scored on the first three categories of the TATT. One of the key signs that students are engaged in knowledge building is making references to the text. When students are knowledge building, they make references to the text to clarify what the author is saying or to share a section of text that is relevant to the discussion. You might hear phrases such as these:

- In the text, it said . . .
- Well, I think it [the text] said . . .
- The author wrote . . .
- Right here, it says . . . (student reads from the text)
- In here it says . . .

Because the text is the primary source of information, there are few extratextual questions that prompt students to go beyond the text. However, in Instructional Conversations, you may hear questions that elicit affective responses as students draw on their background knowledge to make sense of the text. In Instructional Conversations, students grapple with the language of the text, offering interpretations of the author's words based on their own background knowledge and experience.

As for the reasoning categories, the three approaches differ somewhat. In Instructional Conversations and Questioning the Author, students will at times use the text as evidence to support a claim they are making, perhaps in the form of an elaborated explanation, but this occurs less frequently in these discussions than in some of the other approaches we look at (especially those that emphasize critical, analytic thinking and argumentation). Similarly, you will rarely see much in the way of

Figure 9.5 Typical Knowledge-Building Talk

	1 Not Yet	2 Emerging	3 Developing	4 Blooming
Questions				
Authentic	____ None	____ Some	✓ Many	____ Almost all
Uptake	____ None	____ Some	✓ Many	____ Almost all
Analysis/ Generalization	____ None	____ Some	✓ Many	____ Almost all
Speculation	____ None	____ Some	✓ Many	____ Almost all
Textual Connections				
Reference to text	____ Do not use text evidence	____ Once or twice	____ Some of the time	✓ Many times
Extratextual Connections				
Affective response	____ Do not make connections	✓ Once or twice	____ Some of the time	____ Many times
Intertextual response	____ Do not make connections	✓ Once or twice	____ Some of the time	____ Many times
Shared-knowledge response	____ Do not make connections	✓ Once or twice	____ Some of the time	____ Many times

exploratory talk; in these discussions, the teacher plays an important role in guiding the discussion and prompting students to clarify what the text said and build on each other's ideas. Figure 9.6 shows how the reasoning talk in Instructional Conversations and Questioning the Author might be scored on the TATT.

In Shared Inquiry, the talk displays some features of the more critical-analytic approaches described in Section IV, so the talk varies in a few important ways from the patterns shown in Figures 9.5 and 9.6. You will hear the teacher more frequently ask authentic questions (remember these are called "interpretive questions" in Shared Inquiry) than is typical in knowledge-building approaches, and students' responses may be even more text bound—seldom do students go outside the text to interpret what they read. Students show more reasoning in their talk as well. You will hear students more frequently engage in elaborated explanations to support their claims (e.g., "I agree with Joseph because he keeps annoying them

Figure 9.6 Typical Reasoning Talk in Instructional Conversations and Questioning the Author

	1 **Not Yet**	2 **Emerging**	3 **Developing**	4 **Blooming**
Individual Reasoning				
Elaborated explanations	____ Do not provide reasons or provide only one reason	✓ Once or twice	____ Some of the time	____ Many times
Collective Reasoning				
Exploratory talk	✓ Do not collectively explore a topic or reason together	____ Some of the time	____ Much of the time	____ Almost all of the time

by saying shut up and I think he is trying to just get them to let him play because they wouldn't let him play because he didn't have his glove."). There will also be more instances of exploratory talk, extending over several turns, as students talk to each other and reason together to make sense of the text. Figure 9.7 shows how the reasoning talk in Shared Inquiry might be scored on the TATT.

Figure 9.7 Typical Reasoning Talk in Shared Inquiry

	1 **Not Yet**	2 **Emerging**	3 **Developing**	4 **Blooming**
Individual Reasoning				
Elaborated explanations	____ Do not provide reasons or provide only one reason	____ Once or twice	✓ Some of the time	____ Many times
Collective Reasoning				
Exploratory talk	____ Do not collectively explore a topic or reason together	✓ Some of the time	____ Much of the time	____ Almost all of the time

SECTION IV

Talk About Text to Emphasize Argumentation

If you wanted students to meet standards in the English Language Arts or other subjects where reasoning, making arguments, and determining the best answer were necessary, which approach would you use? You could use any one of the classroom discussion approaches described in this section: Collaborative Reasoning, Paideia Seminar, and Philosophy for Children. The goal of these approaches is to promote critical, analytic thinking about the text or ideas raised by the text. In these discussions, teachers pose big questions to students that prompt multiple interpretations. Students take positions about a character's actions or motives (e.g., "I think Shayne cheated in the competition") or about a controversial or puzzling issue (e.g., "I don't think sending people to Mars is worth the risk"), and they support their positions with reasons and evidence, citing information from the text, examples from their experiences, their beliefs and values, or other information.

When students engage with the text in this way, we say they are adopting a critical-analytic stance toward the text (Wade, Thompson, and Watkins 1994). They are going below the surface of the text in search of the underlying arguments, assumptions, worldviews, or beliefs. This stance engages the reader's querying mind, prompting them to ask questions that delve deeply into the text and the ideas it stimulates.

In these approaches, the teacher shares control of the discussion with students. The teacher chooses the text and usually decides on the topic or issue for discussion, knowing that some texts and topics promote argumentation more than others. However, the students largely control turn taking and decide how to interpret the text or the issue raised by the text (i.e., they have interpretive authority). As we will see, this shared control of the discussion offers a lot of opportunities for students to engage in quality talk. The figure below shows the typical format of these discussions.

The theory to explain how these three approaches work owes a lot to Vygotsky's (1978, 1981) ideas about the role of language in higher-order thinking. When students participate in the discussion, they observe and practice the skills

▌ Typical Format of Argumentation Discussion

Approach	Text	Reading	Grouping
Collaborative Reasoning	literary	before	small group
Paideia Seminar	literary and informational	before	whole class
Philosophy for Children	literary	before	whole class

and strategies of argumentation—taking a position, supporting it with reasons and evidence, challenging other participants, and responding to challenges from others. Over time, students internalize these skills and strategies so that what was once made visible in the group's discussion becomes part of their own thinking. And, as in any discussion, using language to interact with others offers opportunities for students to engage in the social mode of thinking called "interthinking" (Littleton and Mercer 2013; Mercer 2000) that we mentioned in Chapter 1. Sharing ideas through talk, especially around big questions where there is no one right answer, gives students a means for combining their intellectual resources to collectively make sense of the text and their experiences.

10

Collaborative Reasoning

COLLABORATIVE REASONING

Research Support

- Increases student talk
- Improves students' high-level thinking, including argumentation
- Improves students' writing of argumentative essays
- Promotes deeper levels of text comprehension
- Improves students' motivation and engagement
- Benefits English language learners

Learning How

There is no formal professional development available, but the teacher-friendly resources listed at the end of this chapter provide a good starting point.

Goals

To promote critical thinking and reading through a process of reasoned argumentation. To promote engagement with text.

Typical Features

- Literary text
- Small-group discussion
- Heterogeneous group
- Teacher led
- Teacher chooses text
- Students read text before coming to discussion
- Teacher controls topic
- Students control turn taking
- Students have interpretive authority
- Little focus on author intent

Typical Teacher Questions

Is there any evidence in the story that tells us that?

Can you think of another reason?

What are you assuming here?

What do you mean . . . ?

Some people might say . . . What do you think about that?

Did you notice what [student] said?

Typical Student Comments

What do you think [student]?

I agree (disagree) with [student]

Yeah, but . . .

What if . . .

I think . . . because . . .

In the story it said . . .

Teacher's Role

- Formulate a big question about a significant idea raised by the text.
- Establish ground rules for discussion.
- "Step back" from the discussion as quickly as possible, but be ready to facilitate argumentation through use of teacher moves.
- Conduct debriefing after the discussions.

What the Talk Sounds Like

In the following excerpt from a Collaborative Reasoning discussion, a class of fourth-grade students and the teacher are discussing a short story called "What Should Kelly Do?" (Weiner 1980). In the story, Kelly and Evelyn are friends who enter an art contest at school. Kelly really wants to win the contest. Evelyn, who is not that interested in the contest, mistakenly leaves her beautiful (and likely-to-win) painting outside, on the playground. Later that day, Kelly notices the painting as rain begins to fall. Before the discussion, the students read the story quietly at their desks. At the discussion, the teacher asks the big question, "What should Kelly do?"

Kenny: I think she *should* get it because everyone would be hurt if um, if her painting was ruined by the rain.

Tamika: I wanna challenge you because, did it seem like when she was propped up there and she went on the swings did it seem like she really cared about it?

Kenny: Well, not really cared about it, but wouldn't you be sad if *your* painting got ruined by the rain?

Tamika: Yes, but I wouldn't be sad because it got ruined so I couldn't enter the contest.

Sonia: I agree with Tamika.

Tamika: Why?

Sonia: That um, because, if I left my painting out there, and, and I didn't really care about it, I wouldn't be sad if I wasn't in the contest, or if I didn't get first place.

Tamika: Yeah, um, I agree with Sonia and because um, there's no reason for her to be sad. She, she propped it against there and went to go swing and forgot about it. She shouldn't have been in the contest in the first place so she has no reason to be sad. She should be mad. She should be mad at *herself*.

Sonia: For example, if I was, if I was a good drawer, and um, there was somebody better than me, and if they, um, won first place, um, I think it doesn't matter because everybody's not perfect.

Kenny: But wouldn't, but would you be sad if your painting was ruined by the rain? . . . But wouldn't you be glad if someone's um, saved it for you, so you could um, keep it?

(Nguyen et al. 2007, 201–202)

In Collaborative Reasoning, students control turn taking and interpret the story together, but the teacher chooses the text and the topic (the big question that generates the discussion). Students ask a majority of the questions and they talk a majority of the time. When teachers ask follow-up questions, these tend to be authentic and demonstrate uptake, which means that the questions build on students' responses.

The authentic questions tend to generate high-level thinking in the form of analysis, generalization, and speculation, as is illustrated above when Tamika defends her position: she analyzes the story evidence, saying, "because there's no reason to be sad . . . she shouldn't have been in the art contest in the first place, so she shouldn't be sad." Kenny responds to Tamika's challenge, offering

Figure 10.1 Some Examples of Quality Talk

Features	Examples	Why They Are Productive
Elaborated explanation	Tamika: Yeah, um, I agree with Sonia and because um, there's no reason for her to be sad. She, she propped it against there and went to go swing and forgot about it. She shouldn't have been in the contest in the first place so she has no reason to be sad. She should be mad. She should be mad at *herself*.	An elaborated explanation is a claim followed by more than one reason (e.g., evidence, example). Elaborations foster cognitive restructuring and rehearsal, and this makes thinking visible for others in the discussion.
Authentic question	Tamika: . . . Did it seem like she really cared about it? Teacher: What should Kelly do?	Authentic questions tend to generate high-level thinking, reasons, and sometimes, elaborated explanations.

a hypothetical situation to argue his position, essentially saying, "Wouldn't you be sad if. . . ?" Sonia supports Tamika's argument, saying, "I agree." Here Sonia is taking a position, which is common in Collaborative Reasoning because the approach emphasizes argument. So, you will often hear statements that begin with *I agree, I disagree,* and *I think.* When we hear these and other reasoning words (e.g., *because, so, but, might, could, would*), we can be assured that students are learning and thinking in high-level ways during discussion.

A major goal of Collaborative Reasoning is argumentation. This simply means that students exchange arguments, taking positions and supporting their positions with reasons and evidence. Exploratory talk, characterized by students taking positions, giving reasons, and challenging each other's ideas, supports argumentation and is a major feature of Collaborative Reasoning. For example, in the excerpt, Kenny offers an argument that includes a position (Kelly should get the painting) and a reason (Evelyn would be hurt or sad if the painting is ruined). Tamika, however, disagrees with this argument, saying, "I wanna challenge." Her counterargument is premised on text evidence suggesting that Evelyn doesn't care about her painting or the competition. Kenny doesn't let the argument go, however. He rebuts Tamika's challenge, saying, "But wouldn't you be sad if . . . ?" Episodes of exploratory talk are frequent in Collaborative Reasoning, and they tend to be long. With minimal teacher interruption, students share multiple positions, reasons, and challenges to each other's thinking about the text.

In Collaborative Reasoning, you will often hear students use text evidence to support their positions, making explicit references to the text with phrases such as *It said* or *The text said.* Likewise, you will often hear *elaborated explanations,* which are responses that include a position with multiple reasons. In the excerpt, Sonia and Tamika offer elaborated explanations as they dispute the "sad argument." When students refer to the text or elaborate their explanations, they make their reasoning and thinking visible to others.

Affective responses, where students relate the text to their feelings and make connections to their lives, are occasionally heard in Collaborative Reasoning, and they tend to occur when students pose hypothetical questions, such as Kenny's question, "But wouldn't you be sad if?" Sometimes students use such a hypothetical question to bring up their own feelings or experiences to argue a position, as Tamika did, saying, "I wouldn't be sad . . ." as a way to defend her position. Less often will you hear connections to previous discussions (shared-knowledge responses) or connections to other texts or media (intertextual responses).

Research Support

The research support for Collaborative Reasoning is remarkable for its quantity and quality. There have been over fifty studies of the approach, most of which have been published in top tier journals. Richard C. Anderson and students have methodically examined almost every aspect of the approach, conducting fine-grained analyses of the discourse during discussion as well as experiments comparing the effects of Collaborative Reasoning on students' educational outcomes after the discussions with those of some form of traditional instruction (usually recitation). Almost all have targeted students in grades 4 and 5.

So, we know a lot about the impact of Collaborative Reasoning on students as well as how it works. Here is what we know:

- Students' talk almost doubles during Collaborative Reasoning, as compared to traditional discussions.

- Students engage in more high-level thinking during Collaborative Reasoning, as compared to traditional discussions. They make more predictions, give more elaborated explanations, and make more use of analogies and other forms of complex thinking. Notably, their argumentation skills improve; students make more use of text evidence to support their arguments and are more likely to consider alternative perspectives.

- The thinking and argumentation skills acquired during Collaborative Reasoning transfer to students' writing. Studies show that, after participating in as few as four Collaborative Reasoning discussions, students write essays prompted by a new story that contain more arguments, counterarguments, rebuttals, and uses of text evidence, compared to students who receive regular instruction.

- Students' high-level reading comprehension may also improve. Although studies of Collaborative Reasoning have not shown appreciable gains in students' performance on conventional, multiple-choice reading-comprehension tests, some studies have shown gains on tests that measure deeper levels of understanding of text (e.g., the ability to make inferences, to integrate and evaluate information).

- Students' motivation and engagement improves. Students who participate in Collaborative Reasoning discussions show greater motivation and engagement than students who participate in conventional teacher-directed, whole-class discussions.

THE STORY BEHIND
COLLABORATIVE REASONING

Collaborative Reasoning grew out of a program of research launched in the early 1990s by Richard C. Anderson and his graduate students at the Center for the Study of Reading, University of Illinois at Urbana-Champaign. For some years, Anderson had been conducting detailed microanalyses of traditional small-group reading lessons. These lessons were characterized by somewhat lifeless, question-and-answer episodes in which students recited story events and teachers evaluated their answers. The studies themselves failed to garner much interest. As Anderson and his students commented, they "were tedious for the students, tedious for the research team, and evidently tedious for the larger educational research community, as the papers have seldom been cited" (Jadallah et al. 2010, 171). Martha Wagner, a doctoral student at the Center and former elementary school teacher, along with other graduate students, encouraged Anderson to explore ways of engaging students in more stimulating discussions.

At that time, Michelle Commeyras, another student at the Center, was conducting her doctoral dissertation on an approach to classroom discussion she had used when she was a sixth-grade teacher. She called it the Dialogical-Thinking Reading Lesson or D-TRL (Commeyras, 1991, 1993). The goal of the D-TRL was critical thinking—"to engage students in reasonable reflective thinking in order to decide what they believe about a story-specific issue" (Commeyras 1993, 487).

Anderson was enthusiastic about the possibilities of the D-TRL, having read one of Michelle's papers. Armed with several carefully chosen stories and "big questions," he and several students made their first foray into elementary school classrooms; each tried their hand at conducting a small-group discussion. They came away impressed with the ease with which students adapted to the new approach, the richness of the discussions, and the quality of students' thinking. From these fledgling attempts, one could say (at the risk of hyperbole) that a "star was born"—Collaborative Reasoning.

From research spanning two and half decades, Anderson and successive generations of students have refined their approach. Ground rules for the discussions were developed, teacher moves were refined, and post-discussion reflection on the talk became a staple of the design. Evidence supporting the approach has continued to build. As a way of engaging students in reasoned thinking and argumentation, Collaborative Reasoning has earned a well-deserved place in a teacher's discussion repertoire.

There is also evidence that Collaborative Reasoning might be particularly beneficial for English language learners (ELLs). In a small study with four classes of
fifth-grade Spanish-speaking students, Zhang, Anderson, and Nguyen-Jahiel (2013)
compared the effects of Collaborative Reasoning to business-as-usual instruction.
After participating in just two Collaborative Reasoning discussions per week over
four weeks, students showed gains in English listening, speaking, reading, and
writing, relative to the control students. They also showed improvements in their
motivation and engagement and their attitudes toward learning English. Ma et al.
(2017) also found benefits for ELLs when Collaborative Reasoning was embedded
in an extended unit of collaborative group work, compared to direct instruction
or business-as-usual instruction. The language-rich discussions of Collaborative
Reasoning give much-needed opportunities for ELLs to engage in extended meaningful communication with others and to develop their critical thinking skills.
As one teacher commented after her ELLs had participated in a series of discussions, "When we do Collaborative Reasoning, I see my students thinking critically.
They're evaluating what they're reading and they're evaluating what others in
their groups are saying" (Zhang and Stahl 2011–2012, 260).

How does it work? One mechanism at play seems to be (with a light touch)
teacher prompting and scaffolding. Anderson and colleagues have shown that
once a teacher prompts or scaffolds a child to use a particular thinking or argument strategy, students are likely to appropriate it. Whether prompted or spontaneous, once a student uses a strategy (e.g., "I think [position] because [reason],"
"In the story, it said [evidence]"), it *snowballs*—that is, it spreads to other students
who then use it with increasing frequency, both in the discussion and in subsequent discussions. The "snowball phenomenon," as Anderson et al. (2001) call
it, has been observed in discussions among students in the United States as well
as in China and Korea. It has also been seen in online Collaborative Reasoning
discussions (Kim et al. 2007). Lin et al. (2012) reported that students' use of analogies during discussion also snowballs.

Another mechanism at play in Collaborative Reasoning is emergent leadership (Li et al. 2007). When the teacher steps back and gives students space, student leaders emerge to facilitate the discussion, managing turns, keeping students
on topic, inviting students to talk, and asking for clarification. Sometimes a primary leader will step up; at other times, several students will share a leadership
role. In this way, students take on more responsibility for the flow of talk in the
discussion.

COLLABORATIVE REASONING in Practice

Planning for Collaborative Reasoning

QUICK GUIDE

1. **Select a text.** Use literary or informational text that has a clear dilemma or issue and is relevant for the students. Good literary selections often have characters that need to make a decision or that make a questionable decision (e.g., upsetting a friend, cheating in a race). Good informational text selections should be relevant and pose a real issue or problem to sort out (e.g., animal captivity and depression, serious injuries in youth sports, sugary drinks in schools).

2. **Write a big question.** Ask yourself what kind of question will create multiple arguments and differing viewpoints. Questions that begin with *Should* and *Why* are good ways to begin a big question. Focus on central themes of the text, such as honesty, adversity, and responsibility, or problematize a current issue (e.g., a policy that affects immigration).

3. **Plan and manage a flow of activities.** Students read the text independently or in a way that's differentiated for reading levels (e.g., paired reading). They usually read the text or a segment of the text one day and then discuss the text a second day. Sometimes, after the discussion, to elicit transfer of the argument structure, the teacher has students write about the issue. Writing might take place during a third instructional period.

The primary instructional goal of Collaborative Reasoning is critical thinking and reasoning about text through the process of reasoned argumentation (Anderson et al. 1998). Critical thinkers question, doubt, argue, and respect the thinking of others (Ennis 1987), and when these ways of thinking are applied to reading and practiced during Collaborative Reasoning, students make plausible arguments and interpretations of what they read, using text evidence and other kinds of reasons (e.g. an example from their own lives).

During the discussion, the goal is to engage students in argumentation, which is the process of advancing multiple arguments and evaluating them, deciding on the best argument and way of thinking about an issue. Considering which argument is the "best" requires students to question each other, to refute arguments with challenges and the use of text evidence, and to make counterarguments, or take opposing positions, with additional references to the text and other reasons (e.g., hypothetical situations). Moving toward a "best" argument inspires strong interpretations and better comprehension of the text.

Making arguments and thinking critically produce desirable learning outcomes (e.g., argument literacy skills, reading comprehension), but the real high point of Collaborative Reasoning is students working together—controlling the turn taking, asking follow-up questions, constructing interpretations—in a way that draws on the power of modeling. For example, let's say a student makes an argument about the text, referring to a detail in the text as evidence to support the position. The language form would look and sound something like, "I disagree with that idea because in the text it said, [reference to the text]." This statement would convey the message about the argument, but it also models an important structure for *how* to use and order words to make an argument or a counterargument. Once a student uses the structure, in essence, modeling it for other students in the group, his or her classmates use the same or similar structure when they take a turn. One theoretical explanation for this is that students "borrow," or appropriate, the words of their peers as they engage in dialogue, and they do so naturally—no direct teaching is required! As mentioned earlier, this phenomenon is also known as the "snowball phenomenon," and the implication of this is that teachers should introduce, prompt, and model argument strategies when they facilitate Collaborative Reasoning. Figure 10.2 lists examples of the different argument strategies and language forms that have been shown to "snowball" when students participate in Collaborative Reasoning.

As noted earlier, teachers select the text and write a big question, which is central to the text and is likely to generate multiple arguments. The text can be either literary or informational, but it should always pose a dilemma or a problem to solve. For example, in the short story "Victor" by James Howe (1995) that we read about in Chapter 1, Victor is a mysterious main character who visits

Figure 10.2 Different Argument Strategies and the Corresponding Language Forms that "Snowball"

Argument Strategy	The Language Form that "Snowballs"
Structure of an argument	I think [position] because [reason].
Evidence to support a position	I think [position] because in the story it said, [reason in the form of text evidence].
Opposition/counterargument	But what if [scenario]? or But what about . . . ? I disagree with . . . because it said . . ..
If/then scenarios	If . . . then . . .

Cody, a boy who is in critical care at the hospital. The author never really clarifies who Victor is, so the reader is left to interpret and infer from the evidence of the story and the reader's prior knowledge. Victor could be a volunteer at the hospital, an angel, a nurse, or an imaginary figure in Cody's mind. The identity of Victor is ambiguous, and there is plenty of text evidence to defend different positions, so a strong big question for the story would be, simply, "Who is Victor?" Figure 10.3 includes two additional texts and big questions that would elicit argumentation.

Teacher's Role in Collaborative Reasoning

At the beginning of the discussion, the role of the teacher is to frame the discussion with a clear purpose (to make a decision about the best idea or argument, but *not* to debate) and the ground rules for participation. In Collaborative Reasoning, the process of reviewing the rules and setting up the discussion is collaborative, giving students agency and a sense of a group identity; whereas in other approaches, the teacher simply lists and states the ground rules (e.g., "do not raise hands to talk," "give positions and reasons," "challenge ideas and the reasons of others," and "listen to each other"). The teacher might begin with a

Figure 10.3 Examples of Texts, Relevant Questions, and Anticipated Arguments

Texts	Big Questions	Anticipated Arguments
What Should Kelly Do? A short story about two classmates who paint pictures for their school art contest	Should Kelly save Evelyn's painting?	Yes—Evelyn's painting will be ruined in the rain. Yes—It is important to look out for others. No— The teacher said everyone is responsible for their own painting. No—Evelyn does not care about the contest.
Ronald Morgan Goes to Bat by Patricia Reilly Giff A short story about a young boy who loves to play baseball even though he can't hit or catch	Should the coach let Ronald Morgan play with the team?	Yes—His enthusiasm is good for the team spirit. Yes— Everyone should have a chance to play. No—The team loses games whenever Ronald plays. No—It's not fair to the other kids on the team.

prompt, saying; "Let's talk about our last discussion. What were the strengths in talking, and what should we focus on today?" The students would respond with a ground rule or related idea (e.g., give reasons), and the teacher might build on the response, adding a suggestion that provides students with an example; he might say, "Yes, and we also need to listen to each other with our whole bodies so it's easier to connect to the reasons of others and build on or challenge them. This sounds like, 'I want to add a reason to what [Teresa] just said.'"

How does a teacher know to frame the student comments in this way? He is always thinking of the ground rules of discussion and the elements of an argument. Figure 10.4 shows a list of statements a teacher might use to frame a Collaborative Reasoning discussion.

During Collaborative Reasoning, the teacher's role is to step back, listening for places to step in to promote argumentation. Some teachers make notes of the arguments while they listen, which sometimes makes stepping in easier. The idea is to be an alert "instructional bystander," ready to step in to promote argument and argumentation, but not so intrusive that students stop talking to each other. When teachers step in, they use "facilitation moves," such as modeling, encouraging, summarizing, prompting, challenging, and clarifying. Figure 10.5 summarizes some of the facilitation moves used in Collaborative Reasoning.

There is a distinct rhythm in the way the teacher facilitates discussion in Collaborative Reasoning (Figure 10.6). It is not a procedure per se, but there is a natural flow or arc that makes sense for this approach. For example, early in the discussion the teacher would prompt students to state multiple arguments—"getting them on the floor" for others to consider—before asking questions toward the

Figure 10.4 Statements to Frame Collaborative Reasoning and How the Statements Support Argumentation

Statements to Frame Collaborative Reasoning	What They Do
We need to ask classmates questions about how they know something. This sounds like, "How do you know that?"	Students employ active listening skills and provide elaborations of their reasoning.
We need to ask classmates to cite text evidence, if you don't hear a reference to the text. This sounds like, "Where in the text does it say that?"	Students return to the text and refer to the author's language as evidence to support their positions.
We should respond to someone who disagrees with us with another reason or question. This sounds like, "Can I respond to that? I have a question."	Students learn to counterargue respectfully.

Figure 10.5 Examples of Teacher Facilitation Moves in Collaborative Reasoning and the Possible Timing of Using the Moves

Facilitation Move	Examples of What the Move Sounds Like	When to Use the Move
Modeling	"Some people would say . . ." "I think the text says . . ." "I'm not sure everyone would agree with that . . . " "I'd like to respond to that..."	When you don't hear students using the strategies of argument—e.g., referring to the text for evidence—or when students consider just one argument, avoiding others' ideas
Summarizing/refocusing	"So far, we've created a few arguments. They are . . . Are there other positions we haven't discussed?"	When you need to redirect the discussion or when you've exhausted the ideas of an argument or two and need to discuss a different one
Prompting	"How do you know that?" "Is there evidence in the story?" "Do you want to respond to that challenge?"	When students give short, unelaborated answers or when students need to pause to give other students a chance to respond to a challenge
Clarifying	"Do you mean . . . ?" "So, are you saying . . . ?" "Can you say a little more so we can follow your thinking....?"	When students' ideas are not yet clear to the group or the students are not connecting or building ideas—when they are simply sharing their thinking in a round-robin style with unrelated thoughts

Figure 10.6 The Flow of a Collaborative Reasoning Discussion over Time

Get ready!
- State the purpose of the discussion.
- Discuss and establish the ground rules.
- Pose the big, central question.

Early in the discussion
- Prompt to "get the ideas and arguments on the floor."
- Clarify students' arguments.
- "Status check"—summarize the arguments so far.

Middle and end of the discussion
- Prompt to elaborate and build the arguments.
- Prompt counter-arguments.
- Summarize the arguments as a final closure.

Post-discussion
- Debrief the quality of the arguments and the talk—e.g., did students use the ground rules?
- If writing is a learning outcome, state the writing prompt.

middle of the discussion that would have students consider counterarguments, evaluate the quality of the arguments, and probe ideas for further elaboration. The teacher often ends Collaborative Reasoning with *debriefing,* reflecting on the arguments as well as the strengths and the areas of the discussion to improve for next time. At the very end, the teacher might lead a transition from the group discussion to an independent or collaborative writing task, prompting the students to consider the dialogue as they write an argument on the issue.

Approach in Action: Small Reading Group, Grade 4

The following Collaborative Reasoning discussion took place in a fourth-grade reading group with eight students. The group had read a short story titled *My Name Is Different* (Prasad 1987) about a boy who begins using an American name at school instead of his Chinese name to fit in with his peers.

Teacher: Those of you that think he should not have changed his name, I'd like to hear your reasons, some of your reasons. Matthew?

Here the teacher prompts and encourages students to get their arguments on the floor, for others to consider. This is a good example of a facilitation move that can be used early in a discussion.

Matthew: One reason is because Chang-Li is part of his history, his life, his, um, culture, like if, he, just 'cause he changed schools, he didn't have to change his name, and even if they're all American, he lives in a Chinese part of town, and uh, it's his culture, all behind him, what, he does Chinese ceremonies and stuff, and um, he just shouldn't have changed his name, 'cause all his culture and stuff.

Matthew offers an explanation for his position. Note that it is an elaborated explanation because he not only provides a reason, based on Chang-Li's history, life, and culture, he also elaborates on what he means by history, life, and culture.

[Several lines omitted]

Mandy: I don't agree with Matthew, because I thought it would be kinda neat to change your name. 'Cause, um, if you kinda get, your name kinda gets old so you'd probably want to change it for a while.

Mandy challenges Matthew, offering an argument with a reason based on her personal beliefs, showing her involvement in the story. It is not really an elaborated explanation because she offers only one reason, and a fairly rudimentary one at that (having one name gets tiresome so it makes sense to change it, at least temporarily).

Alysia: [uninterpretable]

Teacher: Do you think that's the reason?

The teacher asks a follow-up question in the form of uptake to prompt additional reasoning.

Mandy: Well, that's not why he changed his name, but, thought that'd be neat, to change your name . . . And also, you want to be the same as the people, all the rest of the people around you. You wanna have, you wanna have it, a name that's common, around the other people.

Mandy offers an additional reason to support her position: changing his name helps him fit in.

Teacher: I'd like to hear what Alysia has to say to that. You started in to say something here, I think. I'd like to hear more.

The teacher prompts and encourages Alysia to share her thinking so students can explore other perspectives on the issue.

Alysia: I, um, don't know. I think he shouldn't have changed his name because it was fine the way it was. People didn't like his name. That's their opinion, and . . .

The teacher asks a follow-up question in the form of uptake that elicits further reasoning.

Teacher: Do we have evidence that nobody liked his name?

Alysia: Well, nobody wanted to play with him 'cept Dan.

(Chinn, Anderson, and Waggoner 2001, 402)

This excerpt illustrates features of both Collaborative Reasoning and quality talk. In terms of quality talk, Matthew responds to the initial teacher prompt (first line) with an elaborated explanation about the history and culture reflected in a name. The teacher asks two follow-up questions in the form of uptake: "Do you think that's the reason?" and "Do we have evidence that nobody liked his name?" Both questions prompt additional reasons to support the two positions under consideration. Mandy, for example, builds on her original argument that Chang-Li should change his name because it's fun to be able to do so, responding to the teacher's question with another reason that changing a name is good to do because it helps you fit in. We also see reasoning words and phrases in the excerpt, including taking a position (*I don't agree*) and an indication of high-level thinking (*because, but*).

In terms of Collaborative Reasoning, the excerpt illustrates what happens when the teacher elicits argumentation with two facilitation moves, *prompting* and *encouraging*. The teacher prompts for elements of an argument ("I'd like to hear your reasons."). The teacher also prompts for text evidence in the last teacher question of the excerpt ("Do we have evidence that nobody liked his name?"), which encouraged Alysia to share a reason. The teacher doesn't dominate the conversation, but she clearly contributes to the dialogue to encourage students to consider multiple perspectives ("Those of you who think he should not have changed his name, I'd like to hear your reasons," "I'd like to hear what Alysia has to say to that"). The prompting and encouraging pay off because the teacher elicits better thinking and stronger arguments. Alysia returns to the text for evidence and Mandy goes deeper with her thinking, supporting her position with an additional reason.

At the heart of Collaborative Reasoning, students *argue* in the best possible sense—to state and evaluate reasons and evidence, to hear alternative ways of thinking, and to acquire the dispositions of critical thinkers. Those who make arguments think critically and critical thinkers make arguments. Therefore, Collaborative Reasoning is an approach to language arts and reading instruction that supports the wider literacy-development goals of reading beyond basic details of a text, going deeper with thinking and reasoning about the text, and comprehending at interpretive and evaluative levels. Any teacher who uses this approach could easily argue that "Collaborative Reasoning is a gem of an instructional approach."

READ MORE

Anderson, Richard, Clark Chinn, Martha Waggoner, and Kim Nguyen. 1998. "Intellectually Stimulating Story Discussions." In *Literacy for All: Issues in Teaching and Learning*, edited by Jean Osborn and Fran Lehr, 170–186. New York: Guilford.

Anderson, Richard, Kim Nguyen-Jahiel, Brian McNurlen, Anthi Archodidou, So-young Kim, Alina Reznitskaya, Maria Tillmanns, and Laurie Gilbert. 2001. "The Snowball Phenomenon: Spread of Ways of Talking and Ways of Thinking Across Groups of Children." *Cognition and Instruction* 19 (1): 1–46.

Waggoner, Martha, Clark Chinn, Hwajin Yi, and Richard C. Anderson. 1995. "Collaborative Reasoning About Stories." *Language Arts* 72 (8): 582–589.

Zhang, Jie, and Katherine Stahl. 2011–2012. "Collaborative Reasoning: Language-Rich Discussions for English Learners." *The Reading Teacher* 65 (4): 257–260.

11

Paideia Seminar

PAIDEIA SEMINAR

Research Support

- Fosters positive attitudes toward learning
- Increases student-to-student interaction
- Enhances students' critical thinking and argumentation about and around text
- May enhance students' writing that assesses critical thinking

Learning How

Consult resources and participate in professional development offered by the National Paideia Center (www.paideia.org).

Goals

To enrich students' understanding of the ideas and values inherent in a text and to foster critical thinking. To enhance students' intellectual and social development.

Typical Features

- Literary and informational text
- Whole-class discussion
- Heterogeneous group
- Teacher led
- Teacher chooses text
- Students read text before coming to discussion
- Teacher has control of topic
- Students and teacher control share of turn taking
- Students have interpretive authority
- Moderate focus on author intent

Typical Teacher Questions

- Opening question —What's your opinion about this topic? Which part was most interesting to you?
- Core question—Why does the author write about that? Why is this important?
- Closing question—What's your takeaway from the seminar today? How do you feel about this text?

Typical Student Comments

I think . . .

In the text, the author wrote . . .

Maybe if she would have . . .

Teacher's Role

- Establish ground rules for discussion.
- Facilitate dialogue by asking open-ended questions to prompt and maintain discussion.
- Plan and facilitate pre-seminar and post-seminar activities to support learning.
- Encourage intellectual and respectful discussion.

What the Talk Sounds Like

In the following excerpt from a Paideia Seminar discussion, a class of ninth-grade Government students are discussing the Preamble to the Constitution. Before the discussion, the teacher prompted the students to identify a single concept in the Preamble that was most important in a democracy (e.g., "We the people," justice, union, common defense). The question the teacher asked to generate the discussion was, "Why is the concept (chosen from the opening prompt) the most important to democracy?"

Jeremy: It's like no one of these equals a democracy. It's as if you had, say, "domestic tranquillity"; tranquility could exist under a dictator. That one element alone doesn't make a democracy.

Maria: I think I see what Jeremy means. We could "provide for the common defense" with a military government. Maybe even better than with a democracy. So it takes all of these working together to produce democracy.

Mr. Anders: Okay, but how? How are they related to each other?

Monte: For one thing, liberty and justice are related.

Mr. Anders: How?

Monte: A strong justice system protects us from each other. It's what keeps us from beating each other up in the halls, stealing from each other. It's what keeps me from taking someone else's liberty away.

Juanita: Or someone else from taking yours.

Monte: Exactly.

George: It's as if in a democracy we're all connected somehow. What's good for you is also good for me.

Janin: Is that why nine of us said "we the people" was the most important concept in the whole thing?

Will: Has to be. I voted for it, but I was never able to explain why. It's strange, but none of those concepts work if we're at war with each other. It's only when we work collaboratively that any of these ideas have a chance.

Juanita: Yeah. Look at the board: "union," "common defense." It's like the whole theme of the Preamble is that somehow we are all tied together.

(Roberts and Billings 1999, 83)

Paideia Seminars are teacher-led discussions. The teacher chooses the text and topic and generates several questions to facilitate the discussion. The questions the teacher asks are organized into three categories: opening questions, core questions, and closing questions. The question "Why is the concept the most important?" is a core question. Most of the time in Paideia Seminars, the teachers'

Figure 11.1 Some Examples of Quality Talk

Features	Examples	Why They Are Productive
Elaborated explanation	Maria: I think I see what Jeremy means. We could "provide for the common defense" with a military government. Maybe even better than with a democracy. So it takes all of these working together to produce democracy.	An elaborated explanation is a claim followed by a chain of reasons (e.g., evidence, example) or an extension of the idea in a step-by-step way. Elaborations foster cognitive restructuring and rehearsal on the part of the student giving the explanation. Students hearing the explanations benefit from others making their thinking "visible."
Authentic question	Janin: Is that why nine of us said "we the people" was the most important concept in the whole thing?	Authentic questions create space for students' high-level thinking about text. This authentic question elicits high-level thinking in the turn that follows where Will makes a generalization.
Uptake	Mr. Anders: Okay, but how? How are they related?	A follow-up question builds onto a previous comment. In this case, the teacher's follow-up question elicits high-level thinking on the part of students.

and students' questions are authentic and demonstrate uptake, which means the questions are genuine and build on the responses and thinking of other students. During the discussion, the teacher and students share control of turn taking but the students have most of the interpretive authority.

During Paideia Seminars, authentic questions tend to generate high-level thinking in the form of speculation, as illustrated above where Jeremy, George, and Juanita speculate about the Preamble with the words *as if* and *like*. The reasoning words you will most often hear in Paideia Seminar are *if* and *would,* which indicate speculation, and *I think,* which indicates position taking. Authentic questions also prompt analysis and generalization, as when Monte explains the relationships between liberty and justice in response to the teacher's "how" question. So you will hear *because* quite a lot too.

In Paideia Seminars, you will hear both cumulative and exploratory talk. In the excerpt here, the students are engaged in cumulative talk, which means that they move back and forth in their conversation, sharing ideas about the concepts of the Preamble in productive ways, but without any real disagreement or argument. Exploratory talk is defined by putting forward alternative ideas and reasoning with challenges and counterchallenges. Because we don't hear students saying, "But, what about?" or "I disagree" or "I don't think that is true" or "How do you know that?" in the previous excerpt, we would say the talk is more cumulative. Nonetheless, it is productive cumulative talk as the students are working together to construct an understanding of the Preamble.

The goal of a Paideia Seminar is to think deeply about the text. You will often hear students give text evidence (e.g., "Look at the board. . .") and give elaborated explanations to substantiate their ideas or claims. In the excerpt, there are four elaborated explanations. Jeremy makes the claim that all the concepts in the Preamble are important for democracy, citing the example of domestic tranquility and explaining why it supports his claim. Maria essentially does the same but uses the example of the common defense. Monte then makes the claim that a strong justice system protects us from each other, and he supplies three reasons to support his claim. Toward the end of the excerpt, Will articulates his reasoning as to why "we the people'" was chosen as the most important concept in the Preamble, providing a reason and then elaborating on it to explain his thinking. In all four cases, students are making their thinking visible.

Affective responses, where students share their feelings about the text and make connections to their lives, are sometimes heard in Paideia Seminars. However, seldom will you hear connections to previous discussions (shared-knowledge responses) or connections to other texts or media (intertextual responses). There is usually no express need to look outside the text when there's much to consider and explore within the text.

Research Support

There have been some forty studies of Paideia. Approximately half the studies are investigations of the Paideia program as a whole (didactic instruction, coaching, and seminar), and half are investigations of the Paideia Seminar alone. Most studies of the program describe the experiences of various schools and school districts that have implemented Paideia. These studies invariably report positive outcomes from the program in terms of student achievement, attitudes, and, notably, school climate. Studies of the Paideia Seminar itself have examined students' and teachers' perceptions of the seminars, and students' interactions in the discussions and critical thinking. In what follows, we describe the research that has focused on the seminars.

Students who participate in Paideia Seminars hold very favorable attitudes toward the seminar and report enjoying the experience. Indeed, the seminars seem to be the most popular part of the Paideia program (Heipp and Huffman 1994). Students value being able to voice their opinions, being listened to, and having the opportunities to learn about others' ideas (Gellatly 1997). In a study of tenth graders' perceptions of Paideia (Heipp and Huffman, 1994), one student commented, "I love being able to get in a group and discuss ideas and opinions on different subject[s] where you do not have to worry about being put down because of how you feel" (211). Another student in the study noted: "The seminars help you understand the central concept of the document. You get deeper into the document and understand it better" (211). Students also report that the seminars help them develop their thinking skills (Robinson 2006) as well as their skills in resolving conflicts and respecting others' opinions and feelings (Polite and Adams 1997).

A dilemma facing researchers who are interested in examining the effects of the Paideia Seminars is how to assess students' critical thinking—one of the purported goals of Paideia. One way that researchers have attempted to do this in some studies is by examining students' interactions and talk in the discussions. These studies have shown that **students who participate in Paideia Seminars, as compared to regular discussions, question each other more, challenge and expand on each other's ideas more, and generally show a higher level of complexity in their thinking.** In one particularly interesting study with tenth and eleventh graders, Orellana (2008) showed that the more teachers asked open-ended questions that prompted extended discussion, the better the quantity and quality of students' argumentation.

Interestingly, some studies of the interaction and talk in Paideia Seminars suggest that the increased engagement of students may come at a price. Wortham (1994, 1995) has shown that students can become so involved with interpreting a text in terms of their own lives that the discussion veers off track and loses the desired intellectual rigor. Prompting students to make connections between the text and their own lives can be beneficial for student engagement and comprehension, especially with challenging text, but it is important to keep the discussion from digressing too far from the topic at hand.

Paideia Seminars may enhance students' writing that assesses critical thinking. Another way researchers have tried to tap into students' critical thinking is by examining their scores on relevant test measures. Chesser, Gellatly, and Hale (1997) examined the writing test scores of eighth-grade students in a middle school in North Carolina that implemented the seminars over three years. The test asked students to state main ideas, support them with details, and organize their ideas coherently—all critical thinking skills that Paideia Seminars are meant to support. Chesser and colleagues found that students' writing scores increased over the three years at a rate that was far greater than the state average. Many of the teachers often required their students to complete a writing assignment after each seminar, so the increase in writing scores might have reflected this component. Still, the results are impressive.

THE STORY BEHIND THE PAIDEIA SEMINAR

The story behind the Paideia Seminar is really the story behind the Paideia program. In 1982, Mortimer Adler (whom we met in the chapter about Shared Inquiry), working with a network of scholars known as the Paideia Group, published *The Paideia Proposal: An Educational Manifesto*—a blueprint for the reform of American education. The proposal had its roots in the classical Greek teachings of Socrates, Plato, and Aristotle (the term *Paideia* is a Greek word meaning "the upbringing of a child"). It combined the conservative ideas of a liberal arts education of Robert Hutchins (remember the "Great Books") with the progressive ideas about active teaching of John Dewey. Adler (1982) and his colleagues' motto was "the best education for the best is the best education for all" (6). To accomplish this ideal, they advocated three kinds of teaching: didactic instruction in subject matter, coaching of intellectual skills, and Socratic questioning of ideas and values—the Paideia Seminar.

The Paideia Proposal inspired substantial interest among educators, but it was somewhat abstract; teachers and principals wanted more concrete guidance as to how to implement the ideas. In response, Adler and colleagues followed up with two other landmark publications that laid out the ideas in more detail: *Paideia Problems and Possibilities* in 1983 and *The Paideia Program* in 1984.

Still, schools struggled with how to implement the program, and many educators viewed it as elitist—not something that was suitable for all students. Even with the founding of the National Paideia Center (NPC) at the University of North Carolina in 1988, the program failed to gain traction with schools.

It was not until the early 1990s that Paideia began to be adopted more widely. With new leadership at the NPC, the Center sought to broaden the program's appeal and redefine what counts as text worth discussing. Working with K–12 teachers, staff at the Center identified texts and devised seminar plans that were relevant to teachers' curricular needs. Largely because of the NPC, Paideia Seminars became less about interpretive reading (as with Junior Great Books discussions) and more about critical communication and thinking skills.

Since the founding of the NPC in 1988, some five hundred schools in twenty-five US states have adopted Paideia or at least some aspect of the program. Elementary and middle schools, especially, have been keen to adopt Paideia. The Paideia Seminar, or Socratic Seminar as it is often called, is the most popular aspect of the program. Today, the seminar is viewed as a means of engaging students in close reading and of addressing many of the literacy skills in the Common Core State Standards.

In one of the few experimental studies of Paideia Seminars, Tarkington (1988) examined the effects of the seminars on seventh-grade students' critical thinking skills as measured by the Cornell Critical Thinking Test. Students in the experimental group engaged in discussions once a month for seven months, whereas students in two control groups covered the same texts ostensibly without participating in seminars. Results were mixed: students in the experimental group made substantial gains in critical thinking skills in comparison to one control group but not to the other. (Perhaps tellingly, the teachers in the latter control group had participated in a one-day training in the Junior Great Books program—see Chapter 9—the previous spring.) The results also showed that girls made larger gains than boys did.

It is easy to be impressed with the diverse array of research on Paideia and the generally positive outcomes from the seminars and from the program overall. Comprehension has not been an explicit focus of the research as the goals of the seminars are to enrich students' understanding of the ideas and values inherent in text and to have students think critically about them. But it is reasonable to infer that the heavy focus on critical thinking should result in a rich payoff for students' comprehension.

PAIDEIA SEMINAR in Practice

Planning for Paideia Seminar

QUICK GUIDE

1. **Select a text**. "Text" is considered very broadly in Paideia Seminars. In addition to traditional literary and informational texts, videos, poems, graphs, maps, primary sources, and word problems qualify as texts to study more deeply. When selecting a text, consider its relevance, complexity, and ambiguity. Simplified texts that have "all the answers" are not interesting for seminars.

2. **What's the big idea of the text?** Paideia Seminars foster deeper understanding of a central issue, value, or moral that the text inspires. Big ideas about issues such as progress, power, wisdom, desire, compassion, and citizenship can be used by seminar facilitators to formulate questions and to plan pre- and post-seminar activities. Identify the big ideas.

3. **Determine the goals of the discussion.** Paideia Seminars are mostly about improving *thinking* and *communication*, so identify one or more objectives related to these broad goals. Do you want students to work on a communication goal such as asking each other questions to clarify? A thinking goal would be to use text evidence to explain their thinking during seminar.

4. **Write several kinds of questions to ask at the seminar.** Think of questions in terms of opening questions or those that generate brief brainstorming or sharing, core questions that are meaty and support interpretation of the text, and closing questions that elicit the students' personal takeaways from the discussion.

5. **Plan, manage, and implement a three-part structure.** The flow of Paideia Seminars is to conduct pre-seminar activities, the seminar itself, and post-seminar activities. The activities support the quality of the discussion and the transfer of knowledge from the group to the individual.

Paideia Seminar is an approach to discussion that is part of a structured sequence of activities in reading, writing, speaking, and listening that fosters students' deep thinking about text. The primary goal of a Paideia Seminar is to teach thinking through communication. Paideia Seminar proponents describe "thinking" as the ability to explain and manipulate ideas (Roberts and Billings 2006). The more adept students are at explaining their thinking, elaborating their thoughts, and manipulating their ideas to account for alternative perspectives, the more the experience reflects meaningful learning and the more students comprehend text at a high level. A second important aspect of the seminars is the focus on equality among participants during the seminars. Nobody is an expert at the seminar; nobody railroads the conversation with a long-winded display of prior knowledge; and nobody desires a debate. Seminar participants convene to seek greater understanding of the text through hearing the ideas of others. Gray (1988) perhaps said it best, writing, "A seminar is a high road to thoughtfulness" (6), and it is such because it's a conversation among equals—all learners stand before the text together, wanting to grow together and to understand the text better through dialogue.

When planning Paideia Seminar, you need to think about engagement with and comprehension of the text in a three-step instructional sequence comprised of pre-seminar activities, the seminar, and post-seminar activities (see Figure 11.2). All of the activities relate either to the *content* (topic) of the text or to the *process* (the approaches to preparing for the seminar, discussing the text, and reflecting

Figure 11.2 Example of Paideia Seminar's Instructional Sequence in a Typical School Week

Monday Pre-seminar content activity:	Tuesday Pre-seminar reading:	Wednesday Seminar:	Thursday Post-seminar content activity:	Friday Optional post-seminar content and process activities:
Teacher builds background knowledge and interest in the text. Teacher uses explicit strategy instruction to support comprehension.	Students read and make notes while reading and/or write summaries or opinions after reading the text.	Teacher organizes a whole-class seminar in one large circle or two circles, an inner and outer. Teacher prompts goal-setting. Teacher asks the opening, core, and closing questions.	Teacher sometimes prepares a writing prompt related to the core questions and students write a short explanation or argument to show the transfer to their independent thinking.	Students sometimes continue to revise and edit their writing for an assessment. As a process activity, teacher prompts reflection on the quality of the seminar.

on the quality of the seminar). The seminar is the main entrée while the pre- and post-seminar activities are the important side dishes to the entire experience. It's the side dishes that complete the meal even though the main entrée provides the wow factor.

You have to be prepared to ask several kinds of questions—opening, core, and closing questions—in order to promote thinking and productive dialogue. Read the text with an eye toward the *central idea* or a value that informs the text (e.g., progress, conflict). The idea is to build on the central idea or value and to formulate questions. One value evoked in the Preamble of the Constitution is "liberty," for example. An *opening question*, or one that serves as a warm-up and gets ideas onto the floor is, "Which idea in the Preamble do you think is most important?"

A core question that follows the opening might be, "Is *liberty* the most important idea in the Preamble?" Another core question is, "Why do you think the Preamble is important for the average American?" After asking a core question, the teacher lets students talk and listens for places to step in and elicit elaborated thinking (e.g., "What in the text makes you think that?"), an interpretation (e.g., "Why do you think that?"), or a communication skill (e.g., "How does your idea connect to the previous comment?").

A *closing question*, which is written to provoke a personal takeaway and to support the post-seminar activity at the very end of the seminar is, "How do you feel about this document?" The three kinds of questions are summarized in Figure 11.3.

Within the three-step sequence, the teacher must also plan activities related to the *content* of the text (the topic or big idea) and the *process* of using dialogue in specific ways and either preparing for or reflecting on the outcomes of the

Figure 11.3 Three Kinds of Questions for Paideia Seminar

Question Type	What It Does for the Seminar Discussion
Opening question	"Primes the pump" and warms up the group for dialogue; gets everyone to share aloud. Creates comfort in the setting and equality among the students. This is the first question that's asked.
Core question	Elicits interpretations of the text, students' positions about the text, and evidence from the text to support positions. This is asked early in the seminar, after students share their thoughts in response to the opening question.
Closing question	Supports personal takeaways from the discussion and the text. This question is asked at the end of the seminar.

seminar. Figure 11.4 shows examples of activities that relate to the content and process of the seminar. Figure 11.5 shows examples of lesson ideas in each part of the three-step structure.

Figure 11.4 Activities for Planning Lessons Related to the Content and Process of Discussion

Activities Related to the Content of Paideia Seminar	Activities Related to the Process of Paideia Seminar
• Build background knowledge about the topic of the text with a lecture, video, or group activity. • Provide supplementary materials for the text—paired texts, visual aids, or websites to support comprehension of the text. • Provide a short lesson on a strategy to support comprehension of the text.	• Watch a video of a seminar discussion, identifying the positive communication behaviors. • Identify ground rules and use mini-lessons to explain and practice the ground rules. • Develop goals before the seminar. • Reflect on the quality of thinking and communication after the seminar.

Figure 11.5 Sample Lessons for the Three-Step Sequence of Paideia Seminar

Suggested Lessons for Paideia Seminar		
Pre-Seminar		
Lesson Title	Example Lesson	What It Does for Learning
Talking back to the text (a content lesson)	Say: When reading this text, it is important to have your own ideas and thoughts about the author's ideas. This will help us have a good seminar discussion later this week. So, here's what it sounds and looks like: listen to my thinking as I "talk back to the text" when reading (model with the first part of the text). [Teacher reads some of the text]. Okay. I'm going to stop here and write a note about what I'm thinking.	Since the texts for seminar are somewhat complex and ambiguous, comprehension tools, such as annotating or making connections, are important for learning. "Talking back to the text" stimulates thinking about the text, fostering interpretation, connections, inferences, and conclusions.
Stopping for meaning—Monitoring comprehension (a content lesson)	Say: Our seminar texts are challenging, so we need to use a thinking strategy to make sure we comprehend. What we *can't* do is just read the words, passing right by the meaning. We need a strategy to help us stop and think. The strategy is called, "read-stop-retell—reread or read on." Listen to my thinking as I use this strategy. (Teacher reads, stops, and models retelling *and* the thinking to decide that she knows enough to *read on* or not enough and needs to *reread*).	As the text gets harder, the need for monitoring strategies becomes important. Complex texts demand close or analytical reading— the slow, deliberate reading where the reader stops and interprets the text in small chunks.

continues

Figure 11.5 *continued*

Introduction to the Seminar		
Go for a goal! Setting goals and reviewing round rules (a process lesson)	Say: Today, in our seminar, we are going to focus on these ground rules for our dialogue—listening carefully to our classmates, giving reasons, challenging ideas, and connecting our comments to each other and to the text. Let's choose just one ground rule to really make sure we do well, and we will talk about it after our seminar. Which one? (Students throw out ideas and the teacher chooses one.) Now, I want you to think of your personal goal for your participation in the seminar.	When students use ground rules and a group goal is established, they have a common understanding of their roles and purpose in discussion; this supports quality talk, especially high-level thinking, elaborated explanations, and the co-construction of ideas through exploratory talk.
Post-Seminar		
Micro-writing [index card] makes it your own (a content lesson)	Say: Now we have to make the ideas we heard and shared in the seminar our own. I'm going to ask you to write an argument, first planning your argument with an outline and then writing a short argument on the notecard. The plan and notecard must show your position and reasons— text evidence, examples from the seminar, or other data or personal examples.	Writing after the seminar facilitates the transfer of ideas and thinking from the group context to the individual. Students need time after the seminar to reflect on, restructure, and organize the information into a coherent text of their own.

Teacher's Role in Paideia Seminars

After planning the Paideia Seminar, the role of the teacher is to facilitate the discussion. Rearrange your room just before the seminar discussion, adjusting the seats so everyone is sitting in either one large circle or two concentric circles (an inner circle of students who discuss first, and an outer circle of students who watch and wait to switch roles at the midpoint of the seminar). The purpose of the inner and outer circles is to reduce the number of participants in the discussion in order to increase the participation of more students.

Have your questions ready to go. Asking questions is the most important and hardest job of the teacher in Paideia Seminars. Once the opening and core questions are asked, the idea is to avoid too much teacher talk. Be strategic when stepping in to ask follow-up questions. You know to step in, for example, when students give short responses. Extend short responses with questions such as "How do you know that?" "What's your reason for that?" "Is there something in the text that makes you say that?" Because the goal of a Paideia Seminar is to think critically about the text, questions that prompt referring to the text are always a safe bet. And because the spirit of a Paideia Seminar is egalitarian and democratic, stepping in to ask questions that help connect students' ideas is always good. These include questions such as "How does that connect to something you heard before?" "Are you connecting to Ian's idea?" "So are you disagreeing with what Lucila just said?" "Would anyone else like to build on that idea?" (For other suggestions for promoting equity in discussions, see Chapter 13.)

When you think the students have considered new interpretations and meanings of the text, that might be the time to stop and ask the closing question. The idea is help students think about their personal takeaway; this can be done briefly, simply asking a closing question such as "How does the Preamble make you feel?" and pausing to provide students time to think. The post-seminar activity follows the discussion and is typically a writing activity to support transfer of the ideas of the group to the thinking of the individual. This may be done on the same day as the discussion or on a subsequent day.

Approach in Action: Language Arts, Grade 9

The following whole-class Paideia Seminar discussion took place in a ninth-grade language arts class. The class had read an article from a website titled "School Programs to Prevent Tobacco Use." The teacher planned a pre-seminar content activity, using a selective highlighting or close-reading strategy to support position taking and argumentation. The teacher modeled the strategy, reading aloud and stopping to highlight a fact that supported the ban of tobacco on school grounds. She then used a different color to highlight a detail that could be used to oppose the ban. The students read and prepared for the seminar using this strategy.

At the seminar, the teacher began with an opening question, "Which statistic about smoking in the country is most alarming to you?" The students shared their ideas in a random, rapid-fire way, and then the teacher asked the core question: "Okay. So there are lots of facts and statistics about smoking and smoking bans. Let's focus on the idea in lines 66–67. What does this mean about smoking bans: (reads from the text) *Programs that only discuss tobacco's harmful effects or attempt to instill fear do not prevent tobacco use.*"

Connor: Well, that's kind of the commercials and advertisements about smoking is bad. Anybody knows that teenagers are hardheaded to begin with. And, it's really not going to make a difference to them because most teenagers, teenagers are like, Well, I'm going to die anyway, so what?

Tracey: Exactly. I agree with Connor. That's the way a lot of us think. I mean, I think that way, I'm going to die anyway. I do not smoke, no, but I do think that way. You know, I will die one day. It's just, that's going to happen. But, I think if they was to show maybe diagrams of a lung that has been affected by cigarette smoking. Like lung cancer or something maybe that would be better. Maybe that would change somebody's mind. But, you know, we're pretty thick-headed, if we have our minds made up, you know, that's just the way we're going to feel about it.

> Notice how Tracey gives an elaborated explanation, a long turn that has a chain of reasons and evidence.

Connor: That might affect younger kids, but not kids our age. Because we've already seen that. We've already been through the health classes, and the physical ed., and the . . . and we've seen all that. And we just still don't care.

> Here Connor is posing a slight challenge or qualification to Tracey's argument, saying that diagrams might work only with younger kids, but then he seems to agree that it is hard to change teenagers' minds. Here we are hearing elements of cumulative and exploratory talk.

Tabitha: But for a lot of teenagers, if you tell them not to do something, they're going to turn around and do it anyways. It encourages them. It's like an adrenaline rush. (someone else says "It's like (undecipherable)") I mean if you, if you say it's bad, and you tell them not to, they're just going to do it more.

> Tabitha adds another line of reasoning to support the view that ads won't work: teenagers are unlikely to do what they are told because of their need, presumably, to establish their own identity.

Connor: I have a comment on that. That's true. I believe in that. Like if you was to tell me, "Do not stand on that couch," I might just get mad and do it anyway. Just because you told me not to do it. And if you ask me, you know, "Please do not do this" I'll be, "Oh, she really doesn't want me to do that." You know, it will hit me in a different way, if you was to talk to me like an adult, instead of telling me what I should and should not do.

> Connor agrees with Tabitha, supporting the argument that anti-smoking ads do not work for teenagers: because it's the wrong kind of message for his age group. This is another elaborated explanation.

Tracey: But then we have to look at the matter of respect too, towards your grownups. But that doesn't matter to some teenagers.

> Tracey adds a counterpoint to Connor's example that teenagers do what they want when they are treated like children rather than like adults, saying that perhaps we need to respect what adults tell us.

Teacher: So, should we respect grownups in telling us smoking is bad for us?

The teacher asks a follow-up question. Note how she uses uptake to build on the previous turn.

Roberts, Terry. *Paideia in Action*. 2018. www.paideia.org/paideia-in-action/index.

This excerpt illustrates features of both Paideia Seminar and quality talk. In terms of quality talk, the teacher asks an authentic question and students respond with long turns that demonstrate elaborated explanations. They also use many reasoning words, such as *but, I think, because,* and they engage in cumulative and exploratory talk (challenging ideas, giving reasons, sharing thinking and posing alternative views). Connor, Tracey, and Tabitha offer alternative reasons to support the same argument, and their comments elicit more thinking and reasoning. This is why encouraging students to consider alternative viewpoints is so important. Without alternative viewpoints, it's hard to give reasons that promote deeper thinking about the text. In the last student turn, Tracey pushes back on Connor's position that teenagers ignore adults' messages, so they ignore smoking bans. This is a subtle challenge that appears to offer a new direction in the discussion.

In terms of Paideia Seminar, the excerpt illustrates the role of the teacher in that she asked an opening question and a core question to elicit an interpretation of the text. The students demonstrate good thinking as evidenced by reasoning words that indicate high-level thinking and the orchestration of ideas as a way to discuss several alternatives. Each student turn is connected to a previous one, suggesting that the students know how to communicate in a seminar.

The activities of the three-part sequence, organized around the content and process of learning, are the strengths of Paideia Seminar. The very clever design feature, however, is the focus on the *process* of engaging in the seminar and reflecting on the talk of the seminar. Process routines include goal setting for talk, explicit instruction in how to talk, and reflection on the quality of the talk. The persistent focus on thinking about communication elicits the kind of language that fosters an academic way of knowing and talking. "I am a good thinker" is how we want students to see themselves, and it's the precise way of using academic language in Paideia Seminar, made possible through the process activities, that makes it possible for learners to identify with their academic identities. This deposes the lackluster "going through the motions" that some discussions elicit. In Paideia Seminar, students feel confident in their thinking, know how to talk to each other, and engage with each other in ways that will impress you and affirm your hard work and teaching.

READ MORE

Adler, Mortimer. 1982. *The Paideia Proposal: An Educational Manifesto.* New York: Macmillan.

Billings, Laura, and Terry Roberts. 2019. *The Paideia Seminar: Creative Thinking Through Dialogue.* 3rd ed. Charlotte, NC: The National Paideia Center.

Roberts, Terry, with Laura Billings. 1999. *The Paideia Classroom: Teaching for Understanding.* Larchmont, NY: Eye on Education.

Roberts, Terry, and Laura Billings. 2012. *Teaching Critical Thinking: Using Seminars for 21st Century Literacy.* Larchmont, NY: Eye on Education.

12

Philosophy for Children

PHILOSOPHY FOR CHILDREN

Research Support

- Fosters critical thinking during discussion
- Enhances students' reasoning when used consistently
- Benefits may transfer to reading and math
- Appropriate for use with children as young as age four
- Can benefit students who struggle with reading

Learning How

Attend the Summer Seminar and other programs offered by the Institute for Advancement of Philosophy for Children (IAPC). Consult materials published by the IAPC.

Goals

To explore philosophical questions on topics related to the human experience (e.g., truth, friendship, right and wrong). To promote critical, creative, and caring thinking.

Typical Features

- Literary (philosophical) text
- Whole-class discussion
- Heterogeneous group
- Teacher-led
- Teacher chooses the text
- Students read text before the discussion
- Students and teacher share control of topic
- Students and teacher share control of turn taking
- Students have interpretive authority
- Little focus on author intent

Typical Teacher Questions

Why do you think that?

What is your reason?

Do you have an example of what you're saying . . . ?

Does your suggestion fit with our question?

Is that the way it is for everyone?

Are you jumping to a conclusion?

How are you agreeing (disagreeing) with [student]?

Typical Student Comments

I think . . .

I'm agreeing (disagreeing) with . . .

If . . . , would . . . ?

I have a question for [student] . . .

Teacher's Role

- Prompt students to say or write puzzling questions about a text.
- Support students in collaborative and rigorous inquiry around the selected question(s); build a community of inquiry.
- Ask follow-up questions to help students explore and evaluate arguments.
- Facilitate but not direct the dialogue; be "procedurally strong, but substantively self-effacing" (Splitter and Sharp 1996, 306).
- Conclude the dialogue with a prompt to take action.

What the Talk Sounds Like

In the excerpts from a Philosophy for Children discussion that follow, twenty-two first-grade students are having a whole-class discussion about *Elfie* (Lipman 1988), a story about a young girl who is shy and speaks little at school. Before the discussion started, the students and teacher read chorally this paragraph from the text:

> Maybe I don't talk that much, but I think all the time. I even think when I sleep. I don't have fancy dreams. I just think when I'm asleep about the same things I think about when I'm awake. Last night I woke up in the middle of the night and I said to myself, Elfie, are you asleep? I touched my eyes and they were open. So I said, no, I'm not asleep. But that could be wrong. Maybe a person could sleep with her eyes open. Then I said to myself, at this moment am I thinking? I really wonder. And I answered myself, dummy, if you can wonder, you must be thinking. And if you're thinking then no matter what Seth says, you're for real.
>
> (Lipman 1988, 4–5)

After reading, the teacher and students brainstormed several puzzling questions the text elicited, listing the questions on chart paper. Then the teacher selected one of the students' questions for discussion, which was about what makes something real: "If Elfie wasn't a real person, how could she think or talk?"

Jordan: If, if she—if Elfie wasn't real then, then she wouldn't be able to—she'd be able to *talk* because then she might be what we were discussing yesterday [they were discussing "real," "fake," "artificial," and "imaginary"]. But if she wasn't real, then she wouldn't be able, she wouldn't be able to *think!* And she wouldn't, she wouldn't be able to move every part of her body and stuff like that.

Heather: I agree with Jordan 'cause if you're not *there* you can—you can't *do* anything. You, you won't be able to think and move and stuff, and learn stuff.

Alex: I agree with Jordan because if you weren't real you, you couldn't, you wouldn't—you'd be like—you'd just be a model and you wouldn't be able to hear and everything like that.

Teacher: Alex, what did you say? What would you just be if you weren't real?

Alex: Well if you weren't real, you'd just be a model and you wouldn't be able to hear and everything.

Teacher: You'd just be a model.

Alex: And you wouldn't be able to hear.

Owen: Well, I disagree with Jordan because of—well he wouldn't—What do you mean he wouldn't like not be able to move any part of his body? Maybe—What if like it was a *robot*?

Teacher: Well, that's an interesting question.

Owen: A robot can move every part of his body and a robot isn't real!

Teacher: Now, is a robot a person?

[Chorus, No! No!]

Laura: I agree with Jordan because if you weren't real then you couldn't talk. You would just be still, and you wouldn't be able to hear and talk and move at all.

Matthew: Well if, if—I agree with [looks at Laura]

Teacher: Laura

Matthew: Laura. Because if, if you weren't *real* you wouldn't be able to, to like move around. And you would be, you would—You wouldn't be able to *think*, you wouldn't be able to *hear* and you wouldn't be able to do *anything*.

Later in the discussion, the students examine whether sticking the robot with a needle might be a good test to see if it is a real person:

Teacher: Why, why couldn't you throw a needle at it?

Marsha: Because, because if it's—if it sticks you really deep then you would bleed. And to a robot it would—wouldn't bleed.

Matthew: I agree with Marsha. Because if you, if you, if you throw a ro- if a robot—if *somebody* walked in the door right, and someone- and we thought it was a robot, we wouldn't, we wouldn't be able to *know*. And if you threw, if you threw- and if you threw a needle at it, the pers- and *if* it was a real person, wherever you threw it, it would start bleeding. And, and if it was a rusty needle—*if* it was a rusty needle it could, it could, it could hurt them 'cause it would have rust on it and everything.

Kristen: Well I, I think that that's not really a good idea to find out how it works because if it was a real person it would hurt very badly and the person could get hurt. I think that you could, that it's pretty good, but you *shouldn't* do it. You should pick a different way to disc-, to find out.

(McCall 1989, 26, 28)

Figure 12.1 Some Examples of Quality Talk

Features	Examples	Why They Are Productive
Shared knowledge	Jordan: . . . she'd be able to *talk* because then she might be what we were discussing yesterday [they were discussing "real," "fake," "artificial" and "imaginary"].	References to previous knowledge or to a previous discussion indicate high-level thinking because students pull things together, synthesizing ideas across contexts.
Elaborated explanation	Matthew: Well if, if—I agree with . . . Laura: Because if, if you weren't *real* you wouldn't be able to, to like move around. And you would be, you would—You wouldn't be able to *think*, you wouldn't be able to *hear* and you wouldn't be able to do *anything*.	A response that indicates a position or claim and multiple reasons shows high-level thinking.
Uptake	Teacher: Now, is a robot a person?	A follow-up question that builds onto a previous comment facilitates an elaboration of ideas previously shared.

Philosophy for Children is an approach to discussion that uses texts and philosophical questions as tools to examine puzzling aspects of the human experience (e.g., What does it mean to be a good person?). The teacher and students share control of the topic and they share turn-taking responsibilities. In the excerpt above, the teacher and the students worked together to select the questions to discuss. Notice how Jordan and Hannah take turns without the teacher calling on them, but the teacher calls on Alex. The students, however, control the direction of the discussion. The teacher steps in judiciously to help move the discussion forward, as in the follow-up questions, "Now, is a robot a person?" and "Why couldn't you throw a needle at it?"

The teacher and the students' questions (e.g., "What makes something real?") are almost always *authentic,* having multiple right answers. Questions that demonstrate uptake are also a feature of the discussions. *Uptake is* where a follow-up question builds on the responses of others, fostering elaboration of the ideas already shared. For example, in the excerpt, Owen's question about robots builds on Jordan's argument in the first line of the excerpt, and the teacher's question, "Now, is a robot a real person?" picks up a part of what Owen had said and builds on it. Uptake helps the group stay on topic and connect their ideas.

During Philosophy for Children, the authentic questions tend to generate both high-level thinking in the form of speculation (e.g., Owen's speculation about robots) and analysis, which is illustrated with Alex's deduction ("you'd just be a model"). The reasoning words you will hear most often are *because,* which suggests analyzing or synthesizing, *if* and *would,* which suggest speculation, and *I agree* or *I disagree,* which suggest position taking.

Philosophy for Children discussions are characterized by long, elaborated explanations that display students' thinking about how something works or why something is the way it is. They include a position and multiple reasons, such as the use of examples, text evidence, or beliefs to justify a position. In the excerpt, Jordan gives an elaborated explanation for why Elfie is real. He argues that Elfie is real because she talks, and if she didn't talk, she would be imaginary, and he goes on to reference how the group had discussed this example the previous day.

The discussions are also characterized by short, frequent episodes of exploratory talk. In the first part of the excerpt, the teacher intervenes more times than might be desirable for it to be considered exploratory talk. Later in the discussion, Marsha, Matthew, and Kristen engage in a brief episode of exploratory talk (also giving elaborated explanations) as they wrestle with the idea of sticking a robot with a needle to test whether it is a real person. Marsha and Matthew give reasons for why it might be a useful test though they recognize the risks; but Kristen clearly challenges the idea, again giving her reasons. In exploratory talk, you will hear students disagree, challenge each other, and suggest alternative ideas in a back-and-forth way.

During discussions, students often connect the text or the discussion to their own lives, previous lessons, or other texts. Affective responses, where students share the way the text arouses feelings or evokes connections to personal experiences, are sometimes heard in Philosophy for Children. Likewise, shared-knowledge responses, or connections to previous lessons or discussions, are sometimes heard (e.g., Jordan's first turn in the excerpt). References to the text (e.g., "In the text it said . . .") may be heard in the talk of Philosophy for Children, but they are used mostly to anchor the discussion. For the most part, the text serves as a stimulus to inspire philosophical questions about enduring issues (e.g., "Is stealing ever right?"); it is not an object of analysis or a focus of study in its own right. Similarly, you won't often hear students connecting to other texts or media (i.e., intertextual responses).

Research Support

Research on Philosophy for Children is vast and varied. Countless reports describe various implementations of the program, as well as other versions of the program, in schools in the United States and abroad. The quality of the studies varies widely. Some are best described as anecdotal accounts that provide few details about how the program was used or how it was studied. Many of these were published in Philosophy for Children's own journal, *Thinking* (no longer published), and use outcome measures specially designed to assess the reasoning skills encouraged in Philosophy for Children. Others are more rigorous studies, published in peer-reviewed journals, that tease out the depth of children's thinking when they engage in philosophical discussion, and document the benefits for children's cognitive development and their social and emotional well-being.

THE STORY BEHIND
PHILOSOPHY FOR CHILDREN

It was the 1960s. The United States was embroiled in the Vietnam War and there was a growing mistrust of government and much political upheaval on university campuses. Matthew Lipman, then professor of philosophy at Columbia University, was becoming increasingly concerned about the quality of education in American institutions. His students seemed to lack the critical thinking skills needed for reasoning effectively and making informed choices. And university administrators seemed unwilling or unable to engage students in open, critical dialogue. He viewed the turmoil he saw on college campuses as a further sign that radical reform of the education system was needed.

His solution was no less radical. He wanted to infuse the teaching of thinking skills throughout K–12 schooling so that students would learn to think for themselves and exercise good judgment. He believed that the best way of achieving this was to teach children philosophy and that even very young children were capable of thinking abstractly and engaging in philosophical dialogue.

So in 1967 Lipman wrote *Harry Stottlemeier's Discovery,* a philosophical novel for children. It told of a boy and his classmates who grapple with everyday situations and, as they do, model thinking skills and bring to life various philosophical concepts. In 1970 Lipman conducted the first experimental trial with the novel to determine if it was feasible to engage fifth-grade students in philosophical dialogue. The results were promising. After just nine weeks of twice-weekly discussions, students demonstrated improvements in their logic and reasoning compared to students in the control group. When tested two and a half years later, the children who had taken part in the program showed greater gains in their reading scores.

Lipman left Columbia in 1972 to take up a position at Montclair State College (now University) where he thought he could better realize his vision. It was there that he met Ann Margaret Sharp, and together they founded the Institute for the Advancement of Philosophy for Children and developed the Philosophy for Children program. Their collaboration also led to the development of the idea of a "community of inquiry" as an important aspect of discussion. What was initially a single philosophical novel grew into a comprehensive K–12 program comprising seven novels and accompanying teacher's manuals.

Philosophy for Children is now a worldwide educational movement. It is practiced in sixty countries, and the curriculum materials have been translated into twenty languages. Other approaches to engaging children in philosophical thinking have been developed, with some using selected children's literature rather than specially written philosophical novels to stimulate discussion. Philosophy for Children might not have permeated K–12 education as Lipman envisioned, but it has earned an enviable reputation as a way of conducting collaborative and rigorous inquiry to further students' thinking.

In two systematic reviews of research on Philosophy for Children with elementary and high school students, researchers tried to sift out the more rigorous studies. Garcia-Moriyon, Rebollo, and Colom (2005) found eight studies comparing Philosophy for Children to control or comparison groups that passed their litmus test for reliable findings. Most had used Philosophy for Children for a year. All showed that the discussions led to improvements in students' reasoning. Trickey and Topping (2004), in their systematic review, found ten studies that met their criteria for controlled experiments. These studies showed that Philosophy for Children had positive effects on a range of measures including students' reasoning, reading, and math as well as their self-esteem, listening, and engagement.

In recent years, several rigorous experimental studies have been published that provide even more compelling evidence of the benefits of Philosophy for Children. From these "best of the best" studies, we learn the following:

- After participating in a Scottish version of Philosophy for Children discussions for one hour per week over sixteen months, elementary school students showed substantial gains on a measure of verbal, nonverbal, and quantitative reasoning as compared to students in a business-as-usual control (Topping and Trickey 2007a).

- When these students were followed up two years later, after they had moved to high school, the gains in reasoning persisted (Topping and Trickey 2007b).

- Similar positive effects were found in a Texas replication of the Scottish studies. Seventh-grade students who participated in Philosophy for Children discussions in their language arts classes for one hour per week for twenty-two to twenty-six weeks showed substantial gains in reasoning relative to a control group (Fair et al. 2015a). One of the seventh-grade teachers commented that she saw signs of students' high-level reasoning in her reading classes: "I was so impressed that my students started incorporating this style of thinking during our regular reading time. They started asking these amazing philosophical questions. Far beyond just about the plot, they started digging deeper" (28). Interestingly, as mentioned in Chapter 1, eighth graders in the study who had only four to ten weeks of discussions did not show such gains.

- At a three-year follow-up of the seventh-grade students in the Texas study, researchers again found that the gains persisted (Fair et al. 2015b).

- Students may also reap benefits in academic achievement from Philosophy for Children. In a comparison of a British version of Philosophy for Children with a business-as-usual control, grades 4 and 5 students who took part in one discussion per week made gains on national assessments of reading and math (but not in writing) equivalent to two additional months' progress after just over a year in the program (Gorard, Siddiqui, and See 2017). There are indications that the gains were larger for economically disadvantaged students (although a more recent evaluation of the British version by Lord et al. (2021) has cast doubt on this finding).

Even young children can benefit from participation in philosophical discussions. Walker, Wartenberg, and Winner (2013) found that second graders who had participated in a version of Philosophy for Children once a week for twelve weeks showed improvements in their ability to construct arguments and counterarguments compared to students in a comparison group. Some studies suggest that children as young as four and five years of age can engage in discussion of philosophical questions. One five-year-old, for example, was recorded as asking, "Where does time go when it stops?" (Fisher 2007, 620). Philosophy for Children is ideal for capitalizing on young children's natural curiosity!

Another finding from the research is that children who struggle with reading can benefit from philosophical discussion. Yeazell (1982) showed that using Philosophy for Children as a supplement to a regular reading program with fifth graders resulted in below-grade-level readers making greater than expected gains on a standardized test of reading comprehension. A number of case studies also attest to the claim that struggling readers and students who are otherwise disengaged during reading evidence high-level thinking when they participate in Philosophy for Children.

PHILOSOPHY FOR CHILDREN in Practice

Planning for Philosophy for Children

QUICK GUIDE

1. **Select a text.** The Institute for the Advancement of Philosophy for Children archives a collection of novels written specifically for Philosophy for Children. The text in Philosophy for Children is referred to as a *stimulus*, so traditional print (literary or informational), music, visual art, or other media are appropriate as text. When choosing your own text, it should meet two conditions: first, the topic should make sense of our human experience (e.g., breaking rules, being a friend) and, second, the topic should be ambiguous or contestable. Stories that end with a clear message or textbooks may not be good choices.

2. **What's the philosophical point of the text?** Inquiry and dialogue about human experience is the aim of the approach. Students contemplate meaning about puzzling questions that have more than one "right" answer (e.g., Is it ever right to tell a lie?). Students write questions about the text or a segment of the text, and the teacher and students list and organize them on a poster. The students, often with some guidance from the teacher, decide on the question to discuss.

3. **Plan, manage, and implement a five-part structure.** The flow of Philosophy for Children follows the typical approach to organizing discussions (pre-discussion, discussion, post-discussion), and has five distinct parts: reading, generating questions, exploring arguments about the questions, evaluating the arguments, and concluding the discussion (see Figure 12.2). The teacher organizes the five parts across several days or within one long instructional time period. Start to finish, the process takes about seventy-five to ninety minutes, depending on the length of the text.

Philosophy for Children is an approach to discussion that follows a five-part process to engage students in complex thinking about puzzling philosophical questions (see Figure 12.2). The questions reflect topics that most of us find intriguing, no matter our age or where we live. Questions about friendship, fairness, and right or wrong are good ones, as are specific questions, such as "Should I believe what I see?" "Is it ever right to tell a lie?" "What does it mean to be beautiful?" The questions typically relate to branches of philosophy, such as issues of reality, aesthetics, or ethics.

There are no pre-discussion activities, per se, but before the discussion, students listen to or read the text and think on their own about what's interesting to them. After reading, the teacher prompts students to contemplate the puzzling ideas of the text, and the students write questions about these ideas, either in pairs (brainstorming questions together) or independently.

Proponents of the approach refer to talk within the discussion as "inquiry dialogue," since the structure is similar to a scientific inquiry where hypotheses, theories, and suggestions about a problem are offered for the group's consideration. The group then evaluates the arguments and ideas for their soundness and quality. The post-discussion, or the conclusion to the process, is group reflection on the dialogue. At this point, the teacher might ask, "Based on our dialogue today, what should we do or say if we are in this situation next time?" Inquiry dialogue should end with an action or a logical next step, such as doing or saying something different in a situation, taking action on a problem, or trying a new habit.

You don't necessarily need to be an expert in philosophy to facilitate Philosophy for Children, but you will need to "let go" of most of what you know about text-based discussions. In typical discussions about text, analyzing and interpreting the meaning of the story are primary objectives, but in Philosophy for Children the purpose of reading is to prompt philosophical questioning and dialogue to help us make sense of ourselves and the world. Moreover, in typical text-based discussions, a teacher prompts interpretations of the text, asking students to use text evidence, make inferences, or draw conclusions. In Philosophy for Children, these literacy skills are fine if they materialize (and they often do), but they are not the focus of the approach.

The primary instructional focus of Philosophy for Children is to "teach thinking." Lipman (2003) and Lipman's successors at the Institute for the Advancement of Philosophy for Children (IAPC) (e.g., Gregory 2008) define good thinking as *critical, creative,* and *caring* thinking. When we think critically, we evaluate and use reasoning skills; creative thinking manifests as theorizing and speculating,

▌**Figure 12.2** Five-Part Process of the Philosophy for Children Approach to Discussion

PART 1 **Read the Text**	PART 2 **Generate Questions**	PART 3 **Explore Initial Arguments**	PART 4 **Evaluate the Arguments**	PART 5 **Conclusion**
Introduce the topic and text (stimulus). If you are using traditional print, read the text aloud, as in shared reading.	Students reflect on what puzzles them about the text and generate questions independently in writing. Students share their questions and the teacher lists the questions on the board and clarifies; together, the group decides which questions they will discuss, building an agenda for inquiry.	The teacher reviews the ground rules and begins the inquiry dialogue, posing the big question that the group selected. Students share initial ideas, hypotheses, positions, and arguments. These are called "suggestions."	The teacher prompts students to "test" the suggestions, evaluating and identifying alternatives with counterexamples, counterarguments, and additional evidence. Poor reasons and arguments are abandoned.	The teacher prompts students to reflect and consider the next steps (e.g., by asking, "What action, change, or habit should be adopted, as a result of the dialogue?").

Pre-discussion ⟶ *Discussion—Inquiry Dialogue* ⟶ *Post-discussion* ⟶

and caring thinking is expressed with empathy toward others and their points of view. Lipman (2003) argued that these broad modes of thinking generate multidimensional, well-rounded thinking skills, such as reasoning, speculating, and imagining and the dispositions for questioning, listening, and respecting others.

The contemplation of issues within a community of inquirers and multidimensional thinking take center stage in Philosophy for Children. Winning an argument or having a debate are deemed low forms of thinking in the approach; whereas evaluating arguments, proposing alternative ideas, and abandoning poor arguments are valued. It's a duty to the community to share your thinking, and self-correcting, or remedying the errors in your thinking, is expected. Self-correction is made easier when you know that the purpose of the dialogue is to critically examine the quality of reasons, rejecting those that don't measure up. In Philosophy for Children, you have an obligation to the community "to lose" (if warranted) because the truth matters more than anything else!

Teacher's Role in Philosophy for Children

After reading the text, the teacher prompts students to generate questions about how the text puzzled them, since students ask the questions in Philosophy for Children. For example, she might prompt: "To have a good discussion today, we want to think about what puzzles us. So were there parts of the story that made you wonder? Were there parts of the story that made you stop and think or have questions? Write questions about those parts of the story." Students think and write independently for several, quiet minutes. With young children, they share their questions aloud and the teacher writes the questions on chart paper. With older students, the teacher then makes a "call for questions," leading students in listing their questions on the board or on chart paper and organizing them into themes to help the class outline their inquiry (e.g., four to six big questions). The teacher also clarifies the questions, as they are shared, asking students whether it's okay to reword them or to explain their questions with more details.

Perhaps surprising is the quality of the questions that students write when they are prompted to think about the puzzling ideas in the story. The questions tend to be thick or high-level, so you will hear questions like these: "Is it ever okay to lie to a friend?" You usually won't hear a lot of questions, such as "What is the name of the friend in the story?" However, the teacher can always reword or ask students to elaborate a thin or low-level question if it's offered.

Some teachers refer to the process of generating questions as "building a discussion agenda," and sometimes the questions are added to a class "inquiry book," which archives the work of the community and establishes a collective pride in questioning. Finally, the group decides a question for their discussion. A teacher might simply ask students which theme or question they'd like to discuss, or the teacher might have them take a vote. Occasionally, the teacher chooses the question from the list, knowing that the question has potential to generate a lot of good thinking and engagement.

Rearrange the room just before the discussion, adjusting the seats so that everyone is sitting either in one large circle or as a fish bowl, where those in the inner circle begin the discussion while those on the outside circle make notes (after awhile or at the next lesson, the two groups switch places). One of the advantages of using a fish bowl is that it reduces the number of participants simultaneously in the dialogue in order to increase the overall participation of students. The teacher reviews ground rules, emphasizing the norms of participation pertinent to critical, creative, and caring thinking (Figure 12.3). The group pauses to collect their thoughts or to make a few notes, and the teacher begins the inquiry dialogue with the selected question.

After launching the inquiry dialogue, the teacher asks follow-up questions to facilitate the group's progress toward the "truth," ideally allowing the best argument to rise to the top by eliminating the weaker arguments. The overarching role of the teacher is to be a co-inquirer, procedurally strong by asking good follow-up questions (after all, you are invested in the truth, too!) but substantively weak, seldom making comments about the content of the discussion or asking leading questions. This is accomplished when you align the questions you ask to the process and phases of inquiry dialogue: exploring suggestions and initial arguments, evaluating the arguments, and concluding the dialogue.

Figure 12.3 Example Ground Rules for Critical, Creative, and Caring Thinking

Example Ground Rules of Philosophy for Children
1. Respect the ideas of others.
2. Change your thinking or position if you hear better reasons.
3. Ask each other questions.
4. Listen carefully, so you can connect to the ideas of others.
5. Challenge ideas, asking for evidence or examples.
6. Yield to others, so you hear different points of view.

Ask follow-up questions to elicit multiple suggestions and arguments (the exploring phase) and provoke the evaluation of imperfect ideas by prompting counterexamples and counterarguments (the evaluating phase). Toward the end of the dialogue, ask a concluding question to support the group's reflection on the outcomes and to take action (the concluding phase). And it is perfectly fine, when facilitating, to alternate between exploring an argument and evaluating an argument, moving back and forth, as needed, as the dialogue unfolds. Figure 12.4 shows examples of the kinds of follow-up questions teachers ask to elicit the goals of each part of the process and indicates why the questions are important.

Examining flawed arguments and poor-quality reasons is hard to do in a discussion because the conversations moves fast! Many teachers think they need to sit back in discussions to let the students sort things out, but this isn't true. Your goal is to listen for the ideas that need to be "tested," so you're ready to step in to ask follow-up questions. Students will eventually evaluate and test the arguments on their own, but only after much practice. Therefore, at least at first, asking follow-up questions is vital, and if you're procedurally strong and substantively weak, you won't take over the dialogue. To know when to step in, many teachers find it helpful to "map" the arguments as they hear them, either making an outline or sketching a concept map, noting the main points of the students' thinking. Mapping the dialogue makes it easier to track the arguments and to identify when and where to step in.

For example, let's take a hypothetical story about friendship and a related philosophical question, "What does it mean to be a best friend?" Imagine exploring the question in a discussion with fifth graders; a student takes the position and makes the suggestion, "Best friends do what you like to do." In shorthand style, you write this on your discussion map, noting that it is a position without reasons. Then to prompt the students to elaborate with reasons, you might use uptake, saying, "Can you say more about that?" The student would likely elaborate; for example, saying: "Best friends do what you like to do because best friends hang out with you and stuff, so when you're hanging out, you do things that each person likes. If I like to play soccer a lot, my best friend will probably want to play soccer." Perhaps another student agrees, taking the position: "Yeah. I agree. My best friend and I always play Xbox because we both like it."

Figure 12.4 Parts of the Inquiry-Dialogue Process and Corresponding Follow-up Questions

Inquiry Dialogue	Questions a Facilitator Might Ask	What the Questions Do
Exploring suggestions Establish and explore different arguments and hypotheses; clarify the arguments offered.	• Can you say more about that? Is there a reason? • What do you mean by . . . ? • Do you mean . . . ? • So, are you saying . . . ? • Do you have an example of what you're saying . . . ? • How is . . . different than what [Jonah] said? • Does your suggestion fit with our question? • What is your reason? • Is there evidence to support your opinion? • How do you define . . . ? • Does anyone disagree (agree) . . . ? • Let's stop and summarize—does anyone wish to summarize the different arguments?	Elicit multiple suggestions and arguments. Support students' position taking and arguments (position with reasons). Clarify and build coherence across arguments to keep students connected as one community in their progress toward a more reasonable answer.
Evaluating and testing the suggestions Evaluate and test the arguments and reasons with examples, counterexamples, and definitions.	• Is that source a good one? • Is that the way it is for everyone? • Are you jumping to a conclusion? • Is that a fact? • Can we trust that source? • Can anyone offer a counter-example? • What are you assuming? • Is that true? • Is that true for everyone or in all cases? • Is that the only reason? • How do you know that's true? • Does everyone agree? • Some people might say [interject with the opposing or alternative view].	Promote argumentation or disagreement, drawing out assumptions, counterexamples and counterarguments. Move students away from total agreement with each other ("Some people might say . . ."). Facilitate the evaluation of reasons, determining good reasons from bad ones so the group is able to abandon the bad ones.
Concluding Wrap up and take action.	• Based on our dialogue today, what could we do? • Could we do anything differently? • Could we say something differently in the situation? • What's our next step?	Support taking action.

Either through listening carefully or making a couple of bullet points on your discussion map, you hear the elaboration and argument, but it's also easy to see when an assumption needs to be tested: in this example, the underlying belief that activities define a friendship. You ask yourself, "Is this true?" or "Is this always true?" This is the place to be procedurally strong, identifying and asking a follow-up question that probes the assumption and tests the suggestion. You could ask, "Is that true for all best friends?" Alternatively, you might paraphrase to clarify the argument (exploration question) and follow up with a question to elicit evaluation: "So, are you saying best friends do activities together, and this is what it means to be a best friend?" Then after pausing for a response, you might add, "Does everyone agree?"

Basically, the idea is to have follow-up questions ready to ask. Many teachers find it helpful to have a list of questions in front of them during the discussion. While the students talk, ask yourself, perhaps as you map the discussion, "Do I need to step in, and, if so, how?" The decision as to when to step in is hard at first, but when you set your "uptake compass" to two directions, the decisions get easier: (1) Does the group need to hear alternative ideas (exploring)? (2) Has the group covered the different arguments and do they need to reject the ones that are less defensible (evaluating)? (See Figure 12.5.) With practice, your ear for the talk will improve, you will know how to respond and when, and you will be able to support the group's thinking.

Figure 12.5 Two Main Parts of Inquiry Dialogue and their Associated Decision-Making Points and Example Follow-Up Moves

Approach in Action: Elementary Grade, Whole Class

The following whole-class discussion using Philosophy for Children took place in an elementary grade. The teacher read aloud Aesop's fable, "Mercury and Axe," which is a story that typically prompts questions about honesty and truth. Here are some questions the students generated about the text: "What is a lie?" "Is it okay to lie?" "Is it better to tell the truth or to lie?" "Is it ever wrong to tell the truth?" "What's the harm in a lie?" In the excerpt, students are discussing the question, "How do you know something is true?"

Evan: Sometimes you say something you think is true. It's not a lie if you think it is true.

> Evan takes a position with a reason (that seems to be a personal example). This is a simple argument.

Keisha: I disagree with that because you could think something was true and say it was true when it was not true.

> Keisha challenges Evan's argument, offering a counter-position (something is not true when you say it is)

Teacher: Can you give an example?

> Here the teacher uses uptake to connect to what Keisha said in the previous turn. This question prompts an additional reason and example.

Keisha: Well, if you could say it is raining because you thought it was raining and it was only birds on the roof. You can say something you think is true, although in fact it is not true.

> A sound argument. Keisha offers a position (You can say something is true but it's not), supporting it with an example (you can say it's raining when you hear something on the roof, but it might just be birds).

Jordan: You can only tell if something is true if you or somebody sees it with their own eyes and ears. That is why there are many people think things are true, like ghosts or witches, that sort of thing. But you might be wrong, so you have to check it first before you say it's true.

> Jordan offers an elaborated explanation to flesh out Keisha's argument in clearer terms. Something is true when you see it with your own eyes. You have to check things first and see them. People who don't do this believe in witches and ghosts.

Chase: It's not true because you say it is, but it might be.

> Chase is in a subtle way challenging Jordan here. Something that's true and not a lie is not about what the person thinks, sees, or hears. What makes something true is something else.

(Fisher 2007, 621)

This brief excerpt illustrates features of both Philosophy for Children and quality talk. In terms of quality talk, the teacher asks a follow-up question that involves uptake, and the students respond with long turns that include an elaborated explanation (Jordan's turn). The students use several reasoning words and phrases, such as *if, I disagree, because,* which indicate position taking and high-level thinking. Aside from the teacher's prompt for an example, the talk is exploratory (e.g., giving reasons, sharing thinking, challenging ideas, and posing alternatives). Keisha challenges Evan's position that if you believe something is true, then it is not a lie. Keisha believes being mistaken is a lie, and she gives an example of her position, noticing that when you make a mistake about something, such as sounds on a roof, and you're wrong, it makes it a lie. The teacher's use of uptake ("Can you give an example"?) extends her thinking. Jordan builds on Keisha's example with another way of thinking about seeing something with your own eyes.

In terms of Philosophy for Children, the excerpt illustrates the role of the teacher in that she asks an appropriate question for the exploring phase of the dialogue. The point of this initial phase is to share, provoke, and clarify several hypotheses, theories, and arguments before teasing out the good arguments from the bad ones. In the excerpt, the teacher elicits reasons and clarifies with the question, "Can you give an example?" The question clarifies the argument, giving Keisha a chance to support her position with a reason, and she provides a creative example.

Likewise, the students demonstrate critical and creative thinking, as evidenced with an interesting example of believing in ghosts and witches (Jordan's turn). Caring thinking is evidenced in the way each turn is connected to the previous ones, showing that students are a community of inquiry, respecting each other, the different examples they offer, and the process of their inquiry.

John Dewey (1966) wrote, "All which the school can or need do for pupils, so far as their minds are concerned, is to develop their ability to think" (152). Have we perhaps lost this tenet of education in our push to have students meet dozens of standards in any given subject? We ask students of all grade levels to meet hundreds of standards each year, and almost all of them are premised on students thinking in high-level, critical, and complex ways. Most standards begin with the terms *analyze, determine, explain,* or *cite evidence,* but there's little guidance in the standards on what to do when students need more time to develop these ways of thinking. We assume that if we teach students to analyze literature, as an example, through modeling and with guided practice, they'll be able to analyze literature. But is this true for all students? Does it work this way all the time? Philosophy for Children centers learning around *thinking*—deeper, more robust thinking with the emphasis on critical, creative, and caring thinking. Giving students an authentic context to practice thinking, such as inquiry dialogue and Philosophy for Children, is a way to give students a relevant, authentic context for practicing thinking in ways that help them reach the standards.

Some refer to the thinking goals of Philosophy for Children as the "fourth r" for *reasonable* thinking, claiming the ability to reason is just as important as reading, writing, and math. Others contend that critical, creative and caring thinking are the seeds of democracy since good decisions about society's biggest challenges are made when those who make the decisions think critically and have the capacity to self-correct a viewpoint when warranted. There may be truth to these important claims, but the truth that matters the most right now in Pre-K–12 education is the need to support teachers with professional learning in facilitating deeper, more-rigorous thinking. Philosophy for Children is an approach that accomplishes deeper student thinking admirably, so give it a try if you don't know it already, and spread the word about it.

READ MORE

Fisher, Robert. 2007. "Dialogic Teaching: Developing Thinking and Metacognition Through Philosophical Discussion." In *Early Child Development and Care* 177 (6–7): 615–631. https: doi.org:10.1080/03004430701378985.

Gardner, Susan. 2016. "Commentary on Inquiry is No 'Mere' Conversation. *Journal of Philosophy in Schools* 2 (1): 71–91.

Lone, Jana Mohr, and Michael D. Burroughs. 2016. "Children's Philosophical Encounters: Taking Seriously the Role of Privilege in Classrooms." In *Philosophy in Education: Questioning and Dialogue in Schools*, edited by Jana Mohr Lone and Michael D. Burroughs, 209–218. Lanham, MD: Rowman and Littlefield.

Topping, Keith J., Steven Trickey, and Paul Cleghorn. 2019. *A Teacher's Guide to Philosophy for Children*. New York: Routledge.

SECTION **IV**

How Do I Know Students Are Engaged in Argumentation?

As we have seen in this section of the book, when students are engaged in argumentation, they are interrogating the text or the issues raised by the text. They are searching for the best interpretation of the characters' actions and motives or the assumptions, worldviews, and beliefs underlying the text. There is a lot of back and forth between students as they take positions on an issue (e.g., "I think that . . . "), challenge each other's positions (e.g., "Well, I disagree. I think sometimes it's okay to lie, if you're protecting someone else"), and respond to challenges (e.g., "But it didn't say that in the story") in an effort to sort out the issues. Their questions are authentic and relate to the text or topic under discussion. They share their thinking and speculate about a character's actions or the issues raised by the text (e.g., "I think it's never okay to lie, like Marie did, because people expect the truth"). You might hear them theorizing and thinking creatively (e.g., "I wonder if . . . "), supporting a position with reasons and evidence (e.g., "I think he did that because . . . "), and pulling details together to try to make sense of the text (e.g., "It's not really lying when you don't tell the other person because the mom in the story . . . "). As well, there are many references to the text, especially in Collaborative Reasoning and Paideia Seminar where text evidence is highly valued as a way of supporting a position (less so in Philosophy for Children).

Figure 12.6 shows how the three approaches described in this section—Collaborative Reasoning, Paideia Seminar, and Philosophy for Children—might be scored on the TATT. A key feature of the talk in these approaches is that students frequently engage in individual and collective reasoning as they grapple with ideas in, and raised by, the text and explore different perspectives together. Because teachers share control of the discussions with the students, they have the opportunity to model and scaffold quality talk while providing space for students to wrestle collectively with the ideas. So, you will hear a lot of elaborated explanations as students explain their thinking, justify their positions, and respond to challenges. And you will hear quite a lot of exploratory talk as the students explore their ideas together and evaluate each other's arguments. The combination of abundant elaborated explanations and exploratory talk is a telltale sign that students are engaging in argumentation.

Figure 12.6 Typical Argumentative Talk

	1 Not Yet	2 Emerging	3 Developing	4 Blooming
Questions				
Authentic	___ None	___ Some	___ Many	✓ Almost all
Uptake	___ None	___ Some	___ Many	✓ Almost all
Analysis/ Generalization	___ None	___ Some	___ Many	✓ Almost all
Speculation	___ None	___ Some	___ Many	✓ Almost all
Textual Connections				
Reference to text	___ Do not use text evidence	___ Once or twice	✓ Some of the time	___ Many times
Extratextual Connections				
Affective response	___ Do not make connections	___ Once or twice	✓ Some of the time	___ Many times
Intertextual response	✓ Do not make connections	___ Once or twice	___ Some of the time	___ Many times
Shared-knowledge response	___ Do not make connections	✓ Once or twice	___ Some of the time	___ Many times
Individual Reasoning				
Elaborated explanations	___ Do not provide reasons or provide only one reason	___ Once or twice	___ Some of the time	✓ Many times
Collective Reasoning				
Exploratory talk	___ Do not collectively explore a topic or reason together	___ Some of the time	✓ Much of the time	___ Almost all of the time

Overall, in the three approaches described in this section, there is a real sense that students are digging into each other's thinking to determine the best possible answers to the question confronting the group. Because students orient their talk and participation toward making arguments, they have vested interest in the text and the issues raised by it, often using it as a source of evidence to support their thinking. This means students return to the text, reread, analyze, and think critically in order to evaluate the text as well as their own and each other's thinking. These are highly desirable outcomes to aim for when you are trying to help students meet dozens of English Language Arts standards. And, of course, this is good for comprehension too.

SECTION **V**

Your Turn

13

Getting Started with Quality Talk

Fostering a Culture of Dialogue

An important first step in implementing productive discussions is to foster a culture of dialogue in your classroom. A classroom culture that supports dialogue encourages inclusive and robust student participation, supports quality talk, and inspires strategic ways of using talk to meet learning goals. The teacher's primary role in cultivating a supportive classroom culture is to create opportunities for students to participate in whole-class or small-group discussions where they have considerable control over the talk and more agency in their own learning. When you have established a culture of dialogue in the classroom, students readily use quality talk.

Classrooms that don't yet have a fully developed culture of dialogue tend to have strict rules about who talks and when, few guidelines about participation in discussions, and room arrangements where students sit in rows facing the teacher. These conditions offer little, if any, opportunity for quality talk. By contrast, classrooms that have a culture of dialogue feature open participation on the part of students (they can talk without the teacher intervening), ground rules for talk to establish norms for participation, and flexible room arrangements.

The teacher uses talk in specific ways to promote high-level thinking (e.g., asking a follow-up question to promote elaboration), emphasizes talk as a tool for learning, and makes explicit the ways in which students use quality talk in their discussions.

Checklist for Fostering a Culture of Dialogue

To get started, reflect on your own teaching. Check to see whether you have implemented these steps to build a culture of dialogue in your classroom.

Do you have ground rules for discussion that are posted for students to see?

Setting up ground rules is the best and most useful investment of your time in building a culture of dialogue and inspiring quality talk. Establish ground rules or norms for how we talk, think, and listen in discussions and emphasize open participation, whereby students talk directly with each other and are free to build on each other's ideas. Early in the year, or after a break in the school year, start fresh and describe, model, reflect on, and practice the ground rules. We recommend having students and the teacher co-construct a set of ground rules together. To do this, brainstorm what students already know about having good conversations and then distill the list together, paring it down to a set of seven to eight guiding principles or norms for participation. Ground rules set up an inclusive participation structure that will lead to engaging and productive conversations among students.

The ground rules should reflect two modes of participation: talking in ways that indicate high-level reasoning and critical thinking (e.g., "we give reasons," "we evaluate our ideas"), and using appropriate social skills for academic settings (e.g., "listen with your whole body"). The number of ground rules is up to you, but we think six to eight ground rules cover a lot of the bases (Figure 13.1). Sometimes, though, you might adjust a ground rule from the main list, depending on the discussion approach you use or the needs of a particular class. For example, in Philosophy for Children, there is an emphasis on *caring* about the ideas of others, so one ground rule in this discussion approach might be, "Show kindness and respect toward others when asking questions and listening."

We recommend practicing the ground rules a few at a time because each requires some explanation and modeling. Before each discussion, reintroduce the ground rules and call attention to one that is the focus for the upcoming discussion. We like placing a sticky note directly on an anchor chart to indicate the ground rule that is the focus of the upcoming discussion. Figure 13.1 shows the ground rules that we like for upper-elementary through high-school grades. Can you spot those that reflect norms related to social skills and those that reflect goals for high-level thinking? Figure 13.2 shows an anchor chart of ground rules that a colleague used in her fourth-grade classroom but that could be used with any elementary grade.

Based on our recent experiences with online, video-based discussions during the pandemic in 2020, we believe that the ground rules still have an important role and that the cultivation of an online learning community is as necessary in an online space as it is in an off-line space. For your video-based discussions, we recommend the standard, "off-line" ground rules listed in Figure 13.1. However, we think four additional ground rules are important for a productive online, video-based discussion (see Figure 13.3).

The fourth ground rule in Figure 13.3, "be courageous," needs a bit of explanation. In our experience, we have found that video changes the participation structure of the discussion. When you talk on a videoconference tool, your face is directly centered in the middle of the screen. Talking on camera means that you just went from being an engaged but obscure listener (perhaps even off the screen, depending on the video tool you're using) to being the "star" of the discussion—onstage, front and center in the screen. After making small adjustments with the four additional ground rules and encouraging students to "be courageous," we noticed that our online discussions had similar qualities as our off-line discussions. At the end of our online discussions, we reflected on the online ground rules, just as we would the off-line ones. It's important, no matter where you hold discussion, to make students part of the post-discussion reflection and to empower them to improve the quality of their discussions.

Do students reflect on the ground rules, and do you provide post-discussion feedback?

Prompt your students to reflect on the ground rules after discussions and other lessons and highlight features of quality talk, calling attention to the goal of using talk to think together. After the students share their reflective comments, build on and provide feedback, saying, for example: "I heard a lot of reasons in our talk. This was a great part of our discussion today. But I don't think we used reasons based on the text. Next time, when we talk, let's work on using text evidence to back up our ideas." Making shifts in the culture of the classroom takes a lot of

Our Class Ground Rules

1. "Jump in" if there's a space to talk—you don't need to raise hands.

2. Share ideas and give reasons (e.g., text evidence, examples).

3. Listen with your whole body and look up to make eye contact with each other.

4. Challenge others' ideas—ask a question or share a different idea!

5. Build ideas together, connecting your idea to someone else's.

6. Yield to others—hold back if your idea doesn't build on someone else's or if you're taking a lot of turns and missing the ideas of others.

7. Respect the ideas of your classmates, noticing reasons that are better than your own, and be willing to change your thinking!

Figure 13.1 Ground Rules for Promoting Quality Talk

Figure 13.2 Ground Rules Anchor Chart Used in a Fourth-Grade Classroom

Figure 13.3 Ground Rules for Promoting Quality Talk in Videoconferences

Our Videoconferencing Ground Rules

1. Leave your camera on, if possible; use your microphone like a walkie-talkie.

2. Turn off the chat features for discussions—this is about our conversation!

3. Yield to others and sit back for longer to give others time to enter the video space (e.g., time for them to turn on the microphone).

4. Be courageous! Step in to share your thinking, build on others' ideas, and move our discussion forward. Your ideas matter!

deep reflection, feedback, and action. But it doesn't have to take a lot of time. Some other short, two- to five-minute, post-discussion reflection ideas include:

- **Quick response.** Have students give a thumbs up/down/sideways on how well the group used the ground rules. Follow up with a short discussion with the whole group and ask, "Which ground rule should be our focus next time?"

- **Exit ticket with specific ground rule prompts.** Create a rating scale about the ground rules (or a specific ground rule, such as connecting ideas) and prompt students to rate how well the group did on a 1, 2, or 3 rating scale.

  1—We didn't use the ground rules much.

  2—Some of us used the ground rules.

  3—Most of us used the ground rules.

- **Google form or other digital survey tool with prompts for short, constructed responses.** Example prompts: "Did the group use the ground rules?" "Which ground rule stands out to you as the most positive one today?" "How well did we use the focus ground rule?" "Which ground rule do we need to work on next time?" Figure 13.4 shows an example for middle- or high-school students.

Figure 13.4 Example of a Digital Response Form to Support Reflection on the Discussion and Quality Talk

Reflection on our talk

Form description

Think about the talk of our discussion today and reflect on how well we asked each other questions to evaluate the evidence of our arguments. Write about these questions: 1) Did we ask each other questions? Give an example. 2) Did the questions lead us to evaluate the credibility of the evidence and/or the sources of information? Give an example.

Short answer

Short answer text

- **Media apps for short video responses** (e.g., *Flipgrid, Explain Everything, SeeSaw*). Example prompt: "In a thirty-second video, record your reflection, stating which ground rules you think the group used well and which ground rules you think the group should practice." Alternatively, prompt students' individual reflection on the use of the ground rules ("Which ground rules did you use in the discussion?), or focus on the learning by asking: "Did you learn something in the discussion?" "Did you change your position?" For efficiency, rotate the prompts. One day, focus on group participation and the next focus on the individual outcome. By fostering students' reflection on the quality of talk and their participation, you will help improve their discussions and the quality of their thinking.

Do you foster a sense of equity among students?

In a classroom that supports dialogue, a sense of equity, and a belief that everyone has an important contribution to make, need to be defined. When there's a sense of equity, students value the contributions and ideas of others. Without a sense of equity, individuals will hold back, wondering whether their classmates take their ideas seriously, or students will dominate the discussion, talking over their classmates in order to hold the floor. Students will find it easier to disagree, share alternatives, and make arguments when they know their classmates respect their thinking, even when their ideas are challenged.

So how do we encourage equity in discussions? This is one of those classroom situations where your small actions can make a big difference. Before the discussion, use purpose statements that promote a sense of equity. Figure 13.5 shows two examples of purpose statements that you could use to foster a sense of equity during discussions. Once the discussion gets going, reinforce equity, noticing when students share their thinking and encourage each other to speak. It's okay for some students to be quiet in discussions as long as they are engaged and listening, but you can encourage quiet students to share their thinking by asking, "I wonder what [name] is thinking?" When a reticent student shares in the discussion, you can point this out during the post-discussion reflection, saying: "I like the way everyone participated today. Listening to all our classmates is really important." When one classmate asks another what they are thinking, you can quietly praise this: "Good idea to ask others what they think."

Figure 13.5 Introductory Purpose Statements to Promote a Sense of Equity

Purpose Statements to Foster a Sense of Equity	Grade Levels	How the Statements Promote a Sense of Equity
The purpose of our discussion is to use our talk to develop the best answer and take on board everyone's ideas. This means we care about what others think. When we show that we care, we're more likely to offer different ideas or ways of thinking, so we all learn from the discussion.	Upper elementary and secondary grades	Saying "we care about what others think" instills a value of accepting others and their alternative ideas.
When we talk in discussion, we all want to share ideas because our ideas are important and will help us have a good discussion. We care about each other, so we care about each other's ideas.	Pre-K and early elementary grades	Young children often hear how important it is to care for each other, so saying "we care about each other's ideas" will foster a sense of equity in young children.

Have you adjusted your room so that students face each other during discussions?

In a classroom that supports dialogue, everyone needs to be able to see each other in a discussion. If your classroom has moveable tables and chairs, arrange them in circles or squares when you're ready for discussions, or create space to make larger circles of chairs (a fishbowl grouping if involving the whole class). Rows can be the death of dialogue in the classroom. If the seating in your classroom is inflexible, consider scheduling your discussion in another space where you're able to form a circle or square.

Have you made explicit the need to question and challenge others' ideas?

When someone challenges your thinking, what do you do? Most likely you keep thinking, identifying a way to respond with a reason, example, or anything else that will help the person understand your point of view. Students in a classroom that supports dialogue are comfortable with disagreement and feel free to challenge and respond to challenges during a discussion.

Questions such as "Is that true?" or "How do you know that?" are productive ways of challenging ideas, and they stimulate the evaluation of evidence.

However, many people, adults and kids alike, retreat from these kinds of questions, perhaps finding them too uncomfortable. Sometimes, students may have been discouraged from challenging each other's thinking in previous classes. So, we must teach students to accept disagreement and to use their talk to challenge ideas, when warranted, and to eliminate ideas that do not pass muster and accept those that are the best. Getting to the best idea, reason, or argument takes practice with quality talk and lots of commitment to disagreement. You will need to encourage, practice, and reflect on disagreement through the ground rules and model disagreement during the discussion with evaluative questions (e.g., "Did the text say that?" "Can we trust the author?" "Do we know this for sure?").

Choosing an Approach

Because each of the discussion approaches described in this book elicits a different kind of thinking and talk, choosing an approach based on your instructional goal (e.g., making inferences about text), the particular text, and the needs of your students is the primary consideration when planning a discussion. Sticking with a single discussion approach and using it as a matter of routine in your class may feel comfortable, but if your go-to discussion approach and the kind of talk it elicits are not aligned with your goal for the lesson, then what feels comfortable will lack instructional teeth in achieving your aims (see Chapter 3 for an overview of the different discussion approaches and their characteristics). We recommend becoming comfortable with at least one discussion approach from each of sections II, III, and IV, so you have one that foregrounds each of the different stances toward a text.

The best part of knowing about all nine discussion approaches and their respective discourse features is that it enables us to gain control over the kinds of talk and thinking we want to see and hear from our students. Remember, different types of talk serve different purposes. To these ends, teachers must make deliberate, logical, and strategic decisions when planning a discussion.

Using the Text to Guide Your Planning

If you have flexibility in your curriculum, or in what you teach and how you teach it, you can let the text guide your planning process. Often, we have a text that we know would work well for discussion, or sometimes we encounter new topics and texts that make us think of a discussion. We refer to this logic as a "text-driven discussion plan," and it means that the text is the insight for making choices as to the discussion approach you use, the quality talk features you plan to accentuate, and the language arts standard that fits (see Figure 13.6).

To prompt a text-driven discussion plan, you might begin asking questions of the text, for example: "Is the theme of the story complex or contestable?" "Does a character act in an ethically compromising way?" If the text is informational, you might ask: "Does the topic relate to a relevant issue?" "Does the text make readers feel deeply about a cause?" "Is this text chock-full of information that student need to learn?"

Let's explore a couple of examples to build on these initial questions. The book *Ghost*, by Jason Reynolds (2016), often read in grades 6–8, is a story about a seventh-grade student who joins the track team, makes new friends on the team,

Figure 13.6 Sample Planning Scenarios Following a Text-Driven Discussion Plan

Planning Scenario 1	Planning Scenario 2	Planning Scenario 3
1. Consider the text: Is the text literary and is there a major theme that is essential or enduring?	**1. Consider the text:** Is the text literary and does it evoke feelings about a character's action or dilemma?	**1. Consider the text:** Is the text informational and does it have a lot of information, or does the topic relate to an issue of ethics or a cause?
2. Use a discussion approach that emphasizes knowledge-building, such as Instructional Conversations.	**2. Use a discussion approach** that emphasizes personal response, such as Book Club.	**2. Use a discussion approach** that emphasizes argumentation, such as Paideia Seminar.
3. To foster quality talk: Prepare a single authentic question related to a central theme of the story (see Chapter 7; strong thematic focus to the discussion). Be ready to weave follow-up questions (uptake) that relate to prior knowledge, and attempt to evoke connections to previous texts, previous lessons, and previous experiences (e.g., intertextual, shared-knowledge, and affective connections).	**3. To foster quality talk:** Plan a reading-log response prompt to focus students' attention on the character; plan a short lesson about facilitating student-led discussions, such as "asking each other questions" (a feature of exploratory talk). Organize small groups of students who will simultaneously discuss the story while you circulate from group to group. Prepare a closing activity to get students' feedback on the ideas they had about the character.	**3. To foster quality talk:** Plan before-, during-, and after-discussion activities (e.g., a short writing activity before or after the discussion). Write three kinds of questions to ask during the discussion—opening, core, and closing questions. Focus on asking follow-up questions that elicit the evaluation of the quality of the evidence (e.g., "Is that true?" "Can we trust the source?").

and looks up to his coach. More powerfully, however, *Ghost* confronts the themes of emotional trauma and the interplay of class, race, and identity in age-appropriate, culturally responsive ways. If we seek to use literature as a way to develop students' social-emotional capacities, such as building empathy, identity, and the dispositions for anti-racist ways of thinking, books like *Ghost,* and others in Reynolds' Track Series of which *Ghost* is a part, are superb text selections.

In *Ghost*, the coach, an African American and former Olympian, mentors Ghost through a family trauma and a series of poor decisions (e.g., stealing a pair of sneakers). Ghost needs time to process his emotional trauma, and we see how that personal challenge overwhelms his identity and clouds his judgment. With these central themes, the story elicits position taking on the part of the reader about what Ghost could (or should have) done in several points of the story. The more critical-analytic approaches to discussion described in Section IV (Collaborative Reasoning, Paideia Seminar, Philosophy for Children) cultivate position taking and reasoning, so they would be a good fit for a discussion about *Ghost*. With all of the critical-analytic approaches, students take positions, answer big questions related to a central theme or major issue, defend positions with reasons, and put forth arguments for classmates to test and evaluate. We would say in this planning scenario, there's reasonable alignment between *Ghost*, its central themes, and the quality talk features of the more critical-analytic discussion approaches.

In choosing which of the three critical-analytic approaches to use for a discussion with *Ghost*, since all three would align well to the themes of the text, we recommend using a learning objective as the last piece of the planning puzzle before making your final decision. Let's imagine you're working toward the objective "citing text evidence." Of the three critical-analytic approaches, Collaborative Reasoning, with its emphasis on text evidence to support a position, fits beautifully with "citing text evidence," so we have a perfect pedagogical partnership between the discussion approach and the learning objective.

The logic behind text-driven discussion plans is like building anything where layering to build strength is required. You must begin with the text, or your foundation, making sense of the central themes or issues of the text, connecting the themes to the standard you want to address, and making a judgment about the kinds of quality talk that you need to hear to achieve the learning goals. Could you use Literature Circles with *Ghost*? Sure. Would the approach support position taking? Not really, maybe by chance, and not according to what we know about the discourse of Literature Circles, where there is very little exploratory talk (co-reasoning) or use of text evidence. Literature Circles would be a good fit for *Ghost*, however, if the learning goal was to motivate reading and to support student writing about the text after reading. Students ask a lot of authentic questions, use uptake, and make many affective responses during Literature Circles, so these particular features of quality talk would support a level of comprehension that would scaffold students' response writing to, let's say, a prompt like, "How does *Ghost* make you think of your own life?".

Identifying the text, the standard, the discussion approach, and the related quality talk features are just the beginning, albeit, the core of the discussion plan. In most of the discussion approaches that we have described, the other parts of the discussion plan include a focus on reading, or a "during reading" tool or strategy, that would support a modicum of comprehension, a pre-discussion activity or a prompt to engage students with the text just before the discussion begins (writing about the big question in shared inquiry; sharing with a partner or a family member in Grand Conversation), an authentic question or questions to launch the dialogue, and a post-discussion reflection activity or prompt that would allow students to reflect on the discussion, the quality of the talk, and the ideas that transfer into their independent thinking (e.g., writing assignment). Figure 13.7

Figure 13.7 Collaborative Reasoning Lesson Plan Outline for a Sixth-Grade Language Arts/Reading Class with *Ghost* (Reynolds 2016).

During reading	• Focus on character. Use selective highlighting and note making to mark text evidence related to Ghost's feelings, reflective comments that he makes, ideas about who he wants to be, and what he struggles with. As students read, instruct them to create theories about Ghost (cf., Serravallo 2015).
Pre-discussion	• Students review notes and theories about Ghost. Share ideas briefly with a partner. • Teacher frames the discussion as using talk to generate the best idea or argument, yet emphasizing that the discussion is not a debate. • Review the ground rules and identify a focus ground rule (e.g., use of text evidence to support thinking).
Discussion	• Big Question: *Do you think the way the coach punished Ghost for stealing the sneakers was fair?* • Anticipate arguments: YES, Ghost needs grace. NO, stealing sneakers is wrong. • Prepare to model argumentation, offering students a counterargument (e.g., some people might say Ghost showed remorse for stealing the sneakers, and that's what the coach expected to see. Doesn't it matter that he showed remorse?).
Post-discussion	• Debrief the quality of the arguments and the talk. Were the positions supported with *text evidence*? Were other ground rules used? • Students write a short argument related to the big question.

shows the lesson plan outline for *Ghost*, using planning elements of Collaborative Reasoning.

Using the Standards to Guide Your Planning

If you are required to use a curriculum guide that doesn't provide a lot of flexibility, meaning, for example, that in the ninth week of the school year, you need to focus on a particular language arts standard, then a different approach to planning may be needed. In this situation, planning a discussion is still possible with a *standards-driven discussion plan*, such as a standard related to writing an argumentative essay. In a lesson leading up to writing, using discourse related to position taking and citing text evidence would support argument writing. Figure 13.8 shows the logic in selecting a discussion approach after thinking through a standard that is part of a curriculum guide.

In another example with literature, let's look at the Common Core standard: *Reading Literature, Standard 2, Grade 8: Analyze literary text development.* To achieve this standard, readers need to make inferences about the text, especially inferences linking ideas in different parts of the text. Which discussion approach would you use? In Figure 13.9, we lay out examples of the strategic planning decisions for the grade 8 standard.

Shared Inquiry from the Junior Great Books program, which is a knowledge-building approach to discussion (albeit tilted toward a critical-analytic stance), involves a lot of "why" and "how" questions to promote interpretations of the text, references to the text, and elaborated explanations about the text. Shared Inquiry discussions offer many opportunities for making inferences or drawing on specific details of the text. But it's hard to make inferences with too simple

Figure 13.8 Logic Following a Standards-Driven Discussion Plan to Support a Middle-Grades Argument-Writing Standard

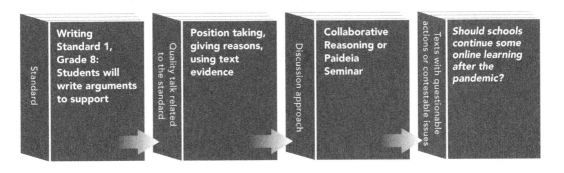

Figure 13.9 Logic Following a Standards-Driven Discussion Plan to Support a Middle-Grades Literature Standard

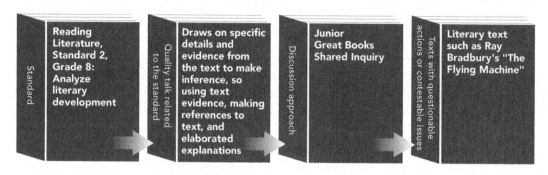

a story. So, in this planning scenario, choose a literary text with rich language, an interesting plot, and thought-provoking themes or characters (e.g., *One Green Apple* by Eve Bunting [2006] for early or intermediate grades or "The Flying Machine" by Ray Bradbury [1953] for middle grades). Once the text is identified in this standards-driven discussion plan, you would then, depending on the discussion approach, decide the pre-discussion activity, the ground rules to focus on, the authentic questions and anticipated follow-up questions or use of uptake, and the post-discussion reflection or other activity.

The examples in this chapter offer guidelines for making big-picture planning decisions about which discussion approach to use. We need to consider the text, students' language and literacy needs, the discussion approach, and the discourse features characteristic of the approach. In language arts teaching, we have the knowledge and tools to make more deliberate and logical decisions about the discussion approach we use, the talk we need to hear, and the text we want students to discuss in order to meet the standards and support the development of high-level thinking and comprehension. Simply stated, we want students to use the kind of discourse that supports the thinking we need in order to meet the desired language arts standards.

14

Troubleshooting: Frequently Asked Questions

We have worked with hundreds of teachers over the years, as they transformed their classrooms and teaching practice with quality talk and we listened to their questions. Below is a list of the most frequently asked questions we hear, followed by our answers.

Q **What should I do when one or two students take a lot of "airtime" in the discussion?**

A Emphasize the ground rule, "Yield to others." Talk about the importance of hearing different viewpoints and ideas and how different points of view always make our thinking even better.

Q **What should I do when there are really quiet students who never talk in discussions?**

A Do we learn by listening? Absolutely. Students do not necessarily have to be verbal to gain from a discussion, but they do have to be engaged. Notice students' engagement. Are they looking at each other when they're speaking or listening? Are they looking back at the text to reread? Also encourage students' participation by revisiting the ground rules, emphasizing that everyone has a stake in building knowledge. Invite students to share their thinking.

Q **What should I do when students seem to just dispute each other?**

A Argument can be good, but talk where students simply dispute each other is not the goal. You will know students are disputing each other when they try to win the argument without giving sound reasons for their ideas. To support productive talk in a discussion, stress the need to consider seriously what others are saying. Return to the ground rules, and focus on "respecting the ideas of others," discussing what this means and what it sounds like. Emphasize the need to think carefully about others' ideas, to accept them if they are well supported, and to challenge them if they are not (with reasons!), reminding students of the purpose of the discussion.

Q **What if students are way off the mark in comprehending the text?**

A Encourage students to take responsibility for checking each other's thinking about the text by challenging the ideas they are sharing. Teach students how to do this with follow-up questions, such as "How do you know that?" If you are part of the discussion, you, too, can prompt students to reread a section of the text and to ask for clarification. If more than a couple of students struggle with the ideas of the text, you might want to support their comprehension through pre-reading, during-reading, and after-reading activities. You want to be sure that students have a modicum of comprehension going into the discussion. Of course, they do not have to understand the text completely—we want to make sure they still have questions and wonderings to fuel the discussion—but students need to know enough about the topic and the text to be able to participate in the discussion.

Q **How do I get students back on topic, after they get off topic?**

A Off-topic talk is normal. In adult discussions, there are tangents and off-topic sidebars, so you can expect students to get off topic sometimes, too. When this happens, you can redirect with a follow-up question related to the text or topic of the discussion, or you can coach students to redirect themselves through the ground rules. You might use this ground rule, for example: "ask questions about the text or topic of the discussion when the focus gets off track."

Q If I conduct an online discussion with a video conference tool, should I use the same ground rules?

A Yes and no. This is new terrain for all of us, and we have explored the question in our own online discussions. Many video conference tools allow for "break-out" or small groups, where the teacher can enter the small groups either to participate or to listen to a small group of students having a discussion. If this is your experience and the kind of videoconference tool you have, we suggest using Book Clubs or Literature Circles, with the ground rules we mentioned in Chapter 13. Book Club and Literature Circles are approaches that feature discussions in small student-led groups, so they are ideal for the break-out groups in many video conference platforms. In our own exploration of video-based discussions, we used Book Club with preservice teachers with some success. Book Club (Chapter 5) organizes discussion into whole-class "community share," followed by small-group, peer-led discussions. The break-out groups in our video conference tool reproduced the face-to-face, small-group discussions well, while coming together as a class before and after the break-out groups took the role of community share. It was in the whole-class sessions that we could establish the purpose for discussion and the ground rules, review any necessary content, and reflect on our talk.

The ground rules for online discussion are basically the same as for off-line, with a few exceptions. When you enter a conversation in a video conference tool, your face may be literally front and center in the screen. To make this sometimes-awkward experience for students seem more natural, we emphasized the need for empathy for each other and sensitivity to the idea that sharing ideas on a video camera takes courage and practice. You can say something like, "When you enter a video space to share your thinking, you're being courageous, and that's really helping the group and supporting our goal to share alternative points of view." We think that "naming" what's happening when students enter the video space as courageous, because it can be uncomfortable, establishes the new normal. Other video-specific ground rules you might include are: "avoid the chat feature during small, break-out groups discussion"; "keep the video turned on, if possible" (so we can replicate face-to-face conversation); "give each other more

wait time to turn on the microphone and to let the video catch up to the audio";
and "yield to others, leaning back a little longer or a little more often so that others can enter the space to share their thinking."

Q **Should I grade the discussions?**

A It depends. Discussion, generally, is a wonderful way to monitor students'
progress toward standards because you hear much of their thinking, so we
can informally assess the quality of the talk and thinking just by listening and using
the Talk Assessment Tool for Teachers (TATT), discussed in Chapter 2 and included
in the Appendix. We know teachers who have implemented discussion midway
through a unit as an informal assessment, using the discussion to promote student
reflection on learning and to formatively assess their thinking about the material
so far. To be deliberate and mindful of the quality of the talk during discussion, we
often have the TATT on our laps and make anecdotal notes and checkmarks to
reflect what we hear as a formative assessment. If you need to take it up a notch
for a grade, consider assessing the quality of the thinking in students' writing after
the discussion, as evidence of their progress toward the standard (e.g., citing text
evidence). If you have a grading routine for these kinds of post-lesson assessments
(e.g., exit tickets), you could grade the individual writing as a way of "grading"
the discussion. As mentioned in the previous chapter, we advocate for informally
assessing students' adherence to ground rules in order to promote reflection on
the discussion and to provide "data" to interpret and create a goal for the group
for the next discussion (e.g., "we need to work on disagreeing with each other").
Fostering a growth mindset with goal-setting and feedback is our preference over
grading discussions.

Q **What should I do if everyone agrees with the same idea or classmate?**

A On your journey toward quality talk and productive discussions, students will
often adopt the same position on an issue; this tendency often appears early
in the year, when you are getting started with discussions. When this happens,
you can step in to prompt alternative ways of thinking, asking, "Does everyone
agree?" Or you can step in to prompt disagreement, saying: "Some people might

Figure 14.1 Discussion Ground Rules and Talk Stems

Discussion Ground Rules	Talk Stems
Share ideas and give reasons (e.g., text evidence, examples)	In the text, it said, . . . I have an example . . . This makes me think of something . . .
Challenge ideas	I disagree because . . . I agree with your position, but I have a different reason . . .
Build ideas together	I want to connect to . . . I can build on . . . I have something else to add to . . . I disagree with that because the text said . . .

say . . ." or "Is that true?" or "If someone were to take a different view, what might they say?" After this happens, you might sharpen your ground rules around disagreement and challenging ideas, restating the purpose of these two moves. You might also show students how to connect their ideas, when they do disagree, giving them talk stems, such as "I disagree with that reason because. . . ." Talk stems are good interventions to use when the ground rules are not taken up after direct explanation and modeling or when you have students who need differentiation for language proficiency (e.g., English language learners). Show students what the talk you want to hear sounds like.

Q How often should I step in? Shouldn't I sit back and let students have their discussion?

A Avoid sitting back too much, especially early in your discussion practice. There's a misconception in some teachers' professional learning that sitting back and not talking equals a good discussion. This may be true in rare cases, but only after students have learned to manage the ground rules well on their own. Quality talk takes practice. Lots of it. Teachers need to model the kind of talk they would like to hear from their students. Over time, students use the quality talk of the teacher on their own. In our experience, this will require discussions on a regular basis (preferably weekly or close to it). If you can plan and facilitate three to four discussions each month, students will learn and grow in their talk and thinking about text.

Closing Thoughts

We can only think through something on our own for so long. Try to remember the last time you made a big decision or had to understand something really hard or new for you (e.g., moving to a new house or learning new technology for teaching). In that situation, at first you might have reflected quietly on it and thought through the decision or challenge on your own, but ultimately you probably found yourself talking about it with someone else, right? A colleague, a friend, or a family member is an essential sounding board and talk partner when we are faced with life's big questions and new or challenging situations. In a classroom, where we and our students are talking to learn, it is no different. Wrapping our thinking around a complex idea or learning a new, difficult skill is made easier when we talk and listen to the ideas of others. Imbued in the language of our classmates and teachers are alternative solutions, fresh perspectives, and important questions, all of which shape how we come to know and learn something. And, as we saw in Chapter 1, talk is a tool for thinking together. When students "chew on" an idea with others and are given the support to do so, they can generate new ways of thinking, new understandings, and creative ideas that extend beyond what each alone is capable of. This is the power of talk!

In this book, we have provided a menu of approaches to classroom discussion about text and offered a lens—the lens of quality talk—to help you understand what the different approaches can (and cannot) do . We hope this helps you to develop an awareness of talk and to become more strategic in using discussion to achieve the educational goals you have for your students. It is only by becoming more sensitive to what is going on in students' talk, by acquiring an ear for talk, that we as teachers can know when to step into a discussion and when to step back, what to scaffold, and what to say or do to improve the quality of the discussion.

Now it's your turn. What do you think?

APPENDIX | Talk Assessment Tool for Teachers

Directions

This assessment tool is designed to help you make judgments about the quality of students' talk during discussions about text in your classroom. Using a video of a whole-class or a small-group discussion, complete the five steps below. The purpose of working though each step is to help you gain both a global understanding of the discussion and a deeper understanding of the specific features of the discourse (e.g., incidence of authentic questions, uptake, elaborated explanations) that indicate high-level thinking and comprehension. It is through understanding the talk at this level that we can begin to understand the quality of students' thinking, learning, and understanding.

1. Before proceeding with the assessment, ask yourself this question: "What was your goal for this discussion?" Write your answer here or discuss your answer with your literacy coach or critical colleague.

2. Select a ten-minute segment from the video that you would like to analyze, and view it. As you view the video segment, record who initiates each turn, and note anything about the turn that strikes you on the worksheet (pages 215–217). For example, you might note the occurrences of elaborated explanations, authentic questions, or affective responses. The Code-as-You-Go notation is provided to help you. Use the worksheet to make notations for approximately fifty turns, or about ten minutes of discussion.

3. View the ten-minute segment again and continue to add notes to your worksheet.

4. Based on your notes from the worksheet, make an assessment of the quality of the talk in the ten-minute sample using the rubrics provided.

5. Based on your viewing of the segment, your notes from the worksheet, and your assessment of the quality of the talk, reflect on the overall value of the discussion by writing responses to the reflection questions provided.

Worksheet

TURN	T/S/Name	
1		
2		
3		
4		
5		
6		
7		
8		
9		
10		
11		
12		
13		
14		
15		
16		
17		
18		
19		
20		
21		
22		
23		
24		
25		

Code-as-You-Go Notation:

AQ	Authentic Question	**AR**	Affective Response (text-to-self)
UT	Uptake	**IT**	Intertextual Response (text-to-text)
GA	Generalization/Analysis Question	**SK**	Shared Knowledge (discuss-to-discuss)
SP	Speculation Question	**EE**	Elaborated Explanation
RtT	Reference to Text	**ET**	Exploratory Talk

Worksheet *continued*

TURN	T/S/Name	
26		
27		
28		
29		
30		
31		
32		
33		
34		
35		
36		
37		
38		
39		
40		
41		
42		
43		
44		
45		
46		
47		
48		
49		
50		

Code-as-You-Go Notation:

AQ	Authentic Question		AR	Affective Response (text-to-self)
UT	Uptake		IT	Intertextual Response (text-to-text)
GA	Generalization/Analysis Question		SK	Shared Knowledge (discuss-to-discuss)
SP	Speculation Question		EE	Elaborated Explanation
RtT	Reference to Text		ET	Exploratory Talk

Worksheet *continued*

TURN	T/S/Name	
51		
52		
53		
54		
55		
56		
57		
58		
59		
60		
61		
62		
63		
64		
65		
66		
67		
68		
69		
70		
71		
72		
73		
74		
75		

Code-as-You-Go Notation:

AQ	Authentic Question		**AR**	Affective Response (text-to-self)
UT	Uptake		**IT**	Intertextual Response (text-to-text)
GA	Generalization/Analysis Question		**SK**	Shared Knowledge (discuss-to-discuss)
SP	Speculation Question		**EE**	Elaborated Explanation
RtT	Reference to Text		**ET**	Exploratory Talk

Assessment of Quality of the Talk

QUESTIONS

Category	1 **Not Yet**	2 **Emerging**	3 **Developing**	4 **Blooming**
Authentic	____ *None* of the questions are genuine or have no known answer; all questions are test questions (i.e., they have a known answer). Test questions dominate the discussion.	____ *Some* questions are genuine or have no known answer, and some questions are test questions (i.e., they have a known answers). There is a mix of questions.	____ *Many* questions are genuine or have no known answer. There are very few test questions.	____ *Almost all* questions are genuine or have no known answer. There are almost no test questions.
Uptake	____ *None* of the questions incorporate a previous student response (i.e., are follow-up questions).	____ *Some* questions incorporate a previous student response (i.e., are follow-up questions).	____ *Many* questions incorporate a previous student response (i.e., are follow-up questions).	____ *Almost all* questions incorporate a previous student response (i.e., are follow-up questions).
Generalization/ Analysis	____ *None* of the questions prompt students to tie ideas together (e.g., "What does the author mean by . . . ?") or to break ideas apart (e.g., "Why do you think that?").	____ *Some* questions prompt students to tie ideas together (e.g., "What does the author mean by . . . ?") or to break ideas apart (e.g. "Why do you think that?").	____ *Many* questions prompt students to tie ideas together (e.g., "What does the author mean by. . . ?") or to break ideas apart (e.g. "Why do you think that?").	____ *Almost all* questions prompt students to tie ideas together (e.g., "What does the author mean by . . . ?") or to break ideas apart (e.g., "Why do you think that?").
Speculation	____ *None* of the questions prompt students to consider alternative possibilities or to consider what might happen about topics or ideas related to the text (e.g., "What might happen . . . ?" or "What if . . . ?").	____ *Some* questions prompt students to consider alternative possibilities or to weigh up what might happen about topics or ideas related to the text (e.g., "What might happen . . . ?" or "What if . . . ?"). You only sometimes hear students say words or phrases such as *if, she would, I might, maybe.*	____ *Many* questions prompt students to consider alternative possibilities or to weigh up what might happen about topics or ideas related to the text (e.g. "What might happen . . . ?" or "What if . . . ?"). You hear students say words or phrases such as *if, she would, I might, maybe.*	____ *Almost all* questions prompt students to consider alternative possibilities or to weigh up what might happen about topics or ideas related to the text (e.g., "What might happen . . . ?" or "What if . . . ?"). You often hear students say words or phrases such as *if, she would, I might, maybe.*

TEXTUAL CONNECTIONS

Category	1 Not Yet	2 Emerging	3 Developing	4 Blooming
Reference to Text	____ Students *do not* use text evidence to bolster an argument, support a position, or clarify ideas.	____ Students *once or twice* use text evidence to bolster an argument, support a position, or clarify ideas. You might hear the students say, "On page x, it said . . ." or "In the story, it said . . ."	____ Students *some* of the time use text evidence to bolster an argument, support a position, or clarify ideas. You might hear the students say, "On page x, it said . . ." or "In the story, it said . . ."	____ Students *many* times use text evidence to bolster an argument, support a position, or clarify ideas. You might hear the students say, "On page x, it said . . ." or "In the story, it said . . ."

EXTRATEXTUAL CONNECTIONS

Category	1 Not Yet	2 Emerging	3 Developing	4 Blooming
Affective Response	____ Students *do not* make connections between the text and their feelings or their own lives (i.e., text-to-self connections).	____ Students *once or twice* make connections between the text and their feelings or their own lives (i.e., text-to-self connections). You only sometimes hear students say, "One time I . . ." or "It made me feel . . ."	____ Students *some* of the time make connections between the text and their feelings or their own lives (i.e., text-to-self connection). You might hear students say, "One time I . . ." or "It made me feel . . ."	____ Students *many* times make connections between the text and their feelings or their own lives (i.e., text-to-self connections). You often might hear students say, "One time I . . ." or "It made me feel . . ."
Intertextual Response	____ Students *do not* make connections between the text and other specific texts, works of art, or other media (i.e., text-to-text connections).	____ Students *once or twice* make a connection between the text and other specific texts, works of art, or other media (i.e., text-to-text connections).	____ Students *some* of the time make connections between the text and other specific texts, works of art, or other media (i.e., text-to-text connections).	____ Students *many* times make connections between the text and other specific texts, works of art, or other media (i.e., text-to-text connections).
Shared-Knowledge Response	____ Students *do not* make connections between the text and previous discussions they have had or previous knowledge they have shared (i.e., text-to-previous discussion connections).	____ Students *once or twice* make a connection between the text and previous discussions they have had or previous knowledge they have shared (i.e., text-to-previous discussion connections).	____ Students *some* of the time make connections between the text and previous discussions they have had or previous knowledge they have shared (i.e., text-to-previous discussion connections).	____ Students *many* times make connections between the text and previous discussions they have had or previous knowledge they have shared (i.e., text-to-previous discussion connections).

INDIVIDUAL REASONING

Category	1 Not Yet	2 Emerging	3 Developing	4 Blooming
Elaborated Explanations	____ Students state their views BUT they either *do not* provide reasons or they provide only one reason to back up their viewpoints.	____ Students *once or twice* individually explain their thinking about their claims, beliefs, or opinions. They state their views and provide two or more reasons or a chain of reasons and evidence to back up their viewpoints.	____ Students *some* of the time individually explain their thinking about their claims, beliefs, or opinions. They state their views and provide two or more reasons or a chain of reasons and evidence to back up their viewpoints.	____ Students *many* times individually explain their thinking about their claims, beliefs, or opinions. They state their views and provide two or more reasons or a chain of reasons and evidence to back up their viewpoints.

COLLECTIVE REASONING

In episodes of student-to-student turn taking, there is Exploratory Talk when students

____ share relevant information

____ * consider each other's ideas and collectively explore a topic, theme, or issue (i.e., students' responses connect to each other)

____ * give reasons for their ideas or opinions (e.g., "I think . . . because . . .")

____ * challenge each other's ideas or opinions (e.g., "but . . . ," "I disagree . . . ," "Why do you think that?")

____ offer alternative ideas or opinions

____ invite other students to speak

Use this checklist as you consider the talk. (Asterisked features are essential.)

Category	1 Not Yet	2 Emerging	3 Developing	4 Blooming
Exploratory Talk	____ Students *do not* collectively explore a topic or reason together about the text or ideas related to the text without the teacher's input during the discussion.	____ Students *some of the time* collectively explore a topic and reason together about the text or ideas related to the text without the teacher's input during the discussion.	____ Students *much of the time* collectively explore a topic and reason together about the text or ideas related to the text without the teacher's input during the discussion.	____ Students *almost all of the time* collectively explore a topic and reason together about the text or ideas related to the text without the teacher's input during the discussion.

Reflection

Based on your viewing of the video, your notes from the worksheet, and your assessment of the quality of the talk, what are your reflections on the quality of the discussion? Write your responses to each of the following questions.

1. How would you characterize students' participation in the discussion? (e.g., Did some students not participate or participate rarely? Did some students hold the floor for too long?)

2. How would you describe the talk? (e.g., How coherent was it? What was the dominant stance? Were there times when students just agreed or disagreed with each other but did not reason collectively?)

3. What do you think the students learned during this discussion?

4. How would you characterize your participation in the discussion (if teacher led)?

5. What will you do in the next discussion to facilitate talk that reflects high-level thinking and comprehension?

Glossary and Notation

Category	Code-as-You-Go Notation	Description
Authentic Question	**AQ**	A question where the person asking does not know the answer or is genuinely interested in knowing how others will answer (i.e., the answer is not prespecified). Almost all student questions are authentic. An authentic question usually allows for a range of responses and generates several responses.
Uptake	**UT**	A follow-up question about something that someone else said previously. Uptake is often marked by the use of pronouns (e.g., "How did it work?" "What causes this?" "What city grew out of this?").
Generalization/ Analysis	**GA**	Student talk that shows evidence of high-level thinking in the form of *generalization* (building up ideas, tying things together, "what's the point") or *analysis* (breaking down ideas, "how or why").
Speculation	**SP**	Student talk that shows evidence of high-level thinking in the form of *speculation* (considering other possibilities, hypothesizing, "what if").
Elaborated Explanation	**EE**	Thinking that is explained in fairly detailed form to others. Elaborated explanations occur in a single turn where a student explains how they arrived at a conclusion by giving a step-by-step description or detailed account of how a conclusion was reached or how a problem might be resolved. These are elaborated descriptions of how things work, why some things are the way they are, or how they should be thought about. These include details of how to think about an issue and justification or rationale for thinking that way.
		Turns in which elaborated explanations occur are typically somewhat longer and more coherent than the average student turn, and contain at least one or more reasoning words (*because/'cause/cos, if, so, I think, agree/disagree, would, could, maybe/might/may be, like, but, how, why*).
		As the phrase *elaborated explanations* suggests, students make some kind of claim and provide either two reasons to support it or one reason and evidence in support of the reason (e.g., "I agree with Joseph because he keeps annoying them by saying shut up and I think he is trying to just get them to let him play because they wouldn't let him play because he didn't have his glove").
Affective Response	**AR**	Students make connections between the text and their feelings or their life (i.e., **text-to-self**) (e.g., "I felt . . . ," "When I was little, I . . .").
Intertextual Response	**IT**	Students make connections between the text and other literary or nonliterary works, other works of art, or media, such as billboards, television, newspapers or magazines (i.e., **text-to-text**) (e.g., *In that other book we read* …).
Shared-Knowledge Response	**SK**	Students make connections between current discussion and previous discussion the students have had, previous topics they have talked about, or previous knowledge they have shared (i.e., **discuss-to-discuss**) (e.g., "This reminds me of last week when we talked . . .").

continues

continued

Category	Code-as-You-Go Notation	Description
Reference to Text	**RtT**	Students refer to the text in order to bolster an argument or opinion.
Exploratory Talk	**ET**	A kind of "co-reasoning," where students (sometimes with the teacher) *over several turns* share knowledge, evaluate evidence, and consider options in a reasonable and equitable way. In essence, it is a way of using language to "chew on an idea," to think collectively, to "interthink." A key feature of exploratory talk is students giving reasons for their ideas or opinions. Hence, exploratory talk typically contains lots of reasoning words (*because/'cause/cos, if, so, I think, agree/disagree, would, could, maybe/might/may be, like, but, how, why*). E.g., **Joanna:** Angelique, *why* do you think she wants to be a kid? `— Invitation to speak` **Angelique:** *Because* she likes to swim and she likes to be around a lot of kids. `— Reasons` **Tamika:** And she likes playing a lot, with the kids and stuff? `— Reasons` **Angelique:** Yes. **Joshua:** And I *agree because if* she wasn't swimming *she'd* probably be sitting back rocking chair. She's having a lot of fun, some fun like [the] children. `— Reasons` **Joanna:** *I think* the same thing as Angelique was saying that *she'd* probably like to be a kid again, and um, probably she had a good life *because* she did a lot of stuff and you know how we, um, how we are now . . . `— Reasons` (several turns deleted) **Brian:** I *disagree.* I *disagree* with Angelique. . . *'Cos* my grandma, she cleans up the house, she goes swimming and everything else, *but I don't think she'd* like to be a kid again. `— Challenge with reason` **Angelique:** Brian, that's different, *but* she still probably wants to be a kid again, this Grandma in the story. `— Challenge` **Brian:** *If* I was that age, I wouldn't want to be a kid again *because* I'd have to go through all that, getting my license again, getting more money to get the house, then I've got to go get a job again, and everything over and over. `— Alternative idea` **Angelique:** *But* that's probably what she wanted to do. It doesn't mean trying to be a kid again. `— Challenge`

▌ Example 1 of Worksheet Notes

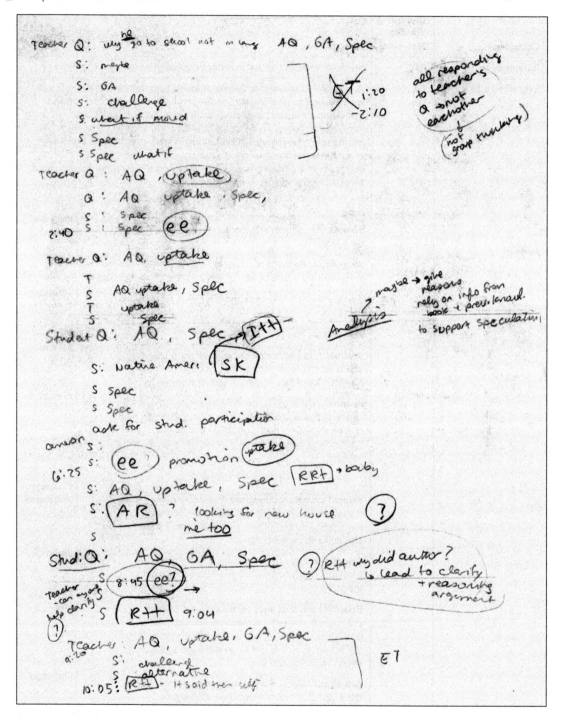

▌Example 2 of Worksheet Notes

<u>Inside Out</u>   ①

T. Why would he be going to a school?   **AQ**

T. OQ
S.

S.   S —   spec.

S.   GA Spec   alternative

S.   S · speculation

S.   S

S.   S

S.   GA — But if they moved. . . . .   ((challenge)

T.   So you think they moved? A OQ   TQ, UT

S   GA

T.   Why would that cause somebody to move? AQ, ∪

S.   S.   }
                                        cumulative
S.   GA   }
                                        ↓
S.   S

S.   S

T.   summarizes - Francisco's dad . . . . get a job . . . .

S. AQ, UI   why would they move · live in a tent

S.
T.   Why would they? AQ, UT

S.   GA # GA

S.
T.   S

S.   What was the meaning ? AQ
S.   are we done ? OQ
S.   SK, IT, GA

S.   Spec.

Example 3 of Worksheet Notes

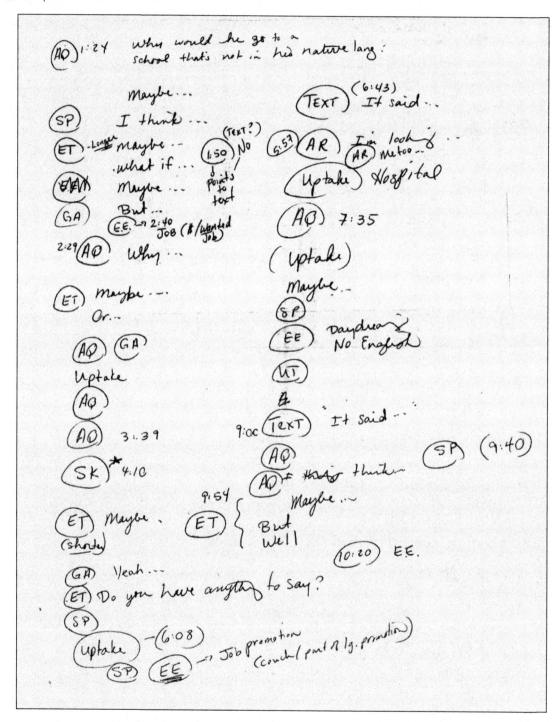

References

Adler, Mortimer. 1982. *The Paideia Proposal: An Educational Manifesto*. New York: Simon and Schuster.

Adler, Mortimer, and Charles van Doren. 1972. *How to Read a Book*. Rev. ed. New York: Simon and Schuster.

Alexander, Robin. 2017. *Towards Dialogic Teaching: Rethinking Classroom Talk*. 5th ed. York, UK: Dialogos.

———. 2018. "Developing Dialogic Teaching: Genesis, Process, Trial." *Research Papers in Education* 335: 561–598. http://doi.org/10.1080/02671522.2018.1481 140.

Allen, JoBeth, Karla Möller, and Dorsey Stroup. 2003. "'Is this Some Kind of Soap Opera?': A Tale of Two Readers Across Four Literature Discussion Contexts." *Reading & Writing Quarterly* 19 (3): 225–251.

Almasi, Janice, Margaret McKeown, and Isabel Beck. 1996. "The Nature of Engaged Reading in Classroom Discussions of Literature." *Journal of Reading Behavior* 28 (1): 107–146.

Anderson, Richard, Clark Chinn, Martha Waggoner, and Kim Nguyen. 1998. "Intellectually Stimulating Story Discussions." In *Literacy for All: Issues in Teaching and Learning*, edited by Jean Osborn and Fran Lehr, 170–186. New York: Guilford.

Anderson, Richard, Kim Nguyen-Jahiel, Brian McNurlen, Anthi Archodidou, So-young Kim, Alina Reznitskaya, Maria Tillmanns, and Laurie Gilbert. 2001. "The Snowball Phenomenon: Spread of Ways of Talking and Ways of Thinking Across Groups of Children." *Cognition and Instruction* 19 (1): 1–46.

Au, Kathryn Hu-Pei. 1979. "Using the Experience-Text-Relationship Method with Minority Children." *Reading Teacher* 32 (6): 677–679.

Beck, Isabel, and Margaret McKeown. 1998. "Transforming Knowledge into Tangible Resources to Support Pedagogical Change: Final Report to the Spencer Foundation." Unpublished manuscript.

———. 2006. *Improving Comprehension with Questioning the Author: A Fresh and Expanded View of a Powerful Approach*. New York: Scholastic.

Beck, Isabel, Margaret McKeown, and Erika Gromoll. 1989. "Learning from Social Studies Texts." *Cognition and Instruction* 6 (2): 99–158.

Beck, Isabel, Margaret McKeown, Rebecca Hamilton, and Linda Kucan. 1997. *Questioning the Author: An Approach for Enhancing Student Engagement with Text*. Newark, DE: International Reading Association.

———. 1998. "Getting at the Meaning: How to Help Students Unpack Difficult Text." *American Educator* 22 (1–2): 66–71, 85.

Beck, Isabel, Margaret McKeown, Cheryl Sandora, Linda Kucan, and Jo Worthy. 1996. "Questioning the Author: A Yearlong Classroom Implementation to Engage Students with Text." *The Elementary School Journal* 96 (4): 385–414.

Beck, Isabel, Margaret McKeown, Gale Sinatra, and Jane Loxterman. 1991. "Revising Social Studies Text from a Text-Processing Perspective: Evidence of Improved Comprehensibility." *Reading Research Quarterly* 26 (3): 251–276.

Beck, Isabel, and Cheryl Sandora. 2015. *Illuminating Comprehension and Close Reading*. New York: Guilford.

Benner, Susan. 2010. "Dialogue and Instructional Conversation as an Instructional Strategy. "In *Promising Practices for Elementary Teacher: Make No Excuses!*, 95–96. Thousand Oaks, CA: Corwin.

Billings, Laura, and Jill Fitzgerald. 2002. "Dialogic Discussion and the Paideia Seminar." *American Educational Research Journal* 39: 907–941.

Billings, Laura, and Terry Roberts. 2019. *The Paideia Seminar: Creative Thinking Through Dialogue*. 3rd ed. Charlotte, NC: The National Paideia Center.

Bird, Jan. 1964. "Effects of Fifth Graders' Attitudes and Critical Thinking/Reading Skills Resulting from a Junior Great Books Program." PhD diss., Rutgers, The State University of New Jersey.

Biskin, Donald, Kenneth Hoskisson, and Marjorie Modlin. 1976. "Prediction, Reflection, and Comprehension." *The Elementary School Journal* 77 (2): 131–139.

Bradbury, Ray. 1953. "The Flying Machine." Woodstock, IL: Dramatic Pub. Co.

Brewer, Pam, and Edward Brewer. 2015. "Pedagogical Perspectives for the Online Education Skeptic." *Journal on Excellence in College Teaching* 26 (1): 29–52.

Brock, Cynthia, Mary Birgit McVee, Angela M. Shojgreen-Downer, and Leila Flores Dueñas. 1998. "No Habla Inglés: Exploring a Bilingual Child's Literacy Learning Opportunities in a Predominantly English-Speaking Classroom." *Bilingual Research Journal* 22(2–4): 175–200.

Brock, Cynthia, and Taffy Raphael. 1994. "Mei: Constructing Meaning During a Sixth-Grade Social Studies Unit." *Yearbook of the National Reading Conference* 43: 89–100.

Bulla, Clyde. 1989. *A Lion to Guard Us.* New York: HarperCollins.

Bunting, Eve. 2006. *One Green Apple.* New York: Clarion Books.

Burnett, Frances Hodgson. 1911. *The Secret Garden.* Illustrated by Charles Robinson. New York: F.A. Stokes Co.

Cashman, Richard. 1997. "The Effects of the Junior Great Books Program at the Intermediate Grade Level (4–5–6) on Two Intellectual Operations, Verbal Meaning and Reasoning Ability." PhD diss., Boston College.

Chapin, Suzanne, and Catherine O'Connor. 2012. "Project Challenge: Using Challenging Curriculum and Mathematical Discourse to Help All Students Learn." In *High Expectation Curricula: Helping All Students Succeed with Powerful Learning,* edited by Curt Dudley-Marling and Sarah Michaels, 113–127. New York: Teachers College Press.

Chesser, William, Gail Gellatly, and Michael Hale. 1997. "Do Paideia Seminars Explain Higher Writing Scores?" *Middle School Journal* 29 (1): 40–44.

Chinn, Clark, Richard Anderson, and Martha Waggoner. 2001. "Patterns of Discourse in Two Kinds of Literature Discussion." *Reading Research Quarterly* 36 (4): 378–411.

Choi, Yangsook. 2001. *The Name Jar.* New York: Alfred A. Knopf.

Cisneros, Sandra. 1984. *The House on Mango Street.* Houston, TX: Arte Público Press.

Coerr, Eleanor. 1977. *Sadako and the Thousand Paper Cranes.* Illustrated by Ronald Himler. New York: Puffin.

Commeyras, Michelle. 1991. "Dialogical-Thinking Reading Lessons: Promoting Critical Thinking Among 'Learning-Disabled' Students." PhD diss., University of Illinois at Urbana-Champaign.

Commeyras, Michelle. 1993. "Promoting Critical Thinking through Dialogical-Thinking Reading Lessons." *The Reading Teacher* 46 (6): 486–494.

Creech, Sharon. 1994. *Walk Two Moons*. New York: HarperCollins.

Criscuola, Margaret. 1994. "Read, Discuss, Reread: Insights from the Junior Great Books Program." *Educational Leadership* 51 (5): 58–61.

Dalton, Stephanie, and June Sison. 1995. "Enacting Instructional Conversation with Spanish-Speaking Students in Middle School Mathematics." Research Report No. 12. Washington, DC: Center for Applied Linguistics/National Center for Research on Cultural Diversity and Second Language Learning.

Daniels, Harvey. 2002. *Literature Circles: Voice and Choice in Book Clubs and Reading Groups*. 2nd ed. Portland, ME: Stenhouse.

Daniels, Harvey. and Nancy Steineke. 2004. *Mini-lessons for Literature Circles*. Portsmouth, NH: Heinemann.

Danticat, Edwidge. 2015. *Mama's Nightingale: A Story of Immigration and Separation*. New York: Dial Books for Young Readers.

Davidson, Margaret. 1969. *Helen Keller*. New York: Scholastic.

Davin, Kristin. 2013. "Integration of Dynamic Assessment and Instructional Conversations to Promote Development and Improve Assessment in the Language Classroom." *Language Teaching Research* 17 (3): 303–322.

DeFelice, Cynthia. 1991. *Weasel*. New York: Avon.

Dewey, John. 1933. *How We Think*. Boston, MA: Heath.

———. 1966. *Democracy and Education: An Introduction to the Philosophy of Education*. New York: Free Press of Glencoe.

Doherty, R. William, and R. Soleste Hilberg. 2008. "Efficacy of Five Standards in Raising Student Achievement: Findings from Three Studies." *Journal of Educational Research* 101 (4): 195–206.

Dudley-Marling, Curt. 2014. "Insisting on Class(room) Equality in Schools." In *The Poverty and Education Reader: A Call for Equity in Many Voices*, edited by Paul Gorski and Julie Landsman. Sterling, VA: Stylus.

Dudley-Marling, Curt, and Sarah Michaels. 2012. "Shared Inquiry: Making Students Smart." In *High-Expectation Curricula: Helping All Students Succeed with Powerful Learning*, edited by Curt Dudley-Marling and Sarah Michaels, 99–110. New York: Teachers College Press.

Echevarria, Jana. 1995. "Interactive Reading Instruction: A Comparison of Proximal and Distal Effects of Instructional Conversations." *Exceptional Children* 61 (6): 536–552.

Echevarria, Jana, and Renee McDonough. 1995. "An Alternative Reading Approach: Instructional Conversations in a Bilingual Special Education Setting." *Learning Disabilities Research and Practice* 10 (2): 108–119.

Eeds, Maryann, and Ralph Peterson. 1991. "Teacher as Curator: Learning to Talk About Literature." *The Reading Teacher* 45 (2): 118–126.

———. 1995. "What Teachers Need to Know About the Literary Craft." In *Book Talk and Beyond: Children and Teachers Respond to Literature,* edited by Nancy Roser and Miriam Martinez, 10–23. Newark, DE: International Reading Association.

———. 1997. "Literature Studies Revisited: Some Thoughts on Talking with Children about Books." *New Advocate* 10 (1): 49–59.

Eeds, Maryann, and Deborah Wells. 1989. "Grand Conversations: An Exploration of Meaning Construction in Literature Study Groups." *Research in the Teaching of English* 23 (1): 4–29.

———. 1991. "Talking, Thinking, and Cooperative Learning: Lessons Learned from Listening to Children Talk about Books." *Social Education* 55 (2): 134–137.

Ennis, Robert. 1987. "A Taxonomy of Critical Thinking Dispositions and Abilities." In *Teaching Thinking Skills: Theory and Practice,* edited by Joan Baron and Robert Sternberg, 9–26. New York: Freeman.

Evans, Karen, Donna Alvermann, and Patricia Anders. 1998. "Literature Discussion Groups: An Examination of Gender Roles." *Reading Research and Instruction* 37 (2): 107–122.

Everett, Gwen. 1993. *John Brown: One Man Against Slavery.* New York: Rizzoli.

Fair, Frank, Lory Haas, Carol Gardosik, Daphne Johnson, Debra Price, and Olena Leipnik. 2015a. "Socrates in the Schools from Scotland to Texas: Replicating a Study on the Effects of a Philosophy for Children Program." *Journal of Philosophy in Schools* 21: 18–37.

———. 2015b. "Socrates in the Schools: Gains at Three-Year Follow-Up." *Journal of Philosophy in Schools* 22: 5–16.

Feiertag, Judy, and Loren Chernoff. 1987. "Inferential Thinking and Self-Esteem: Through the Junior Great Books Program." *Childhood Education* 63 (4): 252–254.

Fillion, Bryant. 1981. "Reading as Inquiry: An Approach to Literature Learning." *English Journal* 70 (1): 39–45.

Fisher, Robert. 2007. "Dialogic Teaching: Developing Thinking and Metacognition through Philosophical Discussion." *Early Child Development and Care* 177 (6–7): 615–631.

Garcia-Moriyon, Felix, Irene Rebollo, and Roberto Colom. 2005. "Evaluating Philosophy for Children: A Meta-Analysis." *Thinking* 17 (4): 14–22.

Gardner, Susan. 2016. "Commentary on Inquiry is No 'Mere' Conversation." *Journal of Philosophy in Schools* 2 (1): 71–91.

Gasser, Judith, Bill Smith, and Ann Chapman. 1996. "A Texas Dilemma: Literature-Based Reading Instruction or Teach to the TAAS." *State of Reading* 3 (2): 21–29.

Geisler, Diana. "The Influence of Spanish Instructional Conversations Upon the Oral Language and Concepts About Print of Selected Spanish-Speaking Kindergarten Students." PhD diss., Texas Woman"s University, 1999.

Gellatly, Gail. 1997. "Students Describe Seminars: Having a Valued Voice in School." MA thesis, University of North Carolina at Chapel Hill.

Goatley, Virginia. 1996. "The Participation of a Student Identified as Learning Disabled in a Regular Education Book Club: The Case of Stark." *Reading and Writing Quarterly* 12 (2): 195–214.

Goatley, Virginia, and Taffy Raphael. 1992. "Non-Traditional Learners' Written and Dialogic Response to Literature." *Yearbook of the National Reading Conference* 41: 313–322.

Goldenberg, Claude. 1992–1993. "Instructional Conversations: Promoting Comprehension Through Discussion." *Reading Teacher* 46 (4): 316–326.

Gorard, Stephen, Nadia Siddiqui, and Beng Huat See. 2017. "Can 'Philosophy for Children' Improve Primary School Attainment?" *Journal of Philosophy of Education* 5 (1): 5–22.

Gratz, Alan. 2017. *Refugee.* New York: Scholastic.

Graup, Leona. 1985. "Response to Literature: Student-Generated Questions and Collaborative Learning as Related to Comprehension." EdD. diss., Hofstra University.

Gray, Dennis. 1988. "Socratic Seminars: Basic Education and Reformation." *Basic Education: Issues, Answers and Facts* 3 (4).

Great Books Foundation. 1987. *An Introduction to Shared Inquiry.* Chicago: Great Books Foundation. www.greatbooks.org/wp-content/uploads/2014/12/Shared-Inquiry-Handbook.pdf.

———. 1992. *Junior Great Books Curriculum of Interpretive Reading, Writing, and Discussion.* Chicago: Great Books Foundation.

———. 2002. *The Junior Great Books Program: An Adventure in Thinking.* Video. Chicago: Great Books Foundation.

———. 2014. *Shared Inquiry: Handbook for Discussion Leaders and Participants.* Chicago: Great Books Foundation. www.greatbooks.org/wp-content/uploads/2014/12/Shared-Inquiry-Handbook.pdf.

———. 2016. "Measuring the Benefits of Junior Great Books—2006–2013." www.greatbooks.org/wp-content/2016/07/Measuring-the-Benefits-of-JGB-2006-2013.pdf.

————. 2020 (June 8). *Inquiry-Based Learning and K–12 Professional Development.* Retrieved June 25, 2020, from www.greatbooks.org/k-12-inquiry-based-learning.

Green, Judith, and Cynthia Wallat. 1981. "Mapping Instructional Conversations—A Sociolinguistic Ethnography." In *Ethnography and Language in Educational Settings,* edited by Judith Green and Cynthia Wallat, 161–207. Norwood, NJ: Ablex Publishing Corporation.

Gregory, Maughn. 2008. *Philosophy for Children: Practitioner Handbook.* Montclair, NJ: The Institute for the Advancement of Philosophy for Children.

Guthrie, John, and Ann McCann. 1996. "Idea Circles: Peer Collaboration for Conceptual Learning." In *Lively Discussions! Fostering Engaged Reading,* edited by Linda Gambrell and Janice Almasi, 87–105. Newark, DE: International Reading Association.

Hait, Nancy. 2011. "Learning to Do Shared Inquiry in a Fourth Grade Classroom." PhD diss., Boston College.

Hart, Shannon, Diane Escobar, and Susan Jacobson. 2001. "The Rocky Road to Grand Conversations: Learning How to Facilitate Literature-Discussion Groups in Fourth Grade." In *Transforming Literacy Curriculum Genres: Working with Teacher Researchers in Urban Classrooms,* edited by Christine Pappas and Liliana Barro Zecker, 307–324. New York: Routledge.

Heipp, Raymond, and Lois Huffman. 1994. "High School Students' Perceptions of the Paideia Program." *The High School Journal* 77 (3): 206–215.

Hill, Bonnie Campbell, Nancy J. Johnson, and Katherine L. Schlick Noe, eds. 1995. *Literature Circles and Response.* Norwood, MA: Christopher-Gordon.

Hill, Bonnie Campbell, Katherine L. Schlick Noe, and Janine A. King. 2003. *Literature Circles in Middle School: One Teacher's Journey.* Norwood, MA: Christopher-Gordon.

Hill, Margaret, and Leigh Van Horn. 1995. "Book Club Goes to Jail: Can Book Clubs Replace Gangs?" *Journal of Adolescent and Adult Literacy* 39 (3): 180–188.

Hoff, Syd. 1959. *Sammy the Seal.* New York: HarperCollins.

Howe, James. 1997. "Victor." In *Birthday Surprises: Ten Great Stories to Unwrap,* edited by Johanna Hurwitz, 74–85. New York: Beech Tree.

Jadallah, May, Brian Miller, Richard C. Anderson, Kim Nguyen-Jahiel, Jie Zhang, Anthi Archodidou, and Kay Grabow. 2011. "Collaborative Reasoning about a Science and Public Policy Issue." In *Bringing Reading Research to Life,* edited by Margaret McKeown and Linda Kucan, 170-193. New York: Guilford.

Jakobson, Roman. 1987. *Language in Literature.* Edited by Krystyna Pomorska and Stephen Rudy. Cambridge, MA: Belknap Press.

Jay, Tim, Ben Willis, Peter Thomas, Roberta Taylor, Nick Moore, Cathy Burnett, Guy Merchant, and Anna Stevens. 2017. *Dialogic Teaching: Evaluation Report and Executive Summary*. London: Education Endowment Foundation with Sheffield Hallam University.

Jiménez, Francisco. 1998. *The Circuit: Stories from the Life of a Migrant Child*. Boston: Houghton Mifflin.

Kendall, Jennifer. 2006. "'Dinosaurs Can't Use Computers, They Don't Have Any Plugs,' and Other 'Grand Conversations:' The Journey Through Book Club with Kindergarten Students." MA thesis, University of Nevada, Reno.

Kim, Il-Hee, Richard Anderson, Kim Nguyen-Jahiel, and Anthi Archodidou. 2007. "Discourse Patterns During Children's Collaborative Online Discussions." *Journal of the Learning Sciences* 16 (3): 333–370.

Kintsch, Walter. 1998. *Comprehension: A Paradigm for Cognition*. Cambridge, UK: Cambridge University Press.

Kong, Ailing, and Ellen Fitch. 2002–2003. "Using Book Club to Engage Culturally and Linguistically Diverse Learners in Reading, Writing, and Talking About Books." *Reading Teacher* 56 (4): 352–362.

Kong, Ailing, and P. David Pearson. 2003. "The Road to Participation: The Construction of a Literacy Practice in a Learning Community of Linguistically Diverse Learners." *Research in the Teaching of English* 38 (1): 85–124.

Kurtz, Jane. 1998. *Fire on the Mountain*. New York: Aladdin Paperbacks.

Li, Yuan, Richard Anderson, Kim Nguyen-Jahiel, Ting Dong, Anthi Archodidou, Il-Hee Kim, Li-Jen Kuo, Ann-Marie Clark, Xiaoying Wu, May Jadallah, and Brian Miller. 2007. "Emergent Leadership in Children's Discussion Groups." *Cognition and Instruction* 25 (1): 75–111.

Lightner, Sarah, and Ian Wilkinson. 2017. "Instructional Frameworks for Quality Talk about Text: Choosing the Best Approach." *The Reading Teacher* 70 (4): 435–444.

Lin, Chen-Ju. 2012. "The Influence of Cognitive Coaching on the Planning and Use of Instructional Conversations, with a Focus on Mathematics Instruction." PhD diss., University of Hawai'i at Mānoa.

Lin, Tzu-Jung, Richard Anderson, John Hummel, May Jadallah, Brian Miller, Kim Nguyen-Jahiel, Joshua Morris, Li-Jen Kuo, Il-Hee Kim, Xiaoying Wu, and Ting Dong. 2012. "Children's Use of Analogy During Collaborative Reasoning." *Child Development* 83 (4): 1429–1443.

Lipman, Matthew. 1988. *Elfie*. Upper Montclair, N.J.: Institute for the Advancement of Philosophy for Children, Montclair State College.

———. 2003. *Thinking in Education*. 2nd ed. Cambridge, UK: Cambridge University Press.

Littleton, Karen, and Neil Mercer. 2013. *Interthinking: Putting Talk to Work*. Abingdon, UK: Routledge.

Lloyd, Rachel Malchow. 2006. "Talking Books: Gender and the Responses of Adolescents in Literature Circles." *English Teaching: Practice and Critique* 5 (3): 30–58.

Lord, Pippa, Afrah Dirie, Kelly Kettlewell, and Ben Styles. 2021. *Evaluation of Philosophy for Children: An Effectiveness Trial*. London: Education Endowment Foundation.

Lowry, Lois. 1993. *The Giver*. Boston, MA: Houghton Mifflin Harcourt.

———. 2009. *Crow Call*. New York: Scholastic Press.

Ma, Shufeng, Richard Anderson, Tzu-Jung Lin, Jie Zhang, Joshua Morris, Kim Nguyen-Jahiel, Brian Miller May Jadallah, Theresa Scott, Jingjing Sun, Kay Grabow, Beata Latawiec, and Sherry Yi. 2017. "Instructional Influences on English Language Learners' Storytelling." *Learning and Instruction* 49: 64–80.

MacLachlan, Patricia. 1985. *Sarah, Plain and Tall*. New York: HarperCollins.

Marshall, Jodi Crum. 2006. "The Effects of Participation in Literature Circles on Reading Comprehension." PhD diss., University of Miami.

Matsumura, Lindsay, Helen Garnier, and Jessaca Spybrook. 2013. "Literacy Coaching to Improve Student Reading Achievement: A Multi-Level Mediation Model." *Learning and Instruction* 25: 35–48.

McCall, Catherine. 1989. "Young Children Generate Philosophical Ideas." *Thinking* 8 (2): 22–41.

McCutchen, Deborah, Anne Laird, and Jan Graves. 1993. "Literature Study Groups with At-Risk Readers: Extending the Grand Conversation." *Reading Horizons* 33 (4): 313–328.

McElvain, Cheryl. 2005. "Transactional Literature Circles and the Reading Comprehension of At-Risk English Learners in the Mainstream Classroom." Ed.D diss., University of San Francisco.

———. 2010. "Transactional Literature Circles and the Reading Comprehension of English Learners in the Mainstream Classroom." *Journal of Research in Reading* 33 (2): 178–205.

McGee, L. M., L. Courtney, and R. G. Lomax. 1994. "Teachers' Roles in First Graders' Grand Conversations." *Yearbook of the National Reading Conference* 43: 517–526.

McGee, Lea. 1992. "An Exploration of Meaning Construction in First Graders' Grand Conversations." *Yearbook of the National Reading Conference* 41: 177–186.

McKeown, Margaret, and Isabel Beck. 1990. "The Assessment and Characterization of Young Learners' Knowledge of a Topic in History." *American Educational Research Journal* 27 (4): 688–726.

———. 2004. "Transforming Knowledge into Professional Development Resources: Six Teachers Implement a Model of Teaching for Understanding Text." *Elementary School Journal* 104 (5): 391–408.

McKeown, Margaret, Isabel Beck, and Ronette Blake. 2009. "Rethinking Reading Comprehension Instruction: A Comparison of Instruction for Strategies and Content Approaches." *Reading Research Quarterly* 44 (3): 218–253.

McKeown, Margaret, Isabel Beck, Linda Kucan, and Cheryl Sandora. 1995. "Second-Year Classroom Implementation of Questioning the Author: New Teachers, New Site." Unpublished manuscript.

McMahon, Susan. 1996. "Guiding student-led discussion groups." In *Lively Discussions: Fostering Engaged Reading,* edited by L. B. Gambrell and J. F. Almasi. Newark, DE: International Reading Association.

McMahon, Susan. 1992. *Book Club Discussions: A Case Study of Five Students Constructing Themes from Literary Texts.* Elementary Subjects Center Series No. 72. East Lansing, MI: Center for the Learning and Teaching of Elementary Subjects.

———. 1994. "Student-Led Book Clubs: Transversing a River of Interpretation." *New Advocate* 7 (2): 109–125.

McMahon, Susan, Laura Pardo, and Taffy Raphael. 1991. "Bart: A Case Study of Discourse About Text." *Yearbook of the National Reading Conference* 40: 285–295.

McMahon, Susan I., and Taffy E. Raphael (with Virginia J. Goatley and Laura S. Pardo), eds. 1997. *The Book Club Connection: Literacy Learning and Classroom Talk.* New York: Teachers College Press.

Mehan, Hugh. 1979. *Learning Lessons.* Cambridge, MA: Harvard University Press.

Mercer, Neil. 2000. *Words and Minds: How We Use Language to Think Together.* London and New York: Routledge.

———. 2013. "The Social Brain, Language, and Goal-Directed Collective Thinking: A Social Conception of Cognition and Its Implications for Understanding How We Think, Teach, and Learn." *Educational Psychologist* 48 (3):148–168.

Michaels, Sarah, Mary Catherine O'Connor, Megan Williams Hall, and Lauren B. Resnick. 2002. *Accountable Talk: Classroom Conversation That Works.* 3 CD-ROM set. Pittsburgh: University of Pittsburgh.

Michaels, Sarah, Mary Catherine O'Connor, and Lauren Resnick. 2008. "Reasoned Participation: Accountable Talk in the Classroom and in Civic Life." *Studies in Philosophy and Education* 27 (4): 283–297.

Murphy, P. Karen, Ian Wilkinson, Anna Soter, Maeghan Hennessey, and John Alexander. 2009. "Examining the Effects of Classroom Discussion on Students' High-Level Comprehension of Text: A Meta-Analysis." *Journal of Educational Psychology* 101 (3): 740–764.

National Governors Association Center for Best Practices, and The Council of Chief State School Officers. 2010. *Common Core State Standards.* Washington, DC: National Governors Association Center for Best Practices, Council of Chief State School Officers.

Nelson, Dawn A. 2007. *DarkIsle.* New York: Delacorte Press.

Nguyen-Jahiel, Kim, Richard Anderson, Martha Waggoner, and Betty Rowel. 2007. "Using Literature Discussions to Reason Through Real Life Dilemmas: A Journey Taken by One Teacher and Her Fourth-Grade Students." In *Talking Texts: Knowing the World Through the Evolution of Instructional Discourse,* edited by Rosalind Horowitz, 187–205. Hillsdale, NJ: Lawrence Erlbaum.

O'Connor, Mary Catherine, and Sarah Michaels. 1993. "Aligning Academic Task and Participation Status through Revoicing: Analysis of a Classroom Discourse Strategy." *Anthropology and Education Quarterly* 24 (4): 318–335.

———. 1996. "Shifting Participant Frameworks: Orchestrating Thinking Practices in Group Discussion." In *Discourse, Learning, and Schooling,* edited by Deborah Hicks, 63–103. Cambridge, UK: Cambridge University Press.

O'Connor, Mary Catherine, Sarah Michaels, and Suzanne Chapin. 2015. "'Scaling down' to Explore the Role of Talk in Learning: From District Intervention to Controlled Classroom Study." In *Socializing Intelligence Through Talk and Dialogue,* edited by Lauren Resnick, Christa Asterhan, and Sherice Clarke, 111–126. Washington, DC: American Educational Research Association.

O'Flahavan, John. 1989. "Second Graders' Social, Intellectual, and Affective Development in Varied Group Discussions about Literature: An Exploration of Participation Structure." PhD diss., University of Illinois at Urbana-Champaign.

Olezza, Ana Maria. 1999. "An Examination of Effective Instructional and Social Interactions to Learn English as a Second Language in a Bilingual Setting." PhD diss., University of Connecticut.

Orellana, Pelusa. 2008. "Maieutic Frame Presence and Quantity and Quality of Argumentation in a Paideia Seminar." PhD diss., University of North Carolina at Chapel Hill.

Patthey-Chavez, G. Genevieve, and Lindsay Clare. 1996. "Task, Talk, and Text: The Influence of Instructional Conversation on Transitional Bilingual Writers." *Written Communication* 13 (4): 515–563.

Pearson, Caroline. 2010. "Acting Up or Acting Out? Unlocking Children's Talk in Literature Circles." *Literacy* 44 (1): 3–11.

Pearson, P. David, and Margaret C. Gallagher. 1983. "The Instruction of Reading Comprehension. *Contemporary Educational Psychology* 8: 317–344.

Peterson, Ralph, and Maryann Eeds. 2007. *Grand Conversations: Literature Groups in Action.* New York: Scholastic.

Peterson, Shelley, and Michelle Belizaire. 2006. "Another Look at Roles in Literature Circles." *Middle School Journal* 37 (4): 37–43.

Polite, Vernon, and Arlin Adams. 1997. "Critical Thinking and Values Clarification through Socratic Seminars." *Urban Education* 32 (2): 256–278.

Prasad, N. 1987. "My Name Is Different." In *Crossroads*, edited by Bernice Cullinan, Roger Farr, William Hammond, Nancy Roser, and Dorothy Strickland, 4–20. Orlando, FL: Harcourt Brace Jovanovich.

Raphael, Taffy, and Cynthia Brock. 1993. "Mei: Learning the Literacy Culture in an Urban Elementary School." *Yearbook of the National Reading Conference* 42: 179–188.

Raphael, Taffy E., Susan Florio-Ruane, Marianne George, Nina Hasty, and Kathy Highfield. 2004. *Book Club Plus!: A Literacy Framework for the Primary Grades.* Lawrence, MA: Small Planet Communications.

Raphael, Taffy, and Virginia Goatley. 1994. "The Teacher as 'More Knowledgeable Other': Changing Roles for Teachers in Alternative Reading Instruction Programs." *Yearbook of the National Reading Conference* 43: 527–536.

Raphael, Taffy E., Marcella Kehus, and Karen Damphousse. 2001. *Book Club for Middle School.* Lawrence, MA: Small Planet Communications.

Raphael, Taffy, and Susan McMahon. 1994. "Book Club: An Alternative Framework for Reading Instruction." *Reading Teacher* 48: 102–116.

Raphael, Taffy E., Laura S. Pardo, and Kathy Highfield. 2002. *Book Club: A Literature-Based Curriculum.* 2nd ed. Lawrence, MA: Small Planet Communications.

Reninger, Kristin Bourdage. 2007. "Intermediate-Level, Lower-Achieving Readers' Participation in and High-Level Thinking During Group Discussions About Literary Texts." PhD diss., The Ohio State University.

Resnick, Lauren. 1999. "Making America Smarter." *Education Week* 18 (40): 38–40.

Resnick, Lauren, and Megan Williams Hall. 1998. "Learning Organizations for Sustainable Education Reform." *Daedalus* 127: 89–118.

Resnick, Lauren B., Christa Asterhan, and Sherice N. Clarke. 2018. *Accountable Talk: Instructional Dialogue that Builds the Mind*. Geneva, Switzerland: International Academy of Education. Available from http://www.iaoed.org.

Reynolds, J. 2016. *Ghost*. New York: Atheneum Books.

Reznitskaya, Alina, and Maughn Gregory. 2013. "Student Thought and Classroom Language: Examining the Mechanisms of Change in Dialogic Teaching." *Educational Psychologist* 48 (2): 114–133.

Roberts, Terry, with Laura Billings. 1999. *The Paideia Classroom: Teaching for Understanding*. Larchmont, NY: Eye on Education.

Roberts, Terry, and Laura Billings. 2006. "Asheville Middle School: A 6–8 Community of Conscience and Intellect." *Middle School Journal* 37 (5): 31–39.

———. 2012. *Teaching Critical Thinking: Using Seminars for 21st Century Literacy*. Larchmont, NY: Eye on Education.

Robinson, Donna. 2006. "The Paideia Seminar: Moving Reading Comprehension from Transaction to Transformation." PhD diss., University of Massachusetts Lowell.

Rogers, Theresa. 1990. "A Point, Counterpoint Response Strategy for Complex Short Stories." *Journal of Reading* 34 (4): 278–282.

Rosenblatt, Louise. 1978. *The Reader, the Text, and the Poem: The Transactional Theory of the Literature Work*. Carbondale, IL: Southern Illinois University Press.

———. 2013. "The Transactional Theory of Reading and Writing." In *Theoretical Models and Processes of Reading*, 6th ed., edited by Donna Alvermann, Norman Unrau, and Robert Ruddell, 923–956. Newark, DE: International Reading Association.

Samway, Katherine Davies, and Gail Whang. 1996. *Literature Study Circles in a Multicultural Classroom*. York, ME: Stenhouse.

Sandora, Cheryl, Isabel Beck, Margaret McKeown. 1999. "A Comparison of Two Discussion Strategies on Students' Comprehension and Interpretation of Complex Literature." *Reading Psychology* 20 (3): 177–212.

Saunders, William, and Claude Goldenberg. 1999. "Effects of Instructional Conversations and Literature Logs on Limited- and Fluent-English-Proficient Students' Story Comprehension and Thematic Understanding." *The Elementary School Journal* 99 (4): 277–301.

———. 2007. "The Effects of an Instructional Conversation on Transition Students' Concepts of Friendship and Story Comprehension." In *Talking Texts: How Speech and Writing Interact in School Learning*, edited by Rosalind Horowitz, 221–252. Mahwah, NJ: Lawrence Erlbaum.

Saunders, William, G. Genevieve Patthey-Chavez, and Claude Goldenberg. 1997. "Reflections on the Relationship Between Language, Curriculum Content and Instruction." *Language, Culture and Curriculum* 10 (1): 30–51.

Schlick Noe, K. L., and N. J. Johnson. 1999. *Getting Started with Literature Circles.* Norwood, MA: Christopher-Gordon.

Serravallo, J. 2015. *The Reading Strategies Book.* Portsmouth, NH: Heinemann

Short, Kathy, and Kathryn Pierce, eds. 1990. *Talking about Books: Creating Literate Communities.* Portsmouth, NH: Heinemann.

Short, Kathy G., and Gloria Kauffman. 1999. "'So, What Do I Do?' The role of the teacher in Literature Circles." In *Book Talk and Beyond: Children and Teachers Respond to Literature,* edited by Nancy L. Roser and Miriam G. Martinez. Newark, DE: International Reading Association.

Smith, Roland. 2014. "Ovatniah." *Storyworks* January: 20–24.

Soter, Anna, Ian Wilkinson, Sean Connors, P. Karen Murphy, and Vincent Shen. 2010. "Deconstructing 'Aesthetic Response' in Small-Group Discussions about Literature: A Possible Solution to the 'Aesthetic Response' Dilemma." *English Education* 42: 204–225.

Stien, Debbie, and Penny L. Beed. 2004. "Bridging the gap between fiction and nonfiction in the literature circle setting." *The Reading Teacher* 57 (6): 510–518.

Takahashi, Etsuko, Theresa Austin, and Yoko Morimoto. 2000. "Social Interaction and Language Development in a FLES Classroom." In *Second and Foreign Language Learning Through Classroom Interaction,* edited by Joan Kelly Hall and Lorrie Stoops Verplaetse, 139–159. Mahwah, NJ: Lawrence Erlbaum.

Tarkington, Stephanie. 1988. "Improving Critical Thinking Skills Using Paideia Seminars in a Seventh Grade Literature Curriculum." EdD. diss., University of San Diego.

Tharp, Roland, Peggy Estrada, Stephanie Dalton, and Lois Yamauchi. 2000. *Teaching Transformed: Achieving Excellence, Fairness, Inclusion, and Harmony.* Boulder, CO: Westview.

Tharp, Roland, and Ronald Gallimore. 1988. *Rousing Minds to Life: Teaching, Learning, and Schooling in Social Context.* Cambridge, UK: Cambridge University Press.

———. 1989. "Rousing Schools to Life." *American Educator* 13 (2): 20–25, 46–52.

———. 1991. *The Instructional Conversation: Teaching and Learning in Social Activity.* Research Report 2. Santa Cruz, CA: National Center for Research on Cultural Diversity and Second Language Learning.

Todhunter, Susan. 1999. "Instructional Conversations in a High School Spanish Class." PhD diss., University of Pittsburgh.

Topping, Keith, and Steven Trickey, 2007a. "Collaborative Philosophical Enquiry for School Children: Cognitive Effects at 10–12 years." *British Journal of Educational Psychology* 77: 271–288. https://onlinelibrary.wiley.com/doi/abs/10.1348/000709906X105328

———. 2007b. "Collaborative Philosophical Inquiry for School Children: Cognitive Gains at 2-Year Follow-Up." *British Journal of Educational Psychology* 77: 787–796.

Topping, Keith J., Steven Trickey, and Paul Cleghorn. 2019. *A Teacher's Guide to Philosophy for Children*. New York: Routledge.

Trickey, Steven, and Keith Topping. 2004. "'Philosophy for Children:' A Systematic Review." *Research Papers in Education* 19 (3): 365–380.

Tsuchiya, Yukio. 1988. *Faithful Elephants: A True Story of Animals, People, and War*. Illustrated by Ted Lewin. Boston, MA: Houghton Mifflin.

Villar, Jeffrey. 1999. "A Model for Developing Academic Language Proficiency in English Language Learners through Instructional Conversations." PhD diss., University of Connecticut.

Vygotsky, Lev. 1962. *Thought and Language*. Cambridge, MA: MIT Press.

———. 1978. *Mind in Society: The Development of Higher Psychological Processes*. Cambridge, MA: Harvard University Press.

———. 1981. "The Genesis of Higher Mental Functions." In *The Concept of Activity in Soviet Psychology*, edited by James Wertsch, 144–188. Armonk, NY: Sharpe.

Wade, Suzanne, Audrey Thompson, and William Watkins. 1994. "The Role of Belief Systems in Authors' and Readers' Construction of Texts." In *Beliefs about Texts and Instruction with Text*, edited by Ruth Garner and Patricia Alexander, 265–293. Hillsdale, NJ: Lawrence Erlbaum.

Waggoner, Martha, Clark Chinn, Hwajin Yi, and Richard C. Anderson. 1995. "Collaborative Reasoning About Stories." *Language Arts* 72 (8): 582–589.

Walker, Caren, Thomas Wartenberg, and Ellen Winner. 2013. "Engagement in Philosophical Dialogue Facilitates Children's Reasoning about Subjectivity." *Developmental Psychology* 49 (7): 1338–1347.

Weiner, Elizabeth. 1980. "What Should Kelly Do?" In *Unfinished Stories for Facilitating Decision Making in the Elementary Classroom*, 13–14. Washington, DC: National Education Association.

Wells, Gordon. 1989. "Language in the Classroom: Literacy and Collaborative Talk." *Language and Education* 3: 251–273.

Wells, Sheila. 2012. "Using Literature to Help 4th and 5th Grade Students with Disabilities Living in Poverty Develop the Problem-Solving Skills They Need to be Successful in Their World." PhD diss., Arizona State University.

Whelan, Gloria. 1991. *Hannah*. New York: Penguin Random House.

White, E. B. 1952. *Charlotte's Web*. Illustrated by Garth Williams. New York: HarperCollins.

Wilkinson, Ian, and Kathryn Nelson. 2020. "Role of Discussion in Reading Comprehension." In *Visible Learning Guide to Student Achievement*, edited by John Hattie and Eric Anderman, 231–237. Abingdon, UK: Routledge.

Wilkinson, Ian, Kristin Reninger, and Anna Soter. 2010. "Developing a Professional Development Tool for Assessing Quality Talk About Text." *Yearbook of the National Reading Conference* 59: 122–132.

Wilkinson, Ian, Anna Soter, P. Karen Murphy, and Sarah Lightner. 2020. "Dialogue-Intensive Pedagogies for Promoting Literate Thinking." In *The Routledge International Handbook of Research on Dialogic Education*, edited by Neil Mercer, Rupert Wegerif, and Louis Major, 320–335. Abingdon, UK: Routledge.

Williams, Karen, and Khadra Mohammed. 2009. *My Name Is Sangoel*. Grand Rapids, MI: Eerdman's Books for Young Readers.

Wolf, Mikyung Kim, Amy Crosson, and Lauren Resnick. 2005. "Classroom Talk for Rigorous Reading Comprehension Instruction." *Reading Psychology* 26 (1): 27–53.

Wortham, Stanton. 1994. *Acting out Participant Examples in the Classroom*. Amsterdam: John Benjamins.

———. 1995. "Experiencing the Great Books." *Mind, Culture, and Activity* 2 (2): 67–80.

Yamauchi, Lois A., Seongah Im, and Nanette S. Schonleber. 2012. "Adapting Strategies of Effective Instruction for Culturally Diverse Preschoolers." *Journal of Early Childhood Teacher Education* 33: 54–72.

Yeazell, Mary. 1982. "Improving Reading Comprehension through Philosophy for Children." *Reading Psychology* 3 (3): 239–246.

Zhang, Jie, Richard Anderson, and Kim Nguyen-Jahiel. 2013. "Language-Rich Discussions for English Language Learners." *International Journal of Educational Research* 58: 44–60.

Zhang, Jie, and Katherine Doughtery Stahl. 2011–2012. "Collaborative Reasoning: Language-Rich Discussions for English Learners." *Reading Teacher* 65 (4): 257–260.

Index

Continuation of credit lines from p. iv: